NEW ENGLAND'S DISASTROUS WEATHER

During the Hurricane of '38, the tanker Phoenix *was swept from the Shell Union Terminal in Somerset, Massachusetts, and came to rest in selectman Adam Gifford's front yard, giving him something to rake around.*

NEW ENGLAND'S DISASTROUS WEATHER

Hurricanes, tornadoes, blizzards, dark days, heat waves, cold snaps . . . and the human stories behind them

Foreword by Donald Hall

YANKEE BOOKS

Camden, Maine

Most of the articles in this book have previously appeared in *Yankee* Magazine. Used by permission.

Edited by **Benjamin Watson**
Art direction by **Amy Fischer**
Photo Editing by **Andrea Meagher and Ann Card**
Type specifications by **Margo Letourneau**

Yankee Books
Camden, Maine 04843

First Edition, 1990
Copyright © 1990 by Yankee Books

Printed in the United States of America

Library of Congress Cataloging-in-Publication Data

New England's disastrous weather / edited by Benjamin Watson.
      p.   cm.
   ISBN 0-89909-184-9
   1. New England—Climate—History. 2. Natural disasters—New England—History.   I. Watson, Benjamin.
OC984.N35N49   1990
   551.6974—dc20   90-12244
                                                                    CIP

This book is dedicated to our friend and colleague

Art Sordillo
(1958–1989)

Who is to say that I am not the happy genius of my household?

Contents

Acknowledgments

The editor in particular owes a great debt to the spirit and life-work of one man—David McWilliams Ludlum. As an author, editor, historian, and meteorologist, Ludlum has contributed more than anyone else to the research and documentation of early American weather. He is the author of several important books on the weather, including *The Vermont Weather Book* (1985), *The American Weather Book* (1982), and *The Country Journal New England Weather Book* (1976), as well as several volumes written for the American Meteorological Society chronicling early American winters, hurricanes, and tornadoes. He is also the author of two of the articles that appear in *New England's Disastrous Weather*.

For editorial assistance, we gratefully acknowledge Barbara Jatkola, John Pierce, and Sharon Smith. For technical assistance, we thank Nancy Fuchs, Rebecca Stevens, and Laurie Seamans. For research assistance, our thanks to Bob Trebilcock, Robin Clark, and Dougald MacDonald.

Our special thanks for research assistance go to Deborah Watson and the reference staff of the University of New Hampshire's Dimond Library. We also are grateful to the Yale University Library and to the Beinecke Rare Book and Manuscript Library at Yale University.

Finally, thanks to all of the authors featured in *New England's Disastrous Weather,* who have contributed to *Yankee* Magazine over the years and who made this book possible.

Good Uses for Bad Weather

BY DONALD HALL

My grandparents nailed two thermometers side by side on the porch of their New Hampshire farmhouse. One registered ten degrees cold, the other ten degrees hot—so that there was always something to brag about. Every morning when my grandmother sat in the rocker under Christopher the canary writing three postcards to three daughters, she could say: "Thirty below this morning. Seems like it might get cold." Or: "Ninety already and the sun's not over the mountain."

In New England we take pride in our weather because it provides us with pain and suffering, necessities for the spirit like food and clothing for the body. We never brag about good weather. Let Tucson display self-esteem over 83 days without rain. Let Sarasota newspapers go free for the asking when the sun doesn't shine. We smirk in the murk, superior.

It's true that we have good weather; we just don't pay it any mind. When summer people flock north to the lakes and the mountains, they do not gather to enjoy our foggy rain. If they're from Boston, they don't come for bright sun and cool, dry air; they migrate north against the soup-kettle mugginess of home. It seems more decent, I suppose.

In good weather—apple days of October, brilliant noons and cool evenings of August—we remain comfortable despite our pleasure by talking about pleasure's brevity, forecasting what we're in for as soon as the good spell is done with.

Winter is best for bragging. For a week or two in March, mud is almost as good. (Mud is weather as much as snow is; leaves are landscape.) "Tried to get the Buick up New Canada this morning. Have to wait for a dry spell to pull it out, I suppose. Of course, we'll have to dig for it first."

Black ice is first-rate, but most of us will settle for a good two feet of snow. We cherish difficulty. We get up about 5:15, make the coffee, check the thermometer: ten degrees. (The warmth accounts for the snow.) Highway department plows blunder down Route 4 in the dark outside. Our cousin Forrest plowed half of our U-shaped driveway at 3:30 A.M. (that's why the dog barked), scooping a trail from the road by the mailbox past the two cars. We get dressed, dragging on flannel-lined chinos, flannel shirt, sweater, down jacket, and boots. Then we broom the car, headlights and taillights, gun it in reverse over the hump of snow the plow didn't get, swing it up Forrest's alley, and swoop it down to the road, scattering ridges of snow.

Only two miles to the store. It's not adventurous driving, but it pays to be attentive, to start slowing for a turn a hundred yards early. The store opens at six. Because this is New Hampshire, somebody's bound to be there by 5:45. We park with the motor running and the heater on—it'll get warm while we pick up the *Globe*— to go inside.

Bob's there with his cup of coffee, and Bill who owns garage and store, and Judy who makes coffee and change. We grin at each other as I stamp my boots and slip my paper out of the pile. We say things like "Nice weather!" "Bit of snow out there!" "Hear we're getting two feet more!"—but what we're really saying is *It takes more than a couple of feet of snow to keep us home!*

Weather is conversation's eternal subject, lingua franca shared by every New Englander with sensory equipment. When Rolls Royce meets junker, they can talk about the damned rain. Weather talk helps us over difficult subjects. On one Monday morning some years ago, Ned said to Will, "Too bad about Pearl Harbor. I hear there's ten feet over on 5A." Will said to Ned, "I suppose we'll win the war. They say a bread truck got through."

In a boring patch when the weather's mild, we talk about disasters and catastrophes of the past. As a child I heard endless stories about the Blizzard of '88. My Connecticut grandfather belonged to a club that met once a year on the anniversary to swap reminiscences— by which, of course, we understand that they met to tell lies.

As I stagger into codgerhood myself, I discover that my own Blizzard of '88 is the great wind of 1938. I was in Connecticut for that one, which first visited our house in my father's disgust over his new barometer. He'd won it in a putting contest, and he was proud of it, pretty in its rich brown wood and bright brass. Then, when he hung it on the wall, it busted; at least, it sank right down until the foolish thing predicted a hurricane.

A few years back we had another New England hurricane. So they called it. Down in Connecticut, it is true, this wind knocked a few trees over, but up in New Hampshire it never mussed our hair. For a good week, traveling in circles that talked about weather, I felt outrage as I grumbled, "You call *that* a hurricane?" I'm ready to join a Hurricane of '38 club.

Most of the time, weather is relative. Every year when an August morning is 40 degrees, we shiver: It's *cold* out there! But when a February morning rises to 40, we walk around with our coats unbuttoned enjoying the heat wave.

Next day an ice storm, and we take relief in the return of suffering: It's true—if you don't have to drive in it—that few things in creation are as beautiful as an ice storm.

Much bad weather is beautiful: dark days when it never quite rains and never quite doesn't, English weather cozy around the fire; wild rains of summer after high heat, compensation and relief; drizzle in autumn that drains color from the trees, quiet and private; the first snow, which steps my heartbeat up; the first *big* snow, which steps it higher; winter thaw, with its hesitant promise; Gothic thunderstorms with bolts of melodrama. We quicken, we thrill, we comfort the dog.

Every now and then we have an open winter, and it's a psychic disaster. It's disaster also for shrubs and bulbs, but it's the soul's woe because we haven't suffered enough. The earth can't emerge because it never submerged. We don't deserve the milder air and the daffodils rising because we haven't lost our annual battles with the snow—fender benders, bad backs from shoveling the mailbox, rasp of frozen air in the lungs, falls on ice, chunks of snow down our boots.

The only bad weather in New England is when we don't have any.

Donald Hall is New Hampshire's Poet Laureate and the author of numerous books, including String Too Short to Be Saved, Fathers Playing Catch with Sons, *and* Seasons at Eagle Pond.

Introduction

One of the oldest of the old saws still told around these parts is the one that goes, "If you don't like the weather in New England, just wait a minute." Like most Yankee folk expressions, it contains a lot of exaggeration and more than a little truth.

In fact, the *only* thing that can be said with any certainty about New England's weather is that it is constantly changing. Rarely will you hear a native describe a season or a year as being "typical." Not that such freak events as normal years don't occur in New England—it's just that a person needs the life span of a Methuselah to witness the recurring themes of our almost infinitely variable climate.

Another thing you won't hear much is, "Oh, we never get snow (wind, earthquakes, etc.) around *here*." That's because, no matter where you happen to be in New England, chances are there's a story about some sudden or unusual weather event that's taken place in recent memory. From Lake Champlain to Aroostook County, from the Berkshires to Block Island, New England has a thousand and one microclimates, each as individual as a fingerprint and as undependable as a two-dollar watch. All of this adds to the delightful uncertainty, even the mystique, of our weather, with which we are so outwardly disgusted and of which we are so secretly proud.

New England's Disastrous Weather celebrates the most famous storms and weather tragedies in our history. The editors have gathered together for the first time their favorite weather-related articles from the pages of *Yankee* Magazine, each story an account of the human drama caused by some great weather event. From the famous Summerless Year of 1816 to the immortal Hurricane of '38, these accounts (and the photos and illustrations that accompany them) reveal an important part of the Yankee character. More than anything else, this book is about survival—about the men and women who lived through fierce storms and devastation to tell their stories to future generations.

To round out this selective and wide-ranging history, the editors have commissioned a few new articles especially for this book and have added some humorous anecdotes and interesting footnotes to history. In the chapter titled "The Prognosticators," we have presented some of the people and institutions behind the art (it's too uncertain to call a science) of New England weather forecasting.

For most of us, no single factor looms larger in our lives than the weather, though much of the time we give it only a passing thought or comment. But on those occasions when the weather controls and dominates us (instead of the other way around), it becomes more than just a topic of idle conversation; deep and lasting memories are made of our experiences with the natural forces that shape our lives. This is a book of memories, and we hope that some of the stories will trigger your own recollections. Fortunately, as Cotton Mather once wrote, "The reading of a storm is not so bad as the feeling of it."

B.A.W.

CHAPTER ONE

Hurricanes

Above: *Mrs. Nellie C. Collins returned to salvage a few personal belongings from her Misquamicut, Rhode Island, home. Of the 500 houses in the Misquamicut area, only five survived the '38 Hurricane.* **Previous pages:** *An intrepid photographer braved wind and water to snap this shot of Providence's Washington Square Yacht Club, destroyed in the Hurricane of '38. The mast of a sunken yacht stands in the foreground.*

The Wind That Shook the World

The Hurricane of 1938

BY JAMES DODSON

For the first time his wife, Irene, could ever remember, Harold Higginbotham decided not to go to work. It had been rainy and muggy all week along the stretch of Atlantic coast from New London, Connecticut, to Point Judith, Rhode Island—a fitting conclusion to a summer that had been pretty much of a washout. Even though school had resumed and it was the third week of September, many families lingered on in cottages at summer beach colonies near the border towns of Westerly and Pawcatuck, hoping for one last break in the dark skies.

All week Harold, a foreman at the American Thread Company in Pawcatuck, and Irene and two of their three sons, Jimmy, 10, and Stanley, 20, had been staying in a small cottage on Montauk Avenue at Misquamicut Beach. Harold had been fighting off a cold, which on the evening of September 20, 1938, grew worse. The family packed up and drove five miles home to West Broad Street in Pawcatuck.

Like everyone else, they had a surprise the next morning. The weather cleared dramatically. There was just a riffle of breeze from the southeast and a benediction of warm sun. It was the kind of fine morning people had been waiting for all summer.

As the fishing fleet put out from harbors up and down the coast, sailboats appeared in Little Narragansett Bay, and college boys hired to close up the big summer houses of Watch Hill stripped off their shirts. Striped umbrellas appeared. Beach outings were hastily assembled.

At Christ Episcopal Church in Westerly, just before ten that morning, a dozen women from the Mothers' Club assembled with their rector for a drive to the beach and a picnic at the Clark cottage. At their handsome house at Watch Hill, Mr. and Mrs. Geoffrey L. Moore, their four small children, a visiting relative, two family employees, and a college boy named Andy Pupillo also were talking about the sudden spell of good weather. There was some talk of strolling down to the Watch Hill carousel to take a ride on the famous carved wooden horses with their real agate eyes.

Sometime before lunch, Stan Higginbotham received a telephone call at the Morris Plan Company, the bank where he worked as a teller. His mother was on the line, and she explained that Stan's father was feeling better. It seemed a shame to waste such fine weather, so she and Jimmy were taking Harold back out to the cottage at Misquamicut. Stan and his girlfriend, Jean, she suggested, could join them there after Stan got off work at five.

Young *Westerly Sun* reporter Bill Cawley was just checking his beat at the Stonington City Hall and cursing his luck at having to work on such a nice day. City Hall was dead, and it would be a slow news day, but he couldn't shake "an eerie feeling . . . something in the air, like a kind of suspension was about to end."

Cawley thought he was merely reading the social weather of the times. There were still 10.5 million Americans out of work, and President Roosevelt had just recently declared the beginning of "the real drive on the Depression."

On that morning, the *New York Times* ran an editorial praising the U.S. Weather Bureau for keeping Americans so well informed about potentially hazardous weather movements, especially tropical cyclones, or Atlantic hurricanes. The forecast for New York on that same day was for cloudy and cool weather with increasing winds.

At the bottom of page one of that day's *Westerly Sun,* however, a small Associated Press wire story mentioned that a "tropical hurricane" would pass far off the coast of Cape Hatteras, North Carolina, "sometime in the next 12 hours." Floridians were boarding up and fetching candles. The storm, which came out of the Cape Verde Islands and had first been sighted on September 16 by the captain of a Brazilian freighter 350 miles northeast of Puerto Rico, was expected to cause high tides in the Carolinas and Virginia before turning harmlessly out to sea.

Fishermen and bathers in Narragansett Bay noticed that the light had developed a peculiar yellow tint and the breeze was clearly picking up. Almost everyone could read the weather signs—yet another line storm was coming. It was almost predictable, they remarked, given the dreary way summer had gone. Some packed up and went home. Others stayed. In faraway Vermont, a dairy farmer paused in his field, marveling. He could actually smell the sea.

Young Westerly Sun *reporter Bill Cawley thought that Wednesday, September 21, 1938 would be a slow news day. Instead, he brought the first account of the tragedy at Misquamicut to the nation.*

In 1938, the U.S. Weather Bureau was but a shadow of its future self. For vital information, historian William Manchester has pointed out, "it relied on the 16th-century thermometer, the 17th-century mercurial barometer, and the medieval weather vane." Meteorologists depended entirely on observations from merchant ships and aircraft to formulate forecasts. It was easier to know where a tropical storm wasn't, it was often said with amusement, than where a tropical storm was.

At about 2:15 that afternoon, a Long Island fisherman saw a huge fog bank rolling in fast from the ocean. He had never seen fog quite so dense, nor a fog bank move so fast. And then he realized his terrible mistake. He wasn't looking at fog but at a churning wall of water.

About the time Stan Higginbotham looked out of the bank and saw people grabbing their hats as they crossed Dixon Square in Westerly, the worst Atlantic hurricane in well over a century was bearing down with 200-mile-per-hour winds on the villages, summer houses, and produce farms of Long Island's fashionable Hamptons. The impact of the storm would register on a seismograph in Sitka, Alaska. In its path lay the richest industrialized seaboard in the world—and 13 million unsuspecting people.

In Westhampton a chicken farmer saw the roof of his chicken house peeled off in an instant and 1,200 hens vanish in a deafening swirl of debris—house shutters, business awnings, tree limbs. Piece by piece, 200 Hampton houses began to come apart like papier-mâché, and the steeple of Sag Harbor's famous Old Whaler's Church smashed to the ground. In seconds, all of Long Island's phones were dead and power was out. In a matter of minutes, 50 people were crushed or drowned under collapsing houses and raging waters that boiled from the sea.

Sucked along by a trough of still, muggy air and a ground surface that had been saturated by days of heavy rain, the eye of the hurricane was advancing at 60 miles per hour—roughly the velocity of a tornado—when it hit Connecticut's shoreline a short time before 3:00 P.M.

In Stonington, Bill Cawley had stopped by the high-school playing field to watch practice and chat with the football coach. Trees around the field, he realized, were suddenly doubled over. The coach abruptly canceled practice, and the reporter raced for the newspaper office.

In downtown Westerly, the large windows of the Morris Plan Company waved as if they were made of sheets of rubber. Staring out, Stan Higginbotham saw bricks flying through Dixon Square. As he watched, trees planted in the town's park before the Revolutionary War were uprooted or toppled over "like bowling pins, one after the other." Right in front of him, a postman was picked up and dashed into a light pole.

At a small grocery store a few blocks away, Stan's next-door neighbor and pal, Don Friend, also 20, watched the roof of the Pawcatuck Congregational Church fly by. He was worried. His mother, Ruth, had gone to Misquamicut with the Mothers' Club from Christ Church.

Stan Higginbotham called home to see if his

mother, dad, and brother had gone back to the beach, praying they hadn't. There was no answer. He called his girlfriend, Jean Meikle, at the telephone company and suggested they use her car to drive to Misquamicut and check on them. His 1929 Essex was parked out at the beach cottage.

By the time the couple reached her family's house on Highland Avenue in Westerly, the Pawcatuck River had spilled over its banks and flooded the downtown area. The presses of the *Sun* were standing in four feet of water. Phones and power were out. The couple decided to wait for the raging wind to subside before heading for the beach. They hoped the situation would be better out there.

Above: *Sandbagging at Rockville, Connecticut.* **Below:** *Houses damaged in the 1938 Hurricane, Noank, Connecticut.*

The Watch Hill Beach Club, before the Hurricane of '38.

At Watch Hill during gales, people sometimes gathered to watch the dramatic breakers. Harold, Irene, and Jimmy Higginbotham did just that. Their folly was compounded by a cruel natural coincidence: Because of the phase of the moon, tides were running a foot above normal. The storm also struck on an incoming tide.

Quickly realizing their mistake, the trio hurried back to the cottage behind the sand barrier in Misquamicut to gather their things and get out. On their flight to higher ground, they stopped at another cottage to pick up a young woman named Alma Bailey, who was dating their third son, Ken. He was at his fraternity house at the University of Rhode Island, 30 miles away, watching trees snap.

Accounts still vary on the size of the tidal wave that struck the unprotected barrier beaches that stretch from Watch Hill to Point Judith. It has been described as anywhere from 30 to 80 feet high. What is known, however, is that 500 cottages sat on or around those normally tranquil beaches. And in those 500 houses, hundreds of people were riding out the storm.

Racing to make the higher ground of what was known as Shore Road, the Higginbothams found themselves trapped when their car stalled in rapidly rising floodwater. Harold shepherded everyone out of the car and into a nearby two-story cottage. They were barely inside the door when an explosion of water chased them up the stairs. On the second floor, Harold smashed out a window. The water rose to their waists. He desperately helped Alma out the window, advising her to grab hold of floating debris. Next, he put Jimmy on a large piece of flotsam, perhaps a door. Then he turned to help his wife. Irene was nowhere in sight. He called her name desperately just as the house began to splinter. The next minute, flailing in the churning water himself, Harold heard Jimmy's terrified voice. Seconds later, Jimmy was thrown from his makeshift raft and disappeared.

In a matter of a few seconds at Watch Hill, the yacht club, a public bathhouse, and 39 large cottages were ripped from Napatree Point and swept toward the Connecticut shore across the mouth of the Pawcatuck River. Forty-two people were inside.

Trapped in their disintegrating house, the Geoffrey

The same beach at Watch Hill, after the storm. In the wake of the hurricane, virtually nothing remained.

Moores and their employees huddled upstairs in the attic and felt the floor begin to buckle wildly. Three of the children wore life jackets. They clutched rosaries, yet were remarkably calm. As the house slid away beneath them, however, the children began to cry. Harriet Moore reassured them. Moments later, the roof blew off the maid's room. It was the best thing they would have for a raft, so with Andy Pupillo's assistance, all ten people clambered aboard. Clutching each other and jagged wall pipes as huge waves broke over them, the Moore party drifted toward the open water of the bay.

The same wave that swept 500 houses from their foundations at Misquamicut Beach sent a massive wall of water up the Providence River toward downtown Providence. The killer wave, 100 feet high, crushed the city's docks and broke near City Hall, drowning dozens of startled pedestrians in shops, doorways, and their own automobiles. The great skylight of the Providence Library came crashing down.

In his dorm at Brown University, junior Bob Perry, whose family kept a summer place near the dunes at Weekapaug, adjacent to Misquamicut, looked out and saw slate shingles from the roof embedding themselves in century-old elms. His first thought was that everyone at home would probably be okay; the intensity of the storm made him think it couldn't possibly be happening anywhere else.

In downtown Providence, a flying sheet of fabricated metal cut a man in half. Display windows blew out of shops. A woman was sucked through a restaurant's plate-glass window. Falling trees crushed people in their cars. A rat floated down the street, bobbing on an empty gasoline can. Living-room furniture, office desks, restaurant tables—a biblical flood of struggling people and everyday objects—swirled down Main Street.

When the wave subsided, the downtown district was under 13 feet of water. The headlights of thousands of automobiles shone eerily underwater. Bob Perry, safe on the hill at Brown, got chills listening to the wail of sirens and shorting auto horns.

Around 6:00 P.M. in Westerly, the wind abruptly died, and the air grew menacingly cold. Bill Cawley

made his way from the newspaper office to the police station where, right on his heels, a pale half-dressed man in the early stages of shock appeared. "Watch Hill is gone," he mumbled dazedly. "It's all washed away." Cawley and a policeman didn't believe him. They decided to go investigate.

Others also were heading to the beaches. Don Friend and his father, Frank, were in their Model A trying to find a way across the boiling Pawcatuck. Also headed to Misquamicut, Stan Higginbotham, Jean Meikle, and a neighbor were stopped by a policeman, who commandeered their vehicle and ordered them to deliver badly needed medical supplies to Westerly Hospital. After that, the group drove toward Watch Hill, but the road was soon underwater. They turned onto Shore Road and came to a halt.

"There, across the road, as high as a house," remembers Stan, "was the largest pile of rubble I had ever seen. It was *unimaginable*. We got out, and a young policeman and I started to climb the mountain of debris. I saw a human hand sticking out. Even though it was utterly shocking, I thought when we got to the top of the pile we would probably find Mom and Dad and Jimmy perching on a roof somewhere."

What they saw instead was a "mountain of rubble of destroyed houses and dead bodies that stretched out of sight." The group went from house to house along Shore Road to search for survivors. Near dusk, they reached the Oaks Inn, which stood on higher ground. The proprietor saw them coming and yelled, "Stan, your father's inside."

Stan found his father in an upstairs room at the inn "sobbing like a baby. They had found him stark naked and full of seawater. Alma Bailey also had survived, with a broken leg. The owner of the inn had pumped my dad full of booze to make him throw up all that salt water. All he said to me between sobs, was, 'Stan, they're out there *somewhere*. Go get 'em.'"

But darkness was falling; there was nothing to do but wait for dawn. Stan and Jean drove three hours over precarious roads to the university, where they picked up Ken and brought him back to Jean's house in Westerly. They huddled around a single gas-jet flame, trying to keep warm until morning.

About the same time Stan found his father, the Geoffrey Moores and their entourage found themselves washed up on the debris-strewn shore of Barn Island, on the Connecticut side of the Pawcatuck. Everyone was bruised, cut, and full of seawater—but otherwise miraculously well. Shoeless, they stumbled through briars to the remains of a barn. While Harriet Moore got her shivering children arranged under the hay, Andy

Opposite page: *Exchange Place in Providence, looking toward the Biltmore Hotel and City Hall. Taken just before the high point of the flooding, this photo shows the floating automobiles and swamped trolley cars that filled the city's streets.* **Above:** *Yachts of all kinds lined both sides of the bridge in Barrington, Rhode Island, after the storm.*

Pupillo went to look for help. He saw lights flickering on the shore, heard voices, and called out, but there was no answer. He returned to the group and cradled one of the small children in his arms.

"The stars came out, and the wind died down," Harriet Moore told a reporter later. They saw light in the southern sky—the glow of New London on fire. They talked and hugged each other, trying to get warm. "We called out intermittently all night long," she reflected. "Of course, we did not know the catastrophe was *so* far reaching."

Harriet Moore was not alone in her ignorance. All over dark, battered New England, thousands of huddling refugees were asking themselves the same questions: How extensive had the great storm been? Why hadn't they been warned?

By the next morning—survivors remember it as being a glorious sunrise—news of the devastation had barely reached New York. From isolated places such as Westerly, it would take days to get the story out to the world.

Units of the National Guard and Civilian Conservation Corps were stationed on roads leading to West-

9

erly's beaches as hastily organized search parties headed that way at dawn. Among them were Bill Cawley and Charlie Utter (whose family owned the *Westerly Sun*), Don Friend, Stan and Ken Higginbotham, and several volunteers from Ken's fraternity who drove down to help search for survivors.

The grim labor of digging through the piled-up houses commenced. There was an aura of unreality about the work: Someone found a woman's severed finger with a beautiful diamond ring on it. Dogs chained to posts had gone mad trying to free themselves. Picking up a board, Stan Higginbotham found the body of his Sunday school teacher, Mrs. Bishop. One by one, bodies were transported into Westerly and lined up in a makeshift morgue in the city high school. Stan identified the body of Don Friend's mother, Ruth; the other ladies of Christ Church were found nearby.

Bill Cawley set out for New Haven around 4:00 A.M. on Friday. Driving over golf courses and through backyards to avoid downed power lines and uprooted

Below: *Sorting through debris at "Hawk's Nest" in South Lyme, Connecticut.* **Opposite page, top:** *The first post-hurricane edition of The* Westerly Sun *told the grim story of the disaster and listed the dead and missing.*

trees, talking his way through police and military barricades, Cawley finally staggered into the office of the Associated Press several hours later. An editor on duty refused to believe the horror story he told about Westerly. As authorizing calls were placed to Washington, Cawley sat down to write his first-person account. His story broke on the front page of the Washington, D.C., *Evening Star* that afternoon.

"I reached the outside world today after witnessing the scenes of horror and desolation that came in the hours after a tidal wave, hurled miles inland by a hurricane, engulfed Westerly, Rhode Island, my home, two days ago.

"I counted bodies—row upon sickening row of them—stretched out in the old town high school after all the city's morgues were filled. When I left at four o'clock this morning, there were 74 dead and almost 100 missing. . . . "

The world now knew about the horror at Westerly.

That same day, Stan and Ken Higginbotham learned the fate of their little brother, Jimmy. He was found, unclothed, under eight feet of rubble, near Brightman's Pond. "At the high school, when I picked him up," recalls Stan, "a photographer wanted to take my picture with him. I picked up a fireman's ax and almost killed the poor fellow. A doctor determined that Jimmy didn't drown. He died of fright."

On Friday afternoon, using an antique handpress, the editors of the *Sun* put out an emergency edition of the paper that listed the local dead and injured. Telegrams were pouring into the newspaper and Red Cross offices from all over the world, inquiring about the fate of loved ones. Doctors, it was reported, were giving emotionally shattered relief workers sleeping pills to permit them to rest.

Four days later, search crews, following the scent of decaying bodies, finally found the remains of Irene Higginbotham, not far from where her husband had washed up on Shore Road.

Oh, the Irony of It All

This editorial from the *New York Times* appeared on Wednesday, September 21, 1938; the weather forecast for New England called for "Rain, probably heavy today and tomorrow, cooler."

HURRICANE

A few miles north of the equator in the West Indies lies a calm, humid region known as the "doldrums." Here heated air rises through cooler in Summer by some process not yet understood. Somehow a twist is imparted to the mass and off it whirls to become what the meteorologists call a "cyclone" and we a "hurricane" that rushes northward at a speed of at least seventy-five miles an hour, to strike terror into the hearts of Floridians and remind even faraway New York that nature is not to be trifled with when she is in one of her angrier moods. Thus interpreted, the cyclone that happily spared our Southern coast is not an extraordinary occurrence. Every year an average of three such whirlwinds sweep the tropical North Atlantic between June and November. In 1938 there was an all-time record of twenty.

If New York and the rest of the world have been so well informed about the cyclone it is because of an admirably organized meteorological service. From every ship in the Caribbean Sea reports are radioed to Washington, Havana, San Juan and other stations. Hour by hour a cyclone is watched, peril that it is, until at last it whirls out into the Atlantic to make passengers on liners wonder why the wind whistles past glass-enclosed decks and why a 50,000-ton hull begins to roll and pitch. In ships and scientific stations are men sending wireless warnings to all the world, caring nothing about nationality or economic prizes. There is a lesson in all those stations and ships of many nations warning the Western world that a cyclone is on the loose. Science is doing its best to teach the world the worth of cooperation.

—Reprinted courtesy of the *New York Times*

These marks on the wall of Providence's Old Market House record the two great tides in the city's history. On September 23, 1815, the water rose 11 feet, 9¹/4 inches above mean high tide. On September 21, 1938, it rose to 13 feet, 9 inches.

The 1938 hurricane was the worst natural disaster in American history—a gale that wreaked more death and havoc than either the Great Chicago Fire or the San Francisco Earthquake. Even today, the numbers are startling. Almost 700 people perished as a result of the storm, and 2,000 were injured. More than 63,000 people lost their homes. Almost 20,000 public and private buildings were destroyed, and 100 bridges had to be rebuilt. The cost of the damage totaled more than $400 million in 1938 dollars. Only about 4 percent of the businesses lost were insured. Many, struggling to stay afloat through the Great Depression, finally sank in the Great Hurricane.

In the "wind that shook the world," as it was later called, New England lost more than 25 percent of its cherished elms. "The greens and commons of New England," lamented one editorial writer, "will never be the same." More than half a million property deeds had to be resurveyed because of storm damage. In New Hampshire alone, 1.5 *billion* board feet of timber were knocked down; the recovery of "storm" lumber would take years. When war broke out in Europe, much of the lumber was used to build military barracks and the interiors of transport ships.

Perhaps the only other good to come from the disaster was when an outraged Congress ordered that the U.S. Weather Bureau be systematically improved so that such a tragedy could never happen again.

In Westerly today, where quarries once produced the granite that was used for most of the monuments at Gettysburg, two generations have come and gone, and there are no monuments to the hurricane that changed every life in town. If you are seeking landmarks, people will send you to the high-water mark on the wall of the *Westerly Sun* pressroom and to a small brass plaque attached to a rock that shows where the raging waters rose on the Misquamicut golf course. The real monuments, people say, are in lives pieced back together after the tragedy.

Bill Cawley was cited by the Associated Press for his "courage and enterprise" in getting the story of Westerly's ordeal to the outside world. After serving with the Air Force during World War II, he returned to Westerly and worked for the *Sun,* becoming sports editor in 1965 and retiring in 1982. "I became, in a way, a kind of celebrity," he reports. "For years, people wrote to me from all over the world wanting to know more or about someone from here they once knew."

No monuments were ever built in Westerly, he

suggests, "because the hurricane acted as a prelude to world war—we were just getting started, turns out." He cannot pass the place where the old high-school gym once stood, now a peaceful town park, without remembering the lines of corpses laid out on the floor.

Bob Perry, a retired banker, still drives to his family house out on Weekapaug Point. He passes million-dollar houses built on the sands of Misquamicut, new cottages, water slides, and penny arcades. He marvels at the wonders of flood insurance, regularly taps his barometer, and ponders the unspeakable: "If it happened today, with ten times the population and so many year-round residences . . . ," he speculates—and draws silent.

Every September, the hurricane's victims, especially the ladies of the Mothers' Club, are remembered in the prayers of Christ Church. On the wall, a small lamp burns in their memory. A move has begun to raise funds for a larger memorial.

Since 1962, Don Friend has lived out at the beach near Brightman's Pond, where his mother perished. He and Ken Higginbotham, he reports, often go sailing on Ken's 24-foot Bristol sloop. "But we never leave the protected bay," he adds soberly. "Never."

Stan Higginbotham, who retired a few years ago after selling Chevrolets in town for 34 years, spends a lot of time thinking about what happened to his father and, oddly enough, his '29 Essex.

Harold Higginbotham lost his job soon after the hurricane when American Thread shut its doors and moved out of town. For a pension, Harold was given a modest $1,000—or about $500 less than he needed to bury his wife and youngest son. He never found a steady job in town again. "He was a proud man. Friends gave him odd jobs to do," says Stan. Finally, near the end of his life, Harold moved to Massachusetts and found a position at a mill. He died in 1978.

A lot of curious stories, Stan points out, came out of the Great Hurricane. Dogs were found alive in closets of shattered houses. A table set with china survived perfectly intact as the house came apart around it. Two babies survived by floating on a door. A man caught a two-pound river trout on Main Street with his bare hands. "Everyone who survived it has a peculiar, singular memory he or she may wish to finally remember it by," Stan says.

His own goes like this: Not long after his mother and brother were buried, he found the remains of his '29 Essex out at the beach. All that was left of his dream car was a chassis, a battery, four tires, and two unbroken headlights.

He looked at it awhile, then picked up a piece of driftwood and knocked out the headlights.   ∞

The *Bostonian*

BY IRWIN ROSS

It was a day set apart for terror. Out of the south an eerie wind howled about the rooftops of New London, Connecticut. It whipped the usually placid waters of the Thames River into a white fury. From skies so close they seemed to hug the earth, a slashing, fitful rain beat down.

Engineer Harry Easton of the *Bostonian,* crack express train of the New York, New Haven & Hartford line, peered anxiously from his cab as the train all but crawled along the shore route toward Boston, more than 100 miles away. Easton was not a man to frighten easily, but he had good reason for caution. In the cars behind him he had 275 passengers, and somewhere ahead of him in this wind-torn chaos between New London and Boston, he had a rendezvous with a hurricane.

All week there had been portents of unnatural things to come. The heat was oppressive for September; day after day rain fell. Somewhere deep in the tropics, born in the vast reaches of the South Atlantic, one of the greatest hurricanes of modern times was roaring northward, gathering momentum as it skirted Florida, sweeping across the sea and hurtling past the Carolinas, Virginia, and Delaware. Now, on Wednesday after-

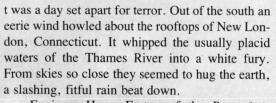

The Bostonian's stranded cars shared the tracks with sea-going cabin cruisers near Stonington, Connecticut.

noon, September 21, 1938, Long Island and Connecticut braced for the blow.

Slowly the *Bostonian* moved past the town of Mystic, half-hidden in the savage gray downpour. Powerful gusts of wind rattled the cars; the train shuddered as engineer Easton throttled down to seven miles an hour.

"Keep that fire going!" he shouted to his fireman.

With every passing moment the storm increased in fury. Peering ahead, Easton felt the skin about his temples grow taut: Telegraph poles were beginning to topple; trees bent almost double and crashed to the earth. But before he could bring his passengers into the comparative safety of the next station—that of Stonington, a mile away—he would have to take the *Bostonian* over a narrow, exposed causeway that stretched 2,000 feet across an expanse of Long Island Sound.

His mouth set grimly, his hand firmly on the throttle, he nursed the *Bostonian* forward. Through the murk he caught a glimpse of the causeway. Water was already beginning to lap at the ties. The train crept out on the narrow ribbon of track and began inching its way forward at five miles an hour. It went 100 yards. Two hundred yards. Now the gale struck with all its power. Hundred-mile-an-hour winds roared across the turbulent sound.

Dr. Aubrey Gould

"An Immense Wall of Ocean Rolled toward Us"

September 21 meant the end of summer vacation for Aubrey Gould and three of his classmates, who boarded the Bostonian *at New York's Grand Central Station that day.*

We had to move away from the windows on the ocean side to avoid flying glass and debris that hurtled into the car. We watched a sedan, its driver still clutching the wheel, blow up into the air and out of sight. An immense wall of dark green foaming ocean rolled toward us with a deafening roar. The wave brought the bowsprit of a 30-foot fishing boat crashing through the window just ahead of us. There was a gigantic jolt, and the coach suddenly lurched over sideways to the left.

My friend Jeff Stockman and I, soaking wet, stumbled along the aisle, finally reaching the platform connecting us to the next coach. I could hear women in the water, screaming. I looked down the metal steps to see two terrified faces in the turbulent water. Jeff and I, grasping the railing with one hand, leaned down and out and pulled the women up. They were frail, elderly ladies, shivering and crying but alive.

We feared that the train would tip over with us in it, so we plunged into rough, cold waves and swam about a quarter of a mile to shore, where we found looters breaking into stores. Somebody told us we were in Stonington. My Aunt Ethel lived there, so Jeff and I found her house, and she sheltered us for three days.   ∞

At that moment he saw the signal tower light. It was red! He uttered an oath and jammed on the brakes. The *Bostonian* ground to a stop.

Easton glanced back. What he saw sent a chill up his spine. The last three coaches were leaning to one side like a child's train derailed by a careless hand. One powerful gust of wind might blow them over.

Easton tugged on his whistle cord. They *must* hear him at the tower. He *must* get a green signal.

The fireman put down his shovel and shook his head. "That whistle won't carry ten feet in this wind," he shouted. Easton suddenly eased himself from his seat behind the throttle.

"All right," he said. "I'm going out there myself. I've got to get that signal changed."

"No, don't try it!" The fireman held his arm. "Harry, you won't make it."

Easton shook himself free and climbed down from the engine. He was up to his ankles in water. The wind was like a solid wall. Head down, bent almost double, pieces of debris swirling about his legs, he forged his way toward the tower.

Minutes later, he reached it. Then he cupped his hands and yelled, "Hey! Hey, there."

A head appeared at a shattered window. Towerman Harry Thomas looked down with amazement at the battered, water-soaked figure.

"Give me a green light!" Easton roared. "I've got 300 passengers. I can't stay out there—we'll be blown away!"

"Okay! But take it easy," came Thomas's voice. "Another train's stalled up ahead."

Easton turned back. Even as he had been standing there, the water had risen with incredible speed. It was now waist-deep as he fought and stumbled his way back toward the train. Halfway there, he lost his footing and fell. He was being swept away; frantically he clutched for a support. His fingers closed on the rail.

He held on with a death grip, managed to pull himself up, and floundered doggedly forward again. Wreckage bruised him, and time and again he slipped and fell, but he finally reached the engine and was helped aboard by the strong arm of his fireman.

Weary and battered, Easton climbed into his seat. As he was about to grip the throttle, George Barton, the conductor, hurried into the cab. "The roadbed under the last three cars is washed out!"

Easton looked back. The cars were now leaning almost at a 45-degree angle. They might topple into the water at any moment.

"Get the passengers into the forward cars!" he

snapped. "Uncouple those last three. We'll go on with-out 'em. Work fast!"

Back in the coaches again, Barton ordered the terror-stricken passengers into the forward cars. Some men and women screamed; others pushed like cattle.

Easton got the go-ahead signal. He pulled the throttle back. The train did not move. The wheels churned the water into a frenzy of foam, but the train would not budge.

Wreckage had become wedged under the wheels of the last cars, smashing the air lines so that every brake had locked.

"All right," said Easton. "Move all the passengers into the head car. We'll have to uncouple the rest of the train."

The crew worked furiously in water now shoulder-deep. The passengers were herded into the first coach. Easton pulled the throttle. The engine started to forge through the high water, drawing behind it the single car jammed with humanity.

Tense, every sense alert, Easton carefully in-creased his speed. One mistake and all might perish within sight of land.

By now the raging wind had torn down every telegraph wire. Draped across the engine, caught in front of the smoke box and pilot, they grew tighter and tighter with every turn of the wheels. Suddenly there was a series of quick, sharp explosions. Telegraph pole after telegraph pole cracked and toppled over.

With wires and poles dragging along on either side, the *Bostonian*, like some prehistoric monster straining to escape from a jungle morass of choking vines and clutching quicksand, moved resolutely on.

Almost at the end of the causeway, Easton saw looming before him the hulk of a wrecked cabin cruiser. It was directly in his path. He slowed almost to a stop,

then drove forward. There was a sound of splintering, and the craft was nudged to one side.

A moment later he saw the top half of a house float majestically into view. Suddenly it swerved and bore down on the train, coming to rest ahead of the engine.

Easton halted a foot from the house. He had no idea how firmly it was wedged onto the tracks. If he tried to push it aside, as he had the cruiser, the *Bostonian* might jump the tracks.

But he had no choice. The sea was now almost as high as the cab. Easton gripped the throttle and pulled it back slowly. The engine groaned and moved forward, driving its nose into the side of the house. Easton added steam. There was a dull crunch and crash.

Now the engine was laboring. Easton, all but hold-ing his breath, dared to pull the throttle back farther . . . farther. . . . The house suddenly gave way. It slipped to one side and careened crazily off toward the distant shore.

Minutes later the *Bostonian* — one battered en-gine, one battered coach, and one indomitable engineer in control — chugged triumphantly into Stonington. The happy passengers cheered the engineer.

Not until later did they realize the ordeal they had undergone. The Hurricane of '38, during the few hours its force was unleashed upon the North Atlantic coast that day, killed more than 600 persons, caused the greatest property damage in hurricane history, and left more than 60,000 people homeless.

It damaged a quarter of a billion trees. It crushed 26,000 automobiles. It completely transformed part of the New England coastline. And for weeks after the storm, home owners in Vermont, 120 miles from the sea, took visitors to see their windows made white with ocean salt—a testament to the great wind that roared out of the tropics that memorable day.

17

The Two *Celias*

BY JOHN B. HAWKINS

The sailing era of the 1930s ended on September 21, 1938, when an unnamed and unheralded hurricane slammed into the New England coast. At the time, my brother Phil and I owned two boats. The *Celia I* was lying to an anchor toward the southeast end of Marion Harbor. She was a gaff-rigged 30-foot sloop on which Phil and I had been sailing since 1927, when I was only 13 and he 10. The other was the *Celia II,* a Friendship sloop we had bought only the year before. She was lying to a mooring near the upper landing off Steve Watt's boatyard.

My brother and I were planning to go for a short cruise that fateful day. By mid-morning, however, wind and sea were pounding into the harbor from the southeast with sufficient force not only to preclude beating out, but enough for us to row out to the *Celia II* and unbend her canvas. While I was sitting on the bowsprit to unsnap the jib, she began to dip me under with each wave. When the canvas was stowed below, it seemed as likely a time as any to get out another anchor. This was no small feat in that sea, though we had done it a thousand times in lesser waves, rowing upwind of the mooring to the limit of the line, then quickly tossing the anchor over. When we had gotten one anchor set, we bailed out the dink and repeated the process with the second anchor.

These activities must have consumed about two hours, bringing us up to noon, though for the next 12 hours time became indistinct—in memory it is all one big simultaneous event. Phil and I had gone below, but by this time the wind was strong enough to make it necessary to crawl out on deck. Waves were continuously breaking over the bow, and visibility was reduced to the nearest shore points. I realized that the tide was getting very high, when in reality it should have been low. I went below to look up high tide in Eldridge just as Phil yelled, "There's a driving float coming down on us; what do we do?"

"Just a minute," I called back. "I'm looking this up in the book." Phil made it explicitly clear that I would *not* find out what to do about it in a book.

The next thing we knew, all kinds of wreckage started drifting toward us—boats, pianos, refrigerators, small houses, anything that would float. We made no effort to fend them off because the weather was too violent for that, but instead watched in a sort of slow-motion stupor as they slid past, breaking the bowsprit, breaking the boom, and gouging our sides as they went. A 30-meter boat tangled her shrouds in our mast, then beat against our side until she sank. That gave us some small measure of satisfaction.

All this time, despite the mooring and the two anchors, we were slowly easing backward toward a stone pier over which the waves were breaking fiercely. We started the engine, a converted Model T, put it in gear, and found that about half throttle would stop the drift. The trouble was that there was gas in the tank for no more than two hours. This fact, plus the proximity of the breaking pier, plus the fear that some piano (they float legs up) would sever our lines, convinced us that the prudent course would be to leave.

Looking back over the years and considering the fact that the hurricane was probably blowing full force at this point, I am not sure just how prudent this decision really was. However, we left the motor going in gear and hauled in the dink flush with the transom. One minute it was above us, the next about ten feet below. By careful timing, I cut the line, then Phil and I jumped as she dropped beneath us. Incredibly, we both landed squarely in the bottom of the dink, which promptly took off backward up the harbor. I got out the oars and by frantic back-watering managed to guide our rush around all the floating debris. We floated right through the woods at the head of the harbor, finally touching bottom at the foot of a large pine tree. There we climbed out, tied the dink to a branch, and started walking back to town to find a vantage point to see how the *Celia I* was doing.

That was a mistake. After walking only a quarter of a mile, we were obliged to swim because the water was rising so fast. Obviously we would need the dink to continue. At that point, the roof of a house came floating by, and we promptly converted it into a raft. Paddling back in the direction of the dink, we were soon joined by rats that came swimming toward us to clamber aboard. Eventually, there were 12 with us on the raft. Incredibly, we paddled straight back through the woods to the pine tree where the dink was tied, though by now her nose was buried under the rising water. We dove down to the base of the tree, uncut the dink, wished the rats good luck, and started rowing back to town.

By now the water was about halfway up the first floor of most houses. As we rowed down the street, people called to us, offering us hundreds of dollars to remove their favorite possessions. Looking back I wonder why we did not take some of the offers, but I suspect we were too intent on getting back somewhere near the boat. We did, however, allow ourselves to be diverted by a man who called down to us that his daughter was ill with pneumonia and he wanted to remove her to dry land, where he had some arrangement to get her to the home of a relative. We rowed right through his front door and across the living room to the top of the staircase where he stood with a little girl in his arms. To my surprise, Phil jumped out of the dink and swam to the stairs, where he asked if he could use the bathroom. In equal surprise, the man pointed to a room on the second floor, and Phil promptly disappeared. After we rowed the man and his daughter to high ground, I asked Phil what had possessed him to ask for a bathroom at that particular moment. "I didn't want to pee in his living room" was the logical answer.

By this time, darkness was beginning to fall. Sometime earlier Steve's boathouse had caught fire, and while the local fire department was being submerged under 13 feet of water, it quietly burned itself down to the high-water mark. As it burned, all the boats stored inside caught fire, then started to float down the streets of the town. That was a scene worthy of Wagner: to be rowing down a street in the gathering darkness and see a blazing boat float around the corner. Luckily, they were all sailboats with no gasoline tanks. We spent the rest of the evening, until the water receded, nudging, poking, and towing burning hulks away from wood-shingle houses. Fortunately, the rain had been so heavy that no other fires started.

It was midnight before we got back to the stone pier, left dry by the receding water. A man was standing in the middle of it, staring at a dark mass that he called his "boat." On closer inspection, it appeared to be an engine block. We could not see the harbor through the murk and gloom, so we retired through the mud on the streets and the hulks of burned-out boats to the local Dutchland Farm, where, by the light of a few dim candles, we ate until dawn.

As we emerged into the dim light, the air was cool from the north and mist rose from the water, reflecting the dawn in grotesque colors. On the water's edge a large house was silhouetted, the ground floor gutted except for the studs, and on its rutted lawn sat two old women, crying. Beyond them, just visible through the mist, swinging to a northwest breeze, was the *Celia II,* and a hundred yards from her, intact, was the *Celia I.* They were the only boats afloat in the harbor. Relaunching the dink, we rowed ecstatically back to the *Celia II.* She looked as though she had been through a war, but she was floating beautifully. The engine, still in gear, had stalled with some gas still left in the tank. With a hacksaw we cut the rigging of two boats still tangled with our mast, then wrestled with the anchors, which were down halfway to China in the bottom. Eventually we got them out, started the engine, and went alongside the *Celia I.* Attached to only a single anchor, which was merely lying on the bottom, she was unmarred. We could only conclude that she must have dragged early in the blow, gone up into the woods, then been washed out again as the water receded. We towed her back to her anchor. When we came ashore, people asked, "How did you do it?"

Despite the devastation and lack of sleep, we were feeling pretty good, and I couldn't resist replying, to my brother's beaming approval, "We've been to sea before."   ∞

Where Were You When the Big Blow Hit?

Memories of Some '38 Hurricane Survivors

On September 20, 1938, John Conover returned from vacation to Harvard's Meteorological Observatory atop the Great Blue Hill in Milton, Massachusetts, where he lived and worked as an observer while attending classes at the Massachusetts Institute of Technology (MIT). When he arrived, he learned that Dr. Charles F. Brooks, director of the observatory, was monitoring a hurricane he believed would threaten New England.

"The Roar of the Wind Exceeded Anything We Had Ever Heard"

In those days, forecasts for New England were prepared in Washington, D.C., but the local office in Boston was permitted to modify the forecasts if they had reason to do so. On the morning of the twenty-first, Charles H. Pierce, a young researcher and former Harvard Observatory employee who was now working in the air mass analysis section in Washington, argued that the hurricane would move straight north and be near Burlington, Vermont, the next morning. However, the official forecasters overruled him by predicting an average track that would carry the hurricane southeast of Nantucket and out to sea. Since winds rotate counterclockwise around North Atlantic storms, the forecast for southern New England was for northeast storm warnings. Hurricane force winds from the south, which would occur if Pierce were right, were not forecast.

After 12:30 P.M. the wind increased from the southeast, and all personnel but Dave Arenberg and me went down the hill. I made a regional weather map from radio signals at two o'clock and found that the pressure had already fallen to 29.00 inches at Lakehurst, New Jersey. The storm was obviously more intense than anyone had imagined and was approaching rapidly. At 3:00 P.M. I started another map, but the power failed, and at 3:31 the windmill anemometer, an instrument to measure wind speed, disintegrated after showing a two-minute average speed of 83 miles per hour. The roar of the wind exceeded anything we had ever heard.

Without the windmill, wind speeds had to be read from a three-cup anemometer that was mechanically connected to a recorder on the third floor of the tower. The inked trace of the recorder showed that the wind averaged 84 miles per hour throughout the hour from 5:00 to 6:00 P.M. Enlarged photos of the trace showed that the highest wind for a five-minute period was 121 miles per hour, from 6:11 to 6:16 P.M. Since the instrument was not intended to record gusts, it was hard to determine how strong they had been. We took numerous readings and established a peak gust of 186 miles per hour, with a margin of error of 30 or 40 miles per hour.

Above: *John Conover.* **Opposite page, bottom:** *White Sands Beach, Connecticut.*

"We Wondered If We'd Ever See the Shore"

Above: *Fanne Case King.* **Below:** *A windswept beach near New London, Connecticut, during the Hurricane of '38.*

Fanne Case King of Orient, New York, was one of eight passengers aboard the ferryboat Catskill *as it made its regular noon crossing between Orient and New London, Connecticut.*

The hurricane caught up with us around 1:00 P.M., just outside New London, and we watched in horror as it pushed us toward the shore rocks. Our captain, Clarence Sherman, turned the boat around, heading back into the wind toward Long Island.

All afternoon that wind kept shifting and tossing us around, and almost everyone got violently ill. We were all scared out of our wits and worried about the crew struggling to control the ship because they were sick, too. When the wind pushed us past Orient, the captain ordered both anchors dropped, but they didn't hold. The wind pushed us back almost to Riverhead, even though the engines were going full steam ahead.

As the winds shifted again, the captain ordered both anchor chains cut and turned the boat once more toward New London. By now it was dark, everyone was exhausted, and we wondered if we'd ever see the shore. The Coast Guard met us at Southwest Ledge Light and told the captain to head for the coal yard at Groton, because the New London dock had been set ablaze by fallen electrical wires.

Finally, after ten hours on the sound, Captain Sherman eased alongside the coal yard dock. As we stumbled ashore, I was amazed to see that the *Catskill*'s only damage was some torn deck awnings. But Captain Sherman never recovered from that awful trip; he died the next year at age 64.

—as told to Linda Goetz Holmes

Frank Smith of Colchester, Connecticut, was to be married on Sunday, September 25, 1938. His mother noticed that he needed new pajamas and, over his objections, insisted that they drive into New London to buy them.

When we arrived and began hunting for a place to park, we noticed that it was rather windy. "The radio said there was a hurricane off Cape Hatteras," my mother remarked. "They thought the fringes of it might even hit the New Jersey coast tomorrow."

"That far north? Impossible!" I said.

I parked the car in front of a huge elm, and we started to walk. I looked back and saw a small branch break off the tree and land on the car roof. I went back and moved the car away from the elm, then rejoined my mother. There was a crash, and we looked back to see the elm going over, taking half the sidewalk with it.

"You'd almost think that this was the hurricane," my mother said.

We continued on to Bank Street, leaning against the gale, and bought the pajamas. When we left the store, it was almost impossible to walk. The air was filled with a kind of roaring shriek, and as we passed the railroad station, we could hear the waves battering the pier just across the tracks.

We headed out of New London in the drenching rain. Branches littered the streets. Some trees were being uprooted, and when I approached one, I would step on the gas to get by it. My mother asked me not to be so reckless.

Three miles outside the city, a fallen tree blocked the road completely. Another car pulled up behind us, and I got out to talk to the driver. "Looks like we're stuck awhile," I said. "Do you suppose this could be an actual hurricane?"

He laughed. "Well, it's pretty windy," he said. "But this is nothing. I've been in *real* hurricanes in Florida."

As we waited, the wind howling, debris flying, and trees crashing down right and left, he began to change his mind. "Maybe it *is* a hurricane at that," he admitted. "Not as bad as we have them in Florida, but pretty fair for Connecticut!"

Editor's Note: *Frank Smith and his mother eventually made it home. The blue pajamas he had bought survived the hurricane and 36 years of shuffling around in bureaus. He never wore them.*

"Pretty Fair for Connecticut"

Above: *Frank Smith.* **Below:** *Toppled trees in New London, Connecticut.*

Dan Fiske

"Apples Filled the Air Like Buckshot"

Dan Fiske was helping his father pick McIntosh apples in a hilltop orchard near Worcester, Massachusetts, when news of the hurricane's approach came over a car radio. The crew retreated to the safety of the storage packinghouse.

At a 1,000-foot elevation, we were exposed to the full screaming fury of the hurricane. A perpetual staccato broadside of everything loose tried to beat our shelter into the ground. At 100 miles per hour, apples filled the air like buckshot. Branches, trees, apple boxes, shingles, windows, and bricks all hammered at our building.

The next day, realization of the tremendous task that confronted us began to sink in. Our entire crop was on the ground, in some places knee-deep. Apple trees with a 30-foot spread were out of the ground, their massive roots exposed to the drying air. Younger trees were found half a mile from their original locations. When we finished our tally, 6,000 trees had been uprooted, about one-third of our plantings. Faced with such heartbreaking devastation, one neighbor went quietly into his cellar and hanged himself. Quite a number of New England orchards were abandoned forever after that disastrous day.

Ever Since Hurricane Gloria the Seagulls and Bugs Like Connecticut

Dick Pealer, manager of Groton-New London Airport, uses a snowplow year-round to keep the runways clear. According to the locals, seed oysters broke loose during the storm and rolled in toward the shallows—now making it possible for even the most unsophisticated gull to pick and choose whenever there's a low tide. "They drop 'em right over my airport on the runway. It's a mess."

Woolly adelgids are insects that destroy hemlocks, and according to Dr. Mark McClure, entomologist for Connecticut, "In the next three years, the entire state should see this insect. Long Island had infestations for years, but we never saw them before. I think Hurricane Gloria may have blown them across the Long Island Sound."

When the storm was over, the cleanup began. Margaret Bancroft wrote to a friend about the aftermath on her family's farm in Tyngsboro, Massachusetts.

W here once stood 75 acres of fine woodlot there now stretched an expanse of almost nothing. The entire acreage had been laid to waste. Trees from saplings to trunks two or three feet thick were lying like matchsticks—crisscrossed, twisted, splintered, and broken—leaving tall stumps in places. It was estimated that there would not be much good timber to salvage, and it would be several months before it could all be cleared and new trees started. It was a most sickening sight. It had been my favorite retreat, but not anymore.

Father remembered that morning that one of the cows was due to calve the day before and was somewhere in the woods. The first thing the men did was go look for the cow and new calf, hoping they were alive. After more than an hour of searching, they found the cow safe, standing quietly in a small clearing. Not far away was the newborn calf, curled into a ball in a circle of broken limbs and tree trunks. The cow was led back to the barn by my brother, and Father carried the little one in his arms, climbing over the tangle.

Above: *Margaret Bancroft.* **Below:** *After the hurricane, this is all that was left of a shed on the Bancroft farm.*

"It Was a Most Sickening Sight"

Even before the hurricane winds reached Weare, New Hampshire, a dam gave way under the weight of three days of heavy rain. Four persons drowned. Chester Colburn watched in horror from a few feet away.

"I Could See the Water Rising Higher and Higher"

Above: *Chester Colburn.* **Below:** *The breached dam at Weare, New Hampshire.*

All morning a gang of men had been attempting to sandbag the road and left wing of the dam, but even though the sand was just across the road in the gravel bank, they could not keep up. I could see the water rising higher and higher as it poured over the sandbags and down the road. It seemed only a matter of seconds before the road was gone. The water rushed at unbelievable speed through the gap, tearing into the gravel bank, sweeping four- and five-foot chunks of earth downstream.

Now that the road was gone, the wing of the dam, which ended at the road, was exposed to the full force of the flood. In 15 minutes the end of the dam was exposed, and the concrete core for the wing broke off and flopped toward the front of the dam. The flood left a gaping hole from the dam itself to the high gravel bank. The hole was more than 100 feet wide and about 40 feet deep.

Below the dam the Drewry Brothers toy shop had disintegrated entirely, water stretching across where it had been, covering the bridge and flowing all around the Drewrys' two-story colonial home. The big house seemed to toss a bit on its granite foundation. To my amazement, it floated up on the floodwater, leaning first one way and then the other, then floated down the river out of my sight.   ∞

The Hurricane Nobody Knew Was Coming

BY EVAN MCLEOD WYLIE

Outward bound from Hyannis on Cape Cod in a light southeast breeze, the *Fair Wind,* a 55-foot offshore lobster boat, sped across Nantucket Sound on Friday afternoon, November 21, 1980. In the pilothouse of the trim green-and-white craft, the 30-year-old skipper, Bill Garnos, checked over his charts, while at the wheel his mate, 33-year-old Ernie Hazard, held a course for the Great Round Shoal channel buoy east of Nantucket. Down in the galley, 22-year-old Rob Thayer whistled as he put together a supper of soup and sandwiches for all hands. On the open afterdeck, David Berry, still a month away from his twenty-first birthday, mended a trap line and shouted an exuberant greeting to the crew of another outbound lobster boat, the *Sea Fever.*

Aboard the *Fair Wind* there was the relaxed atmosphere and easy camaraderie of a seasoned crew, but the mood this afternoon was exceptionally lighthearted because this voyage was to be one of the last of the year. Since early April they had been working a grueling schedule that kept them at sea much of the time. But high market prices for lobster and rich hauls had made many a trip a bonanza. The night before they had celebrated their good fortune with steak dinners at the Back Side Saloon in Hyannis. Soon the *Fair Wind* would be dry-docked for winter overhaul while her crew scattered on winter vacations that ranged from the New England ski slopes to the Florida Keys.

Designed specifically for offshore lobstering, the *Fair Wind* was a rugged, all-steel vessel of 27 gross tons propelled by a 265-horsepower diesel engine, strengthened with five watertight bulkheads, and outfitted with the latest in sophisticated electronic navigational gear, including loran, radar, VHF radio, power steering, and automatic pilot. In equipment and attention to safety, the boat was one of the most highly rated in the New England fishing fleet. In the six years since it had been launched from a Massachusetts shipyard, it had proved itself to be a highly seaworthy craft. It confirmed the belief of its young owner, Charles Raymond of Beverly, Massachusetts, that a truly modern fishing vessel with a top-notch crew could operate safely and turn a profit for all hands. Raymond and his men had lavished so much attention on the boat that it had been nicknamed "the yacht."

Setting out to sea, the *Fair Wind* did not lack for company. Good weather and a favorable marine forecast for the weekend had brought forth scallopers, draggers, trawlers, and lobster boats from Maine to Rhode Island. Many were planning to work within ten to 20 miles of land, but the *Fair Wind* and *Sea Fever* were bound on a course that would take them into vastly different waters. Their destination was Georges Bank.

Lying far out in the Atlantic Ocean, 130 miles southeast of Cape Cod, Georges is one of the world's richest and most extraordinary fishing grounds. Its undersea terrain, spread over an area of 10,000 square miles, ranges from chasms and canyons thousands of feet deep to shoals so shallow that breaking seas often fling fountains of spray high in the air.

Here, near the edge of the continental shelf, the icy

green waters of the Labrador current collide with the warm waters of the Gulf Stream as it sweeps up the east coast of the United States and swings northeasterly toward Europe. The mingling of these two mighty ocean currents creates an upwelling of ocean-bottom water mixed with the minerals and microscopic plankton on which fish thrive. Cod and halibut spawn in the canyons and rise to feed among the layers of plankton that drift toward the upper sunlit waters. Lobsters dwell in the depths and ascend the walls of the canyons and gorges.

Bathed in bright sunshine on a sparkling summer day, Georges Bank can seem like a fisherman's paradise, but the immensity of its riches is matched by the perils of its dense fogs, treacherous tidal currents, and shifting shoals. As autumn wanes, the low atmospheric pressures of the warm Gulf Stream pull the cold air from the interior of the continent out to sea to create savage winter gales.

By dusk the *Fair Wind* had passed through Great Round Shoals channel and was breasting the long swells of the open Atlantic Ocean. As the lights of Nantucket faded on the horizon, night watches were set, and all hands save the man at the wheel settled into their bunks. The overnight run would bring them to Georges by 6:00 A.M. After that they would be hauling their trap lines for 48 hours straight.

In the darkened pilothouse, illuminated only by the faint glow from the loran and radar scopes, Ernie Hazard scanned the gauges of the droning diesel and held his course to the southeast. All seemed snug and serene. The 6:00 P.M. marine weather forecast on Friday, which the *Fair Wind* crew heard as they ate their soup and sandwiches, called for northwesterly winds 15 to 25 knots, shifting to southwesterly on Saturday. This was definitely good fishing weather for a sturdy vessel the size of the *Fair Wind,* and it was on the basis of this forecast that skipper Bill Garnos decided that they were definitely "go" for the weekend.

But at that moment they were, in fact, heading into the path of one of the most violent ocean storms to strike Georges Bank in this century. Far to the south, a gathering storm was heading northeast at 50 miles per hour. Unlike a land storm, which is monitored by dozens of land weather stations whose early warnings are spread far ahead, this offshore storm was moving north at night over the open sea. Clouds obscured it from conventional weather satellites. No ships or weather stations noted its force and progress.

Says Sherrill Smith of the Massachusetts Division of Marine Fisheries, "This was no ordinary winter storm system. It was an ocean hurricane of titanic proportions. When it reached Georges, it struck like an atomic bomb explosion."

As the *Fair Wind* arrived on Georges on Saturday morning, Ernie Hazard awoke to find the boat plunging heavily through the screaming gale. Hurriedly he joined Bill Garnos and Dave Berry in the pilothouse. They had already flooded the lobster tanks to try stabilizing the boat. Hazard and Rob Thayer moved out onto the deck to lash down all gear. The wind was now out of the northwest. It was too late to turn into the teeth of the gale and try to run back toward Hyannis. They were trapped on the Bank, and the seas were building behind them. Reducing speed, they ran with the seas, but the waves were enormous and were taking them on the stern. The *Fair Wind* was plunging deeper into the troughs.

Through heavy radio static they heard calls from another vessel. It sounded like the *Sea Fever,* but the words were garbled.

"Repeat your message," Bill Garnos responded. "We can't hear you. It's going crazy out here."

The *Sea Fever,* a 50-foot, wooden-hulled offshore lobster boat from Hyannis, also had been taken by surprise by the lack of storm warnings. At 5:00 A.M. when it arrived on Georges, the Boston weather forecasts still were predicting winds of 20 to 30 knots, but it was already blowing 50 to 60 knots, and the storm was intensifying fast.

At 11:00 A.M., when Boston finally broadcast a storm warning for all of Georges Bank, winds had reached 80 to 100 miles per hour.

The fury of the winds combined with the shoals and turbulent currents of the Bank produced towering, steep-walled, breaking seas such as most fishermen never see in a lifetime. "Each wave came at us like a mountain," says Richard Rowland, 22, of Danvers, Massachusetts, a crewman on the *Sea Fever.* "It was awesome."

As the *Sea Fever*'s skipper, Peter Brown, 24, of Swampscott, Massachusetts, wrestled to hold his boat's bow into the seas, a monstrous wave rushed toward them. Looking up, Rowland saw the wave cresting overhead. Then with a roar, it smashed down upon them, shattering the thick windows of the pilothouse. A torrent of water surged into the boat, knocking out the navigational equipment and flooding the bilges.

Turning downwind to avoid taking any more seas through the windows, Peter Brown shouted, "We've got to close up the bridge! Gary, take the wheel, and Dick, get me some boards."

As Peter Brown tied a rope around his waist so that he could climb out on deck to fix the broken windows,

The lobster boat Fair Wind, *in fairer days.*

Rowland knelt down to saw up a slab of wood. He heard Gary Brown (no relation to Peter) cry out as a wall of white water picked up the *Sea Fever* and hurled it on its side. The deck lurched beneath Rowland, and he slid into a corner, buried under water and wooden debris.

When he surfaced, he found that the boat was wallowing on its beam-ends with the pilothouse half-underwater and no engine power. Gary Brown had disappeared. At first Rowland thought he might still be buried in the submerged debris, but Gary had been hurled through the wall of the pilothouse, and Rowland caught sight of him drifting in the sea about 15 yards off the stern.

While Peter Brown dove down a hatch to try to start the engine, Rowland scrambled back along the slanting deck and tossed Gary a lifeline. Gary made no attempt to grab it. Peter had the engine going, and he swung the listing boat around to bring the bow over to Gary. He was in plain view off the port side, and they shouted and tossed him more lines, but he did not respond. His face was blank and glassy-eyed as if he had been stunned or was in shock. In another moment he had drifted out of sight.

On the radio, Peter Brown called, "Mayday. Mayday. We have a man overboard. We may be sinking."

On the 65-foot *Broadbill,* about 12 miles east of the *Sea Fever*, skipper Grant Moore of Westport, Massachusetts, heard the Mayday and turned his boat to respond. Taking seas that put his deck underwater from rail to rail, he fought his way through the storm, radioing reports on the *Sea Fever*'s plight to Coast Guard stations on Cape Cod.

The great offshore storm struck the New England coast such a glancing blow that most people were unaware that Saturday was any more than another blustery autumn day. The first persons on shore to discern the magnitude and intensity of the storm were the staff of the operations center of U.S. Coast Guard headquarters in Boston. The center, which directs all Coast Guard operations in the North Atlantic between Canada and Rhode Island, is manned 24 hours a day. Within its oblong, low-ceilinged chamber on the fourth floor of a building near North Station and the Boston Garden are crammed communication consoles, chart tables, a computer, wall maps studded with multicolored tags to mark the positions of ships and aircraft, and radio and telephone hot lines connected to a network that includes the U.S. Navy and Air Force, Canadian armed forces,

20 Coast Guard bases, and the Coast Guard air station at Otis Air Force Base on Cape Cod.

"It is not a place," says Chief Petty Officer James Fay, "where you sit and watch the world go by."

When Chief Fay arrived for a stretch of 24-hour duty at 5:30 A.M. on Saturday, "the telephones were ringing off the walls." One hour earlier, Lieutenant Robert Eccles had received a hot line call from the Coast Guard station at Point Judith, Rhode Island. Its radio room was picking up a Mayday from the 76-foot dragger *Determined,* which reported that it was sinking in heavy seas 30 miles east of Block Island.

On Eccles's list of available rescue craft the nearest large vessel was the Coast Guard cutter *Active,* which was en route to its home port in New Hampshire after a month of law enforcement patrols in Florida waters. It was steaming toward the Cape Cod Canal with a crew that was looking forward to a Thanksgiving holiday at home. But when called by Eccles, the *Active* swung around and sped toward the *Determined.* By 5:15 A.M. it had reached the vessel, which was wallowing close to the waterline in heavy seas, and the crew passed over a pump to try to stem the flooding.

At 6:00 A.M., as Lieutenant Eccles was briefing Chief Fay about this emergency, the Coast Guard station at Nantucket relayed a hot line report that the fishing vessel *Cape Star* was in serious trouble with a split bow off Chatham, Massachusetts. The Coast Guard station in Portland, Maine, came on the line with word that another fishing vessel, the *Sea Rose,* was sinking 15 miles east of the Isles of Shoals, and the Woods Hole station on Cape Cod was relaying a message from the *Nordic Pride* that the *Christina* was sinking on Georges Bank.

The Boston operations center began crackling out orders for patrol craft based in Portsmouth, New Hampshire, Boston, and Chatham to put to sea to aid the stricken vessels and alerted helicopter crews at the air station on Cape Cod to stand by for a rescue launch.

Messages continued to come in from the *Active.* The *Determined* was going down. Seas were too rough for the cutter to come alongside. A team of swimmers donned wet suits, and a cargo net was rigged. The crew of the *Determined,* clad in survival suits, leaped into the seas and were rescued by the *Active*'s swimmers. At 8:15 A.M. all were safe, and the *Determined* disappeared beneath the waves.

In Boston, a continuous stream of distress calls was monitored, and rescue units were being marshaled and dispatched. Lieutenant Eccles, who had been relieved by Lieutenant James Decker at 9:00 A.M. on Saturday, stayed at Decker's side all afternoon. They

were joined by Lieutenant Gary Krizanovic, who had been summoned from Gloucester.

"We had eight search-and-rescue operations going," said Eccles, "including four 'sinkers.' We were getting burned out trying to keep up with the storm."

Behind the *Fair Wind* the seas were building higher and steeper and the boat was plunging deeper into the troughs. Fearful that he might capsize, Bill Garnos maneuvered the boat around to face the towering waves. The wind, rising to a screaming pitch, was sucking the bait out of the barrels, and the surface of the ocean was lashed into such a boiling fury that the *Fair Wind* seemed to be buried in foam. The waves, Ernie Hazard guessed, were now 60 to 70 feet high. The *Fair Wind* rose to meet each one, battling toward the crest. Looking up, Hazard saw a huge wave looming up beyond the bow. It burst thunderously over the top of the pilothouse, and under the avalanche of water, the *Fair Wind* was almost driven beneath the sea.

The next wave was even more gigantic. As the *Fair Wind* fought its way up the slope, a rogue wave broke sideways and spun the boat completely around. Caught on the face of the wave, the *Fair Wind* hurtled

Opposite page: *Captain Bill Garnos, 30, of Beverly, Massachusetts, was finishing his sixth season aboard the* Fair Wind *and his second year as her skipper.* **Left:** *Rob Thayer, 22, of Hamilton had joined the crew only that spring.* **Bottom:** *David Berry, 20, of Marblehead was the most experienced lobsterman in the crew, although he was also the youngest.*

headlong down into the trough. As her bow buried itself in the sea, the stern shot skyward. In a matter of seconds, the *Fair Wind* had "pitch-poled," turning completely upside down.

Ernie Hazard found himself underwater in icy darkness. Groping and struggling, he collided with hard metal and realized that he must still be inside the pilothouse. His head broke out into a pocket of air, and he gulped it down into his lungs. He knew he had to get out, but it was impossible to get oriented. He saw a block of dim light and swam and groped toward it, desperate for more air. He bumped hard on a metal doorway, swam through it, and then suddenly emerged, gasping and choking, in the sea beside the overturned boat. The exposed propeller was screaming as the engine raced out of control. Waves surged over the hull. He had surfaced on the windward side, and the overturned boat was blowing away from him. Alone in the sea, he thought, I've got to make it back to the boat. Maybe the hull will float. Spying a floating bucket, Hazard overturned it to trap its air and, clinging to it as if it were a barrel, kicked and bodysurfed down the next wave to try to reach the boat. As he reached the hull, he was astonished to see that an orange-colored canopy raft was bobbing in the water on the far side of the boat.

It was a Givens Buoy Life Raft, invented and built by Jim Givens of Tiverton, Rhode Island. An all-weather, self-righting raft, the Givens consisted of two rings of heavy-duty neoprene, five feet in diameter, covered by a protective nylon rip-stop canopy supported by three inflated arch tubes. Attached to the bottom of the raft was a submerged ballast chamber with a capacity of 2,900 pounds of water designed to keep the raft stable in high winds or heavy seas. Within the circular shelter of the canopy was space for six people.

Hazard battled his way around the drifting hull until he reached the raft. There was a small door in the side of the canopy, and he pulled himself inside, hoping he would find himself reunited with his crew mates. The raft was empty. Hazard recognized it as the raft that had been stored in a canister on the roof of the pilot-house. When the *Fair Wind* had overturned, the raft had been torn loose and some miracle had yanked the lanyard, which caused it to inflate automatically. Now it bobbed and tugged at the end of the lanyard, which was still attached to the boat. Crouched inside the raft, Hazard caught his breath and waited, praying that he would see one or more of his shipmates rise to the surface. They might still be alive in air pockets inside the pilot-house and might escape at any moment. He was shaking from shock and immersion in the icy cold water. In his fight to stay afloat he had kicked off his shoes and cast aside a wool jacket, and now he was wearing only soaking wet jeans, socks, and a sweatshirt.

Despite the huge seas that surged over the partially submerged *Fair Wind*, the Givens raft was riding well at the end of its tether. The large ballast bag beneath the raft had filled with water and was providing great stability, but the constant yanking and tugging on the line that secured the raft to the boat was placing a great strain on the undersea bag, and it was being ripped open.

About an hour passed, and still there was no sign of life from within the *Fair Wind*. The submerged hull was sinking beneath the waves. Fearful that he and the raft would be pulled under, Ernie Hazard loosened the line, and the raft drifted swiftly away.

As Hazard's raft drifted away from the *Fair Wind*,

it was still engulfed in winds and seas of hurricane force. Only one other life raft is know to have survived passing through the center of a hurricane at sea, and that, too, was a Givens. But the damage that Hazard's raft had suffered while it was tethered to the submerged hull had made it less stable, and as giant seas hurled it from the crests to the troughs, it tipped and pitched so wildly that Hazard considered lashing himself to rings in the canopy's wall. He decided against it, fearing that if the raft overturned, he might not be able to escape. A moment later he regretted his decision as a wave burst in through the door and swept him out of the raft. As the raft drifted away, Hazard swam frantically to overtake it and climbed back inside.

Within a short time another mammoth sea picked up the raft and turned it completely upside down. As the submerged canopy filled with water, Hazard groped his way to the door and swam to the surface, but now he was without shelter from the driving spray and screech-

ing gale. He glimpsed a hole that had been ripped in the bottom of the ballast bag and thrust himself down inside it. He was in water up to his neck, but at least he was protected from the terrible wind.

Another wave rose beneath the raft and heaved it on its side. The wind caught the canopy and flipped it right side up. Hazard was again in underwater darkness inside the ballast bag, and when he tried to swim free, he found that his sweatshirt was snagged. Battling with his last breath as the bag filled with water, Hazard tore off his sweatshirt and left it behind. Kicking and swimming, he wriggled out of the hole in the ballast bag, swam back to the surface, and crawled back inside the canopy. He found himself seated in two feet of water, naked to the waist.

Grimly he told himself, *So long as this thing floats, I'm going to hang on!*

Locking his hands in the straps on the canopy's wall, he braced himself within the raft with his back against the rear wall and his feet toward the front door. Once again he felt another mountainous sea carrying the raft toward its crest. Up it went and then again turned upside down. Briefly Hazard hung upside down, spread-eagled within the canopy, and then the breaking crest of the wave surged past and the raft righted itself.

Hazard was like a man in a barrel going over Niagara Falls. Relentlessly the seas tumbled the raft, spun it, buried it, and sent it careening from crest to trough. Tons of water smashed over the canopy's arched roof and surged in and out of the door hatch, but the raft continued to float. Hazard hung on.

Night had fallen over the Atlantic Ocean when Helicopter 76, piloted by Lieutenants Buck Baley and Joseph Touzin, lifted off from the Coast Guard air station on Cape Cod with pumps for the *Sea Fever*. As they flew out over Nantucket, the moon was shining, but soon they encountered the solid cloud mass of the storm and were forced to drop down to within a few hundred feet of the ocean. The wind, still strong out of the northwest behind them, propelled the big twin-engine helicopter at a fast clip, but its crew was keenly aware that on the return flight they would be bucking that wind as their fuel tanks emptied. If the helicopter went down in the violent seas beneath them, it would probably capsize, and there would be no one to rescue them.

Flying on instruments, they arrived on Georges Bank and began calling the *Sea Fever* and the *Broadbill*, homing in on their radio signals. Two other fishing vessels had joined the *Broadbill*'s vigil over the *Sea Fever*. They were the *Reliance*, commanded by Allan Eagles of Newport, Rhode Island, and the *Stephanie Vaughan*, a long-liner. Finally the helicopter sighted the cluster of white deck lights in the black sea.

Hovering 50 feet above the water, Lieutenants Baley and Touzin inched their helicopter closer until they were directly over the *Sea Fever*. In the glare of the chopper's floodlights, they could see that part of the pilothouse was missing and waves were breaking over the stern.

"Do you wish to remain with your vessel, or do you wish to be lifted off by hoists?" they radioed. It

Lieutenants James Decker (**left**) *and Robert Eccles* (**right**) *were on duty at the U.S. Coast Guard's Boston Operations Center during the hurricane, keeping track of distressed vessels and sending ships and aircraft to their assistance.*

wouldn't be easy: Winds were still over 40 knots, and seas were running 20 feet.

"We will stay with the boat," Peter Brown answered.

"Stand by for the pump," replied the men in the chopper.

Down went a drop line, and Petty Officers Davern and Smith wrestled the pump into the open doorway of the helicopter. Below, on the heaving deck of the *Sea Fever,* Richard Rowland and Peter Brown were grabbing for the line. There was little time for mistakes. Fuel limits would soon reach the point of no return. Now Brown and Rowland had the drop line aboard, and Davern and Smith winched down the pump.

As soon as the pump was safely aboard the *Sea Fever,* Helo 76 veered off and switched on its "Night Sun." In its three-million-candlepower beam, they searched the sea for any sign of Gary Brown, who had been washed overboard that morning. Then, with its fuel gauge dropping, the helicopter swung around and started the long flight toward Cape Cod.

In the Coast Guard's Boston operations center, Lieutenant Robert Eccles reviewed the situation at 11:00 P.M. Saturday. From Georges Bank came reports that the pump that had been delivered to the *Sea Fever* was stemming the flooding. The cutter *Active* was due on the scene at daybreak. The sunken *Christina*'s men were safely aboard the *Nordic Pride.* Motor lifeboats from Chatham and Provincetown were towing in the *Cape Star.* A helicopter from the Cape Cod air station had guided the *Christina Marie,* another disabled fishing boat, through the treacherous shoals north of Nantucket, and the cutter *Cape Horn* was escorting the vessel toward Hyannis. The dragger *Barbara and Christene* had sunk, but her four crewmen had been rescued. No other ships were reported missing. Eccles concluded that one of the most hectic days in the history of the center was winding down, and after being on duty for more than 38 hours, he bade Fay, Krizanovic, and Decker good night and went home.

Out on Georges Bank, Ernie Hazard was still alive in the Givens raft. Before darkness fell, he had discovered that the raft contained a canvas survival kit and two paddles. Using the blade of a paddle as a shovel, he scooped and bailed water out the door until he was exhausted. Outside the storm still raged, and gusts of wind-driven spray hammered on the canopy like machine-gun fire. Alternately bailing and dozing off, Hazard fought to hold on until morning.

Hazard awoke at dawn. It was Sunday, November 23. The wind had dropped, but there was still a heavy sea running with tremendous swells. The raft wallowed in them, and when Hazard craned his neck out the door, he could see nothing.

Taking stock of his situation, Hazard found that he was bruised and sore from being flung about within the raft, but no bones appeared to be broken. Sorting out the contents of the survival bag, he found that it contained six 10-ounce cans of fresh water, a can of high-protein cookies, a can opener, a small bellows pump for the raft's air chambers, two packages of hand-held signal flares, and a small canister of Smith and Wesson flare cartridges. Secured to the canopy outside the door of the raft was a coil of heaving line and a small, blunt-nosed knife.

Hazard marveled at the cans of fresh water, which, although badly dented from the pounding of the seas, were still intact. He opened one and drank it slowly and also allowed himself one protein cookie. He dared eat no more than one because he had no idea how long he might have to wait to be rescued. The sea seemed warmer to him. He estimated it at about 50 to 55 degrees and guessed that wind and current were carrying the raft southeast, toward the edge of the Gulf Stream. Although it would be warmer, it also meant that he must be nearing the edge of the continental shelf, and that the chance of being sighted by a fishing vessel was slim.

A strong, self-reliant man who enjoyed challenges—he had once bicycled from Seattle to Mexico as a vacation jaunt—Hazard realized that endurance was now his only weapon. Although he seemed to have survived the abating storm, it had left him adrift as a solitary speck in a wintry ocean. It seemed quite likely that he was the only one who knew that the *Fair Wind* had been sunk. The boat was not expected back in port until Tuesday, and it would be some time after that before it would be presumed missing and a search begun. By that time the Gulf Stream might have carried the raft far out into the Atlantic toward Europe.

Thinking about all these things and his friends on the *Fair Wind* disturbed Hazard greatly, and he turned to keeping himself occupied. He cut the heaving line into sections and tied up a hammock for his survival kit. With the tip of the can opener, he punched some holes in the canopy around the door and, after scooping and bailing out most of the water, used some more of the line to sew the door shut to keep out wind and water. He massaged his legs and feet, which were numb and blue from the cold water in which he had been kneeling and sitting, finished nibbling on the cookie, and decided to rest until dark. The chance of such a small raft being sighted by day was slight. He would stay awake during the night, and if he heard an aircraft or a boat's engine, he would risk firing a flare into the sky.

He was aroused from his dozing by an ominous hissing. A damaged valve in the neoprene ring that formed the base of the raft was leaking air, and above his head the inflated arches that supported the canopy were sagging. The roof was literally falling in on him. Quickly he seized the small hand pump and began pumping air back into the valve. It reinflated the arches, but now behind him there was another hissing sound, and he found that another valve in an opposite corner of the raft was leaking. With his knife he cut patches from the survival bag and tried to tie off the leaks. But he could not stop them completely, and suddenly it became clear that there would be no time for sleeping. He would have to keep pumping one valve, tying it off, and then turning to pump the other. His legs were numb from kneeling, and there was no longer any feeling in his swollen feet. He was afraid that they were already frostbitten and that, without dry clothing, hypothermia would soon overwhelm him.

"You don't want to admit you're going to get beat," he told himself. "It's better to keep working."

It also helped to keep his mind off the *Fair Wind.* "Better not to think when you're alone," he said. "Keep going. Keep busy." And so, during the blackness of Sunday night, he pumped air, rested, dozed, and then awakened to pump again.

Ernie Hazard, 33, of Peabody, Massachusetts, gave up his job as a machinist to become a lobsterman aboard the Fair Wind.

Arriving on Georges Bank at dawn on Sunday, the Coast Guard cutter *Active* found the *Sea Fever* still afloat. The pump delivered by the Coast Guard helicopter on Saturday evening had been able to stem the flooding. The three fishing vessels were standing by, and the *Broadbill* had passed over hot coffee and nails and plywood to patch up the smashed pilot-house. As the *Active* undertook escorting the crippled *Sea Fever* back toward Cape Cod, there was talk between the ships about other boats on Georges that might be in trouble. No one, it was learned, had heard from the *Fair Wind,* and at 7:30 A.M. Grant Moore, skipper of the *Broadbill,* recalled that he had last had radio contact with the boat at 10:00 A.M. on Saturday.

In his home in Beverly, Massachusetts, the *Fair Wind*'s owner, Charlie Raymond, was aroused by a ringing phone. "This is the radio marine operator," a voice said. "I have a call for you from the fishing vessel *Broadbill.*"

"Charlie," said Grant Moore, "I am out on Georges. We have been in a bad blow. Have you heard from your boat?"

It was the first inkling Raymond had that the *Fair Wind* might be in trouble. So strong was his faith in the boat and her crew that he assumed their radio antenna had been damaged in the storm.

Quickly he notified the Coast Guard. In the Boston operations center, Chief Fay and Lieutenant Decker, who had been looking forward to going home after a hectic 24 hours, found themselves swept up in a new search-and-rescue effort. The cutter *Active* was directed to turn over the *Sea Fever* escort to another fishing vessel and return at once to Georges Bank to resume the search.

Once more helicopters were launched from Cape Cod. A large HU-16-E aircraft out on patrol from Otis Air Force Base was summoned to fly a search pattern that scanned 5,000 square miles. Coast Guard shore stations from New Hampshire to Rhode Island began calling the *Fair Wind* on their radios, and an urgent bulletin about the missing vessel was broadcast.

Sunday passed with no aircraft sighting of debris and no radio signals. The *Fair Wind* and its crew had vanished. By late Sunday, the Boston operations center was convinced that the boat was sunk. The remaining question—were there any survivors—had to be answered quickly, because in late November the life expectancy of a man in the water is short.

Lieutenant Joseph Duncan, search planner, backed by a computer, began calculating the area to search, based on winds and currents. The major offshore search would continue through Sunday night with a C-130 from Elizabeth City, North Carolina, scanning another 10,000 square miles. On Monday there would be the *Active* and three large patrol planes. The search area was now beyond the range of helicopters.

Seeking further assistance, Lieutenant Duncan picked up a hot line and called the U.S. Naval Air Station in Brunswick, Maine. Based there was a squadron of long-range P-3 patrol planes whose anti-submarine and reconnaissance flights carried them far out into the Atlantic Ocean between Nova Scotia and Bermuda. Carrying a crew of eleven airmen and sophisticated electronic scanning equipment, each huge P-3 could stay aloft for a full day or night and search an immense range of ocean. At dawn on Monday, a P-3 from Squadron VP-10, headed by Commander William Lash and Lieutenant Commander Alfred Linberger, was airborne to search an area 350 miles east of New York.

Peering out the door of his raft on Monday morning, Ernie Hazard noted that the skies were clearing. He was alone amidst the long swells of the Atlantic Ocean. The drift of his raft seemed to be toward the rising sun, farther and farther from land. A few birds flashed by, flying close to the water, and he recognized them as storm petrels and shearwaters, which dwell hundreds of miles at sea.

The sun would slowly warm the raft's interior, but Hazard doubted that it would do him much good. Exhaustion and hypothermia were overwhelming him. He was finding it difficult to move his legs. He was now too weak to pump air much longer.

Dimly he became aware of the drone of a large jet aircraft, and craning his neck out the door of the canopy, he saw a plane passing on a course to the west. Lunging for his survival bag, he seized the Smith and Wesson signal flare kit and pressed the trigger, praying

it would fire. There was a sharp pop, and a red flare, trailing smoke and sparks, shot skyward, arching high into the sky before it dropped back into the sea.

Had they seen it? He could not tell, and not daring to wait, Hazard fired again. Another flare rocketed skyward, and this time Hazard saw the wing of the plane dip.

Aboard the P-3, radioman Craig Martin had just reported to the pilots that he thought he had spotted something, possibly a life raft. Commander Lash swung the aircraft around for a closer look and then saw the flares and a man in the raft waving an orange cloth.

It was 8:35 A.M. when their radio message was flashed to the *Active* and relayed back to Boston operations. The P-3 came thundering low over the waves to drop a smoke buoy as Ernie Hazard hung out the raft door feebly waving his orange survival bag.

Soon there were other planes in the sky. A Coast Guard C-130 dropped a portable radio, but it fell some distance from the raft, and before Hazard could retrieve it, another Coast Guard plane dropped a string of orange marker buoys in a scatter pattern. As Hazard's raft drifted close to one, he picked it up. Within it was a message: "If other crewmen aboard raft, wave."

For the first time, Hazard felt deep anguish overwhelm him. It confirmed what he had been putting out of his mind for two days: He was the only survivor.

As the planes circled, he kept pumping to keep the raft inflated. On the horizon he glimpsed a hull, the bow of a white cutter emblazoned with bright reddish orange stripes. The cutter *Active* was steaming in for a pickup.

A whaleboat was lowered over the side, and a crew of three came alongside the raft. "Could I have your name, please," a seaman with a portable radio was saying.

As Hazard mumbled a hoarse reply, the men peered inside and asked, "There is no one with you? There was no one else?"

Aboard the *Active,* Hazard was buried in blankets and revived with mugs of coffee and clam chowder. He was suffering from multiple abrasions, frostbite, and hypothermia and needed hospitalization just as soon as possible.

As soon as the *Active* reported that a raft had been sighted by the P-3, Helicopter 1484, with Lieutenants Baley and Touzin again at the controls, flew from Cape Cod to Nantucket to stand by for a possible transfer of its survivor. When further word was received from the cutter that Ernie Hazard would require medical supervision en route, Linda True, 23, an emergency medical technician with the Nantucket fire department, was out-

Judge Rules Forecasters at Fault
for Failing to Call Storm

Four years after the tragic hurricane on Georges Bank, survivors of the dead sailors aboard the Fair Wind *and* The Sea Fever *went to court in an attempt to prove that the unexpected storm should have been predicted.*

BOSTON (AP)—A federal judge ruled yesterday that the National Oceanic and Atmospheric Administration is liable for the deaths of three lobstermen lost at sea four years ago when weather forecasters failed to predict a violent storm 150 miles off the Massachusetts coast.

"It's very significant because it's the first case in which the United States was held responsible for basically an inaccurate forecast," said Michael Latti, a Boston attorney who represented the fishermen's surviving relatives. "We're delighted."

In a 40-page opinion, U.S. District Judge Joseph Tauro said the federal agency negligently failed for nearly three months to repair a broken weather buoy that could have provided an accurate forecast of the storm that produced 60-foot waves and 100-mph winds.

Latti said previous court rulings have held that the National Weather Service cannot be held responsible for a faulty forecast.

"But here Tauro says there's an exception to that rule—when you don't maintain your equipment properly," the attorney said.

Tauro, who presided over a week-long non-jury trial, must hold a second trial to assess damages. He set January 28 for a pre-trial conference.

"We're obviously disappointed," said Don Witten, public affairs officer for the National Weather Service in Silver Spring, Maryland. "I would assume that the agency will appeal, but that's a decision that will ultimately be made by the Department of Justice."

The $3.2 million lawsuit was filed by the surviving relatives of three of four fishermen presumed drowned November 22, 1980, a day after they set out in fair weather from Cape Cod for a week of lobster fishing on the remote Georges Bank.

According to testimony at the trial, the fishermen were taken by surprise by the fierce storm.

William Garnos, 30, of Beverly, David Berry, 20, of Marblehead, and Robert Thayer, 22, of Hamilton disappeared when their fishing boat, the *Fair Wind* upended and sank.

Another crew member, 33-year-old Ernest Hazard of Peabody, climbed onto a life raft and drifted for 48 hours before he was spotted by a Navy plane and rescued by the Coast Guard.

Less than two hours after the *Fair Wind* went under, 25-year-old Gary Brown, of Plymouth, was swept overboard while trying to steer his vessel, the *Sea Fever*.

Relatives of Berry, Garnos, and Brown claimed the mariners relied on a National Weather Service forecast calling for good weather when they set out from Hyannis on a 12-hour voyage to the Atlantic fishing grounds.

David Hutchinson, a U.S. Justice Department attorney who represented the federal weather agency, claimed in court documents that the storm came up so suddenly that it could not have been predicted when the fishermen set out. He also said that the National Weather Service provides forecasts as a public service and has no liability if they turn out to be wrong.

But in his ruling, Tauro said that once NOAA, the overall federal agency responsible for weather forecasting, decided to undertake the task of providing forecasts for mariners, it had a duty to those fishermen to make sure its predictions were correct. The National Weather Service was unable to get a complete picture of weather on Georges Bank because of malfunctioning wind sensors on a key weather buoy, the judge said.

"Forecasters rely on buoy data because it is more accurate than other available surface observations, such as communications from passing ships," the judge wrote.

He added that even though the National Weather Service was aware of the buoy's importance to a Georges Bank forecast, the buoy "was permitted to remain in disrepair for 2½ months prior to this incident."

Tauro also criticized the weather agency for failing to warn the fishermen that its forecasts for Georges Bank were based on incomplete data.

"Small vessel fishermen had faith that the buoy data, and the forecasts based thereon, provided the most accurate and up-to-date 'snapshot' of weather conditions at various locations where they intended to fish," he wrote.

From an Associated Press wire service article, December 22, 1984. Reprinted courtesy of The Associated Press.

Editor's Note: *The National Oceanic and Atmospheric Administration (NOAA) did appeal the decision. Judge Tauro's ruling was overturned by a higher court.* ∞

fitted with a survival suit for the long-range ocean flight.

At 2:30 P.M. the helicopter was hovering over the *Active* on Georges Bank. Ernie Hazard, reviving after treatment on the cutter, protested when he was carried out on the afterdeck on a stretcher and saw the hoist line dangling from the chopper. The prospect of being plunged once again into the icy ocean terrified him, but in a few moments he had been winched aboard the helicopter and was en route to a hospital in Beverly, with Linda True at his side. Swift medical treatment enabled him to make a complete recovery.

Throughout Monday and Tuesday, the *Active,* assisted by Navy and Coast Guard patrol planes, continued to search the ocean, but no more survivors or wreckage were found. The weather had cleared, and, in the serenity of the long ocean swells, all traces of one of the most violent storms in the history of Georges Bank had disappeared.

The *Fair Wind* is believed to lie in water nearly two miles deep. Its three crewmen and Gary Brown of the *Sea Fever* join the legions of fishermen whose lives have been lost at sea.   ∞

The Yankee Gale

BY ROLAND H. SHERWOOD

The hardy fishermen out of the port of Gloucester learned very early in their fishing experience that one of the richest fishing grounds in the world lay in the Gulf of St. Lawrence, just off the great crescent shape of Prince Edward Island, Canada.

This knowledge, while it brought them rich cargoes of fish, was of little value when hundreds of fishing vessels were caught in a freak storm, the worst in the history of Prince Edward Island. This maritime disaster was to become known as "The Yankee Gale," since the majority of fishing vessels, and those who lost their lives in the storm, were from the New England states.

On those fatal days, October 3–5, 1851, the greatest concentration of American fishing vessels that year was on the gulf's fishing grounds. Although all the men on the schooners were classed as fishermen, the majority were actually college students, teachers, and college professors spending their holidays working on the boats.

Prior to the storm, there was no indication that one was brewing, although Friday, October 3, felt singularly warm for late autumn. The morning sun came up from the sea in a blaze of splendor and during the forenoon was surrounded by a halo of peculiar color and brightness. By afternoon the halo had disappeared, the sun was obscured by a thick haze, and cloud formations were of such extraordinary shape and color as to cause alarm on many of the vessels.

During the spectacle, the waters of the Gulf of St. Lawrence were as still as a millpond, the surface having a glassy appearance as if thousands of barrels of oil had been poured upon the waters. An unusual aspect of the strange calm on that Friday afternoon before the storm was the fact that not a single fish was taken by the hundreds of fishing vessels in the gulf.

As night came on, a heavy swell from the east began to heave the waters. This in itself was peculiar, for there wasn't a breath of wind. Ships far out on the water, and objects at a distance on the land, seemed to float above the sea and the earth, while distant sounds could be heard with amazing distinctness. Thousands of sea birds went winging in toward the land as if fleeing before a gale. And yet there was still no indication of a storm.

By late afternoon, some of the fishing vessels began to make toward the harbors, but the majority stood out to sea. When night dropped over the ships, the darkness was so intense that, it was later reported, "it could almost be felt."

At eight o'clock that evening, a slight breeze began to blow from the northeast, and a fine drizzle of rain relieved the heaviness of the atmosphere. The wind and rain increased in intensity as the night hours advanced. By midnight a vicious gale was lashing the coast of Prince Edward Island, and a driving downpour of rain beat hard upon the land.

There was no letup in the fury of the storm that night, and it continued all day Saturday and into Saturday night. By noon on Sunday, the wind began to abate and gradually die away, leaving in its wake the wreckage of hundreds of fishing vessels and the bodies of many men scattered along the island's shore.

Newspapers of the time carried reports of the

mountainous waves that came thundering in, to break with the sound of heavy gunfire that could be heard for miles inland. They reported that, during the height of the storm on Saturday, October 4, hundreds of vessels were pounded to pieces on the shore, and there were vivid descriptions of the destruction caused by the rain that beat in torrents and by the gale-force winds that shrieked over the sea and the land. Reports told of vessels driven in on every shore, smashing to bits with the impact and hurling dead bodies far up on the land while witnesses stood helpless.

A story from Rustico told how, on the Saturday afternoon of the storm, a dismantled schooner was picked up by a giant incoming wave and flung 300 feet inland from the shore, and how, within a mile of that wreck, three other vessels were hurled into the pastures that skirted the shore. Following the storm, the people of the little village of Rustico found, in one pasture alone, 36 bodies of men from the fishing fleet. Bodies were found lashed to the rigging, fastened to stumps of masts, or half-buried in the sands of the beaches.

The storm damaged more than the ships, for the gale beat every inch of the island, with water rushing in over shore acres that had never before been underwater. Buildings, bridges, milldams, fences, and trees were blown down and carried away by the wind and the water.

When the great storm was over, and the work of finding and checking the large number of wrecked ves-

sels got under way, only 50 hulks could be identified, all the others being just so much broken timber.

From one end of Prince Edward Island to the other, the task of locating and reporting the wrecks went on. Among the fragments of dories and vessels that littered the shore, a great variety of gear and supplies was found. Mixed with the wreckage of the vessels and shredded sails were barrels of flour, broken and soggy; great quantities of fish, trunks, ropes, spars, clothing, and musical instruments; and books, barometers, anchors, chairs, tables, chronometers, clocks, and bedding. Most of the bodies that washed ashore were stripped of clothing by the relentless pounding of the storm-lashed sea.

Within an area of 40 miles of Savage Harbor, 32 vessels lay shattered upon the shore. At Richmond Bay, 24 fishing schooners had been reduced to clusters of broken timbers, while from Richmond Bay to Cape North, another 17 vessels had been beaten to death by the storm and the sea.

A proclamation was issued asking the people of the island to salvage as much as possible for return to the rightful owners, but no such proclamation was necessary. The islanders were hard at work at the storm's end, aiding those who were injured, gathering the dead for burial, and salvaging materials. They opened their homes to survivors, fed and clothed the men, built coffins, and buried the dead.

The Great September Gale

One of the most destructive hurricanes in New England's history struck the region's coast on Sunday, September 23, 1815. After hitting Long Island, the storm tracked inland, bisecting the six-state region from Saybrook, Connecticut, to Canada. Although causing widespread deforestation in central New England, the storm's main fury was unleashed on Providence and Narragansett Bay.

As in the Hurricane of '38, the chief danger to the coastal cities of New England came from flooding associated with the storm and the powerful tidal surge, which carried oceangoing vessels far up into the streets of Providence. The ship *Ganges* skewered its bowsprit through the third floor of the Washington Insurance Building. A bridge joining the two parts of the city was destroyed as ships, loose from their moorings, drifted farther upstream. A General Lippet returned to find a ship in his garden, while a Mr. Webb discovered a wayward sloop sitting upright in front of his door.

Several noted authors have immortalized the Great September Gale and its effects, among them Oliver Wendell Holmes, who wrote a poem celebrating the storm. The twentieth-century horror writer H.P. Lovecraft even slipped in a historical footnote on the ships sailing through the streets of his hometown, Providence, in his famous short story, "The Shunned House."

New England Vessels Lost in "The Yankee Gale"

Fair Play, Portland, Maine . . . 7 lost
Traveller, Newburyport, Massachusetts . . . 8 lost
Statesman, Newburyport, Massachusetts . . . 10 lost
American, Lubec, Maine . . . 9 lost
Belena, Portsmouth, New Hampshire . . . 10 lost
Skip Jack, came in with 12 bodies
Flirt, Gloucester, Massachusetts . . . 13 lost
Mary Moulton, Castine, Maine . . . 14 lost
Franklin Dexter, Dennis, Maine . . . 10 lost

Following the storm, owners of fishing vessels sent a number of trustworthy men to investigate and report on their losses. After a long and exhaustive inquiry, this delegation concluded that of the vessels hailing from Gloucester, 19 were lost or destroyed. The number of people stranded on the shores of Prince Edward Island was estimated at 74, and the number of lives lost was estimated at 160.

A representation based on eyewitness accounts of the Yankee Gale of October 1851.

A grim incident was reported in connection with one fishing vessel out of Gloucester. This was the *Franklin Dexter,* one of the many American vessels fishing in the gulf at the time of the storm. She was driven ashore and totally wrecked at Cavendish. The bodies of her crew were found and buried by the residents.

A short time later, after word of the disaster reached the *Franklin Dexter*'s home port of Gloucester, the owner of the vessel arrived at Cavendish. He had the bodies exhumed and put aboard the *Seth Hal,* another New England vessel, for transport to Gloucester, so the bodies of the drowned fishermen might rest in their home plots. But the gods that guard the fates of fishermen must have decreed otherwise. The *Seth Hal* sailed in the fairest of weather, but was caught in a brief storm of the same intensity as The Yankee Gale—and was never heard from again.

No one ever knew how many vessels were wrecked on the shores of Prince Edward Island in that storm, for, in addition to American and Canadian boats, wreckage was found indicating that foreign vessels also were caught and driven ashore. Of the hundreds of vessels that were on the fishing grounds prior to the storm, only 22 could be salvaged and used again, and of those 22, each and every one had lost all of its crew.

Eighty-five American women were made widows, and 350 children became orphans in the wake of The Yankee Gale, the storm that whipped out of a dead calm and beat with a terrible vengeance over the Gulf of St. Lawrence in October of 1851.   ∞

CHAPTER TWO

Blizzards

Above: *In front of Hartford's American Hotel, a group poses atop the drifts left behind by the Blizzard of '88.*
Previous pages: *A rotary snowplow in action.*

White Fury

The Blizzard of 1888

BY EVAN MCLEOD WYLIE

Saturday, March 10, 1888, was a balmy late winter day in southern New England. The mildest winter in years seemed to be over, and people worked in their vegetable gardens, preparing to plant their first rows of carrots and cucumbers. Stores heralded the approach of spring with announcements of gala sales, and newspapers advertised spring tonics ("One Hundred Doses of Sarsaparilla—Only One Dollar!"). In Danbury, Connecticut, the local paper reported that the earth was sunbathed and the streets thronged with shoppers, loungers, and baby carriages. In Vermont and New Hampshire, farmers made ready for running sap and the maple sugar harvest.

As New Englanders went to bed that Saturday night, a big snowstorm was quite likely the furthest thing from their minds. Yet on its way was the most savage and catastrophic snowstorm ever to strike the Northeast. Without equal in all records, it has come to be known as the "Blizzard of '88." It was a howling cyclone of snow, wind, and bitter cold described by the New Haven newspaper as a "bewildering, belligerent, blinding blitz. Nothing like it ever happened before in this part of North America."

Forecasters of the nation's weather at that time were well aware that a heavy snowstorm had originated in the Rocky Mountains near Utah on Thursday and was slowly traveling eastward. In the South, another front of moist, warm air had brought gale-force winds to Tennessee and Alabama and was moving northeastward. But meteorologists believed that both storms either would dissipate before reaching the East Coast or would blow out to sea. Predictions for the Northeast for

Sunday were for cloudy weather, followed by light rain or snow and clearing.

On Sunday winds along the New England coast veered to the northeast, a sign of an approaching gale and wet weather. In New York City a downpour of rain began on Sunday afternoon. Farther to the north snow was falling lightly, but it was thought to be a "sugar snow" that would bring hogsheads of clear, sweet sap.

Confined by heavier air around it, the western storm grew in intensity and raced eastward into New York. About 4:00 A.M. on Monday, it converged with the southern gale, creating winds of hurricane force, hail, sleet, and snow. The southern edge of the massive storm system struck Washington and the coastal waters of the Chesapeake and Delaware bays, while the northern front shrieked into the Northeast.

At 4:00 A.M. New York was enveloped in a fury of snow and winds that were gusting as high as 84 miles an hour. At dawn in Danbury, Connecticut, snow began flying through the air in great clouds. Temperatures fell sharply, and a ferocious wind snatched away the breath of pedestrians. By 6:00 A.M. New Haven was reeling beneath an onslaught of sleet, snow, and violent winds.

As the raging blizzard swept over the cities and towns of New England, horses refused to face the blinding sleet and snow and had to be unhitched and led to their barns. Horsecars, a principal means of transportation in the cities, soon were blocked, derailed, and buried in drifts. Schools, stores, and factories began closing down, but soon it became too perilous to venture outside to try to reach home.

In Hartford, a group of factory girls, roped together and led by two men, barely managed to reach a

The Origin of the Word *Blizzard*

The best claim among the many theories and speculations about the origin of the word *blizzard* as applied to a violent snowstorm seems to lie with an Iowa newspaper editor named O.C. Bates, who employed the word in 1870 in his spirited story on a crippling snow that buried his local bailiwick of Estherville. Until then the word meant a violent blow, or a rifle shot, rain or shine. Ten years later the country was treated to an unusual series of worse-than-average snowstorms and the term *blizzard* spread from the Middle West to the East in plenty of time for the big show of 1888. Once it was firmly fixed in popular speech the professional weather experts found it necessary to give the term an accurate definition for use in their records, which they proceeded to do without any reference to what the word had originally meant before Mr. Bates had his inspiration and gave it a new meaning.

—*From* The Blizzard of March, 1888 and N.H. Town Meeting Storm *by Samuel D. Lord (Manchester, N.H.: John B. Clarke, 1888).*

nearby home. Two Bridgeport working girls who tried to brave the storm were found dead, locked in each other's arms. A Danbury man died in a drift a few yards from his house. Strong men barely succeeded in reaching their front doors before they collapsed and were dragged inside by their families.

In the country, fields, fences, roads, and paths vanished. Lone travelers were trapped and died on country lanes. Farmers chose to spend the night in their barns rather than risk trying to reach their houses.

The railroads were stricken as never before. During the early hours of the storm, trains looked like solid masses of moving ice and snow, but soon they were slowing down, laboring heavily through the drifts that were mounding up on the tracks, and finally stalling. The most powerful locomotives butted impotently at the mountains of snow and spun their wheels on icy rails.

All across New England, engineers sought vainly to summon snowplows and rescue parties for their passengers. Driving winds piled the swirling snow high around the cars. Tracks vanished and trains could go neither forward nor backward. The vast network of freight, commuter, and mail trains that covered the East was all but paralyzed by the storm.

Not a single train reached New Haven after noon on Monday. Trains that attempted to leave the stations were halted a short distance down the tracks. Passengers were led back to the depots but could go no farther. Crowds huddled around station stoves, and food containers were quickly emptied. In Berlin, Connecticut, travelers trapped in the railroad station subsisted on crackers and cheese and melted snow. Even with four stoves going full blast, the temperature within the station fell below freezing. Early Tuesday morning the wind rose to such force that the entire building swayed and appeared about to collapse, but none dared flee into the blinding storm.

Trains filled with passengers lay isolated all over New England. Train crewmen and passengers pulled down the blinds, caulked the cracks around the windows with newspapers, huddled around car stoves, and prayed that their supplies of coal would last until relief came.

The train from Albany—carrying an opera company bound for Fitchburg, Massachusetts—was caught in a drift near Shelburne Falls and was soon nearly buried beyond sight in the falling snow. Famished passengers and singers broke into the express car and discovered it contained a ton of "Chicago Tenderloins"—rolled beef consigned to Boston. The steaks were cooked on coal shovels over car stoves.

Other train passengers were not so lucky and survived only because farmers came to the rescue with food. Some would accept no payment. Others were more profiteering. Near New London farmers swarmed around one stalled train "like flies around a molasses can, offering sandwiches at prices enough to paralyze a hungry man—25 cents."

Throughout Monday night the blizzard shrieked across New England. "A night of horror—the worst storm that has ever blasted this town," reported the Danbury newspaper. "In fury we doubt if anyone in Danbury ever saw its equal, even in dead of winter. The tempest's roar made hearing impossible. The winds howled and screamed all night." The roofs of school buildings were blown off. Factory smokestacks snapped. A baseball stadium grandstand was reduced to debris. By morning, drifts 20 feet high had transformed the town into a wilderness.

A prominent Danbury citizen was battling his way down Main Street in the snow and darkness when suddenly his feet struck an obstruction that sent him sprawling over what seemed to be a human form. With a yell that could be heard above the storm's din, he rushed into a nearby saloon and shouted that there was a man dead and frozen stiff on the walk. The entire saloon emptied out onto the sidewalk and dug down only to discover a wooden cigar-store Indian.

The storm continued to assault most of New England through Tuesday. In its wake it left silence, bitter cold, desolation, and chaos. Only Boston, among large New England cities, had escaped a major disaster. By good fortune it had been in the eye of the storm and had not suffered as severely as its neighbors to the north, west, and south. Although icebound and isolated, it was able to keep its horsecars running. The *Boston Globe,* a center of communication for news of the Northeast, in banner headlines proclaimed, EMBARGO OF THE FIERCE ICE KING LAID UPON THE COUNTRY. WASHINGTON BESIEGED AND CUT OFF. VERMONT FARMERS IMPRISONED. MAINE ROADS COVERED BY DRIFTS.

With all transportation in and out of New England cities suspended, fears arose that supplies of coal and food would not last. A run on food stores began as people bought enough provisions to last for a week. Only a few grocery stores and saloons were open. Milk had vanished, and there was hardly a loaf of bread to be found.

In northern New England country roads and city streets were impassable. Windsor, Vermont, reported on Wednesday that "no one in this village has been seen or heard from since Sunday. Not a pound of maple sugar was made in Vermont so far this season, and it

Weather forecaster Adolphus Greeley took full blame for the prediction made on March 10, 1888: "Light to fresh easterly winds with warmer, fair weather."

will be impossible to get into the sugar orchards for weeks."

Although Boston escaped lightly, its suburbs and surrounding towns suffered heavy damage. On the North Shore, beaches were strewn with the wreckage of cottages, bulkheads, and fences. High tides swept inland, transforming coastal roads into rock-strewn rubble and washing out the tracks of the Boston-Revere-Lynn Railroad. Along Revere Beach, houses were reduced to kindling wood. Woburn was littered with broken trees and trunks stripped of their branches. Heavily iced telegraph and telephone poles tilted and toppled. In Lawrence, the textile mills closed and all electricity failed, plunging the city into darkness.

As the storm took a northeastward course out over the Atlantic, it dropped less snow but raked the coast with high winds, sleet, and torrents of rain. Long Island Sound was lashed with gales of hurricane force. Block Island was isolated in a tempest of snow and sleet. At Point Judith, Rhode Island, wreckage of schooners and small craft was strewn along the beach. At Newport and on Narragansett Bay there was a terrible storm that the captain of the lifesaving station declared caused the greatest seas he had ever looked upon. The Narragansett Pier was heavily damaged, and Providence was besieged by such torrents of rain, high winds, and sleet that all business was suspended.

Cape Cod, spared the snow, was swept by an easterly gale. "The broad Atlantic," a Chatham newspaperman reported, "was an awe-inspiring sight, a mass of heavy, roaring, foaming, rushing billows and breakers as far as the eye could see. In the afternoon, high tides sent seas bursting over the dunes and rushing over the beaches with tremendous force. Pollock Rip Lightship, anchored in one of the most exposed positions on the Atlantic coast, is still holding, although it's gyrating like a French dancing master."

It was Thursday afternoon before the last of the lingering storm clouds disappeared out to sea. The sun appeared again, and temperatures climbed. With most of the Northeast deep in snow, fears arose that a sudden thaw followed by rain might set off rampaging floods, but moderate weather prevailed, and soon all New England was digging out.

Bodies were found in city streets and along country lanes. In Waterford, Connecticut, two little boys who had started out to meet their mother took shelter behind a stone wall and were quickly buried by drifting snow. A search party led by their father finally found them 22 hours later, badly frostbitten but still alive. They were taken to a nearby farmhouse, and their fingers and noses were wrapped in cloth soaked in molasses to ease the frostbite.

Armies of men were sent into the battle to clear streets and rail lines. Snowplows propelled by heavy locomotives moved out into the country to reach trains that had been trapped since Monday. Frequently they charged such huge drifts that both plow and engine would be buried in an avalanche of snow and crews would be forced to tunnel out.

As mails arrived and telegraph lines were patched together, many learned for the first time about the magnitude of the storm and the vast toll it had taken. There were 400 dead. Nearly 200 ships were wrecked or had disappeared, and 100 lives had been lost at sea.

New York City alone had suffered an estimated $20 million in property damage, and in the aftermath of the storm it resembled "a wreck-strewn battlefield." Trains were snowbound and wrecked in New York, New Jersey, and Pennsylvania. In the Chesapeake and Delaware bays, where many coastal vessels had sought shelter, hurricane winds and blinding sleet and snow had sunk many barks and schooners, driven scores ashore, and drowned sailors floundering in the icy wa-

Locomotives were no match for the deep snow. Here, in Naugatuck, Connecticut, ropes had to be used to hold the engine in place while a crew of workers hurried to clear the tracks beneath it.

The following table of precipitation for the state of New Hampshire was compiled following the Blizzard of '88 by Professor Winslow Upton of Brown University, secretary of the New England Meteorological Society. But apparently the snow is always deeper in the other fellow's yard: Troy, New York, recorded 55 inches of snow in the storm.

How Much Snow Fell in the Blizzard of '88?

Town	Estimated Snow in inches	Town	Estimated Snow in inches	Town	Estimated Snow in inches
Acworth	33	Exeter	18	New Boston	27
Allenstown	24	Farmington	24	New Hampton	32
Alton Bay	18	Fitzwilliam	36	New Ipswich	34
Amherst	36	Goffstown	22	New London	36
Amoskeag Falls	27	Gorham	22	North Conway	15
Antrim	30	Grafton	30	Ossipee	24
Atkinson	24	Great Falls	21	Pittsfield	24
Bartlett	26	Hanover	25	Plymouth	26
Berlin Mills	24	Haverhill	20	Raymond	18
Bethlehem	23	Hillsborough	30	Rochester	22
Boscawen	24	Hooksett	20	Rumney	23
Bradford	28	Hopkinton	24	Shelburne	20
Campton Village	20	Jefferson	24	Stratford	12
Canterbury	22	Keene	36	Suncook	18
Chesterfield	40	Laconia	31	Tamworth	30
Claremont	36	Lebanon	24	Troy	36
Colebrook	24	Littleton	18	Walpole	30
Concord	27	Manchester	24	Washington	36
Contoocook	24	Meriden	36	Weare	28
Derry	20	Milton Mills	16	West Milan	17
Dublin	42	Nashua	30	West Salisbury	24
Enfield	30				

—Reprinted from The Blizzard of March, 1888 and N.H. Town Meeting Storm *by Samuel D. Lord (Manchester, N.H.: John B. Clarke, 1888).*

ters. In Lewes Harbor, at the mouth of the Delaware Bay, 35 of 40 vessels had been destroyed in a gale that struck at midnight on Monday.

Although New York City had suffered the greatest damage, more snow actually fell in New England. New York had 20 inches compared with 30 to 40 inches in Connecticut and Massachusetts, where there were some drifts as high as 30 to 40 feet. April had arrived before communication lines were repaired and railroads and city streets were back to normal. But the damage to New England in revenues, shipping, lost livestock, farm buildings, and fishing fleets was beyond calculation.

Comparing notes on the storm, older inhabitants recalled the gales of 1867 and 1851 [which destroyed Boston's Minot's Ledge Light, see p. 97] and the winter of 1868, when there had been 12 consecutive weeks of sleighing before March 2, with three snowstorms yet to come.

But it was generally agreed then, and ever since, that the Blizzard of '88 stands as winter's worst blow against New England on record. There have been more bitter cold waves and heavier snowfalls, but for swift, overwhelming fury and paralyzing power, nothing like it has ever been seen. ∞

He's
Still Buried by
the Blizzard of '88

BY EDIE CLARK

Judd Caplovich lives in a house whose trees were once shorn by a tornado, a house that has been struck by lightning. Storms come to him. He was six years old when another tornado struck Worcester, Massachusetts, his hometown, in 1953. As it tore its lethal trench just three miles away, the boy wandered outside, arms outstretched, palms upward, to catch the hailstones. A few years later, when Hurricane Donna swept into Massachusetts, he was out on his paper route, hurrying to deliver the last of the papers. The wind howled around him. As he crossed the street, an electrical transformer exploded above his head. He ran home, those last papers still in his bag. In 1973, in an ice storm that left even the major highways of Connecticut hopelessly greased, he and 12 other members of his carpool, stranded by the storm, huddled in a tiny Manchester apartment, the only place that still had electricity. More recently, in another snowstorm, he was stranded in his own house for two days without food. He doesn't keep food in his house—there's no room. The kitchen cupboards bulge with books, piles of papers and folders teeter on the counters, and the sink is filled to the faucet with more papers.

The inside of Judd Caplovich's house, a modest raised ranch in a quiet neighborhood in Vernon, Connecticut,

looks as if that tornado not only grazed the side of the house but hurtled *through* it, uprooting whatever sense of order the rest of us have come to expect of a house. That is not Judd's vision. A collector "since birth," he has twice had to hold auctions to unburden the house, which would otherwise have burst its seams with its mother lode of pianos, typewriters, books, and accumulated what-all, not to mention the 75 years of *National Geographic*s in the living room and the five tons (his calculation) of old phonograph records in the basement. The rooms, of course, are filled—couches, chairs, and floors stacked with *stuff*. There is room for only one visitor, and even then the occasion requires a considerable amount of rearranging to clear a seat in a house that appears to have no seat, even for its owner. Judd Caplovich probably doesn't sit much.

At one time Judd had 550 typewriters shoehorned into the house, on shelves in the living room, kitchen, bathroom and a great number of them in his bedroom. When he sold them at auction several years ago, it was thought to be the world's largest collection of typewriters. He now has only five or six, willy-nilly, on tops of piles.

Judd Caplovich, the authority on the Blizzard of '88.

One of the earliest things Judd collected was considerably less bulky—the headlines of storms. "It's not so much the storms," he says. "I don't really enjoy storms. It's what comes after—the damage and the disaster. I've always been interested in that." He saved the Worcester *Telegram and Gazette* that chronicled the 1953 tornado; then there were the hurricanes in 1954 and 1955, and the accounts of the floods of the same year that virtually destroyed Winsted, Connecticut. Later he found headline editions from the Hurricane of '38, a storm so fierce, his grandmother recalled, that she had seen trees flying through the air. Before long he had a boxful of these newspapers chronicling the aftermaths of disasters. And then he had two boxfuls. But he had nothing on the Blizzard of 1888, the greatest snowstorm of all time. And that kind of got him thinking.

"Around the end of 1986, I realized that the centennial of the storm was coming up," he said. There is a sense of electricity about Judd—his coarse hair stands out on top and at the sides in Einstein disarray, and his eyes pop, as if fresh from the excitement of discovery. "I knew where there was a large collection of photographs of the storm, and I knew there wasn't very much written about it. So I decided to do a book. To fill the void."

He had never "done a book" before. He is not a writer, had spent little or no time in libraries, and knew nothing about "research." "You start out knowing nothing," he says nonchalantly. "And then you learn." But he is a man of entrepreneurial spirit, and the idea of consolidating all that he could find out about the Great Blizzard between two covers seemed a surefire way to make money—that is, if he did it himself. It never really occurred to him to take his idea to a publisher. "I'm funny," he explains. "I can't do it someone else's way. It has to be my way." To be able to do it his way, he took out a $90,000 mortgage on his house and threw himself into the project, which had its own built-in deadline—the anniversary of the storm—giving him about a year to do the work.

He says a lot of all this that surrounds him now in this storm-tossed house is from the book that eventually came out in early 1988. *Blizzard! The Great Storm of '88!* is a hefty three-pounder loaded with pictures of the surprise mid-March blizzard—a storm that buried ten states in 3, 4, and 5 feet of snow that drifted up to 40 feet, just as crocuses had come to bloom and farmers had begun their spring plowing. It is the storm that consumed him for two years, the storm that rolled up 20,000 miles on his car, whose vanity plates (BLIZ*88) announced his mission wherever he went.

He searched out libraries and historical societies all over the Northeast (including Long Island, Pennsylvania, New Jersey, and New York State) that might be able to contribute. In that time, he sorted through huge collections of photographs in search of pictures of the storm and read through countless stacks of newspapers, circa 1888, hoping to find first-person accounts. He'd stay as late as he could, until the libraries shut their doors and sent him home again, where he would continue to work until two or three in the morning. He fit it together like a puzzle, compiling facts and photographs of the storm, and charting its scope, which he had thought, when he first started, hadn't gone much beyond Connecticut and Massachusetts.

"All I knew when I started was that it was big," he says. There was precious little meteorological data available on the blizzard, which is now commonly believed to have been a collision of two massive storm fronts. He wanted this kind of information in the book. In his research, he came across people who knew more about the storm than he did, and he enlisted their help. He read an article about the blizzard in a meteorological bulletin written by Paul Kocin, a NASA research meteorologist. They talked, and before long Kocin was at work with Judd, mapping out the path and progress of the entire storm, something that had never been done before. Similarly, Judd contacted David Ludlum, who has written more than ten books about weather and its phenomena, and he, too, joined in the project. Judd also hired a writer and an editor, who understood it had to be done Judd's way, and he hired a photographer, Wayne Cogan, who traveled with him to some of the libraries and historical societies where Judd had already made preliminary selections of photos to be included in the book. Rather than borrow the photos, which some of the institutions would not allow, Judd and Wayne made copies right there, on the spot.

Arriving at each place, their car loaded with the equipment that constituted their traveling studio, Judd and Wayne would work within whatever space was available, setting up a tent and lights on poles, rephotographing the old pictures that Judd wanted to be part of the book. "By the time I got to that stage, it was summer, and it was the hottest of all summers. Under the hot lights, inside that tent, we sweated, it seems, all summer long." But the pictures were cool—snowdrifts that made men look like toys, steam locomotives buried in drifts, nothing but the stack sticking up out of a wave of white. There were pictures of ships wrecked, their masts and decks laden with a thick coating of ice, and there were buildings with snow piled up to the second-story windows. And everywhere there were wonderful snow tunnels—in Hartford, in New York City, in

Bridgeport, in Brattleboro, Vermont—perhaps the only way to get through the towering drifts (some were 40 feet high) to the other side.

Newspapers of that era still relied heavily on woodcuts and engravings, if they illustrated their texts at all. So almost all the pictures came from private collections, photos taken by a new breed, the amateur photographer. "Thank God," he says, "for historical societies." Without them, the story of the blizzard would have been folklore. These pictures provided the only witness, the only way for him to see for himself what it might have been like.

He also photostated headlines and included them in the book: "Death in the Snowdrift," "The Buried City," "A Night of Devastation," "SILENCE—The Wires All Down." The stultifying experience of an entire region was recounted in paper after paper, but perhaps nowhere as succinctly as in the *Bellows Falls* (Vermont) *Times,* which had only this to say: "No paths, no streets, no sidewalks, no light, no roads, no guests, no calls, no teams, no hacks, no trains, no moon, no meat, no milk, no paper, no mails, no news, no thing—but snow."

He found first-person accounts in some of the newspapers he'd run through on microfilm. In the *New York Times,* he found this account by a woman watching the storm from her apartment window: "I saw a man for one and a half hours trying to cross 96th Street. We watched him start, get quarter way across, and then be flung back against the building on the corner. The last time he tried it, he was caught up in a whirl of snow and disappeared from our view. The next morning seven horses, policemen, and his brother charged the drift, and his body was *kicked* out of the drift."

The newspapers abounded with grim stories—the account of a farmer finding a woman frozen to death in his outhouse, where she had sought shelter, having lost her way in the ferocious storm. And the two children in Waterford, Connecticut, who were making their way to their aunt's house and were quickly buried in the fast-falling snow. They huddled together for hours inside the snow cave until searchers found them by poking though the snow with a stick. They were alive, their hands and ears frostbitten. The icy snow whipped by gale-force winds made being out in the storm like being in a sandstorm or being sandblasted. It was reported,

To penetrate the barriers made by the mountains of snow, shop owners tunneled archways to provide access for their customers. At Curtis and Frasier's candy store in Saratoga Springs, New York, the tunnel was made broad enough for a sleigh to pass through.

here and there, that people had resorted to wearing squares of carpeting on their feet and blankets around their heads, or bags with holes cut for eyes.

For three astonishing days—March 11 to 14—a whirlwind of ice and snow pummeled the region, and when it was over, it had taken the lives of 400 people and caused uncalculated damage. In New York City, where such things were capable of being totted up, there was an estimated $20 million worth of damage. It was the greatest amount of snow ever to have fallen since the formation of the United States. Nothing since has overtaken that record.

In his reading, Judd found that the entire Northeast had been paralyzed by the storm. Telephone and telegraph wires were down from Washington, D.C., to Maine, and the trains, which provided the only *real* transportation in those days, were at a standstill—many smashed to ruin, some stuck in drifts, some never able to leave the station. In Bridgeport, Connecticut, more than a thousand passengers crowded into the station, unable to go home, unable to go anywhere. Among them was a traveling theater group, which had come to perform *Uncle Tom's Cabin* at a Bridgeport theater that week. They did an impromptu performance for the shivering crowd, then and there. Passengers on trains that had become stranded for days in a virtual snow

wilderness fared better or worse, depending on what the baggage cars held. One trainload of starving passengers discovered 5 gallons of oysters and 300 pounds of bacon and sausage when they looted the stock. But the luck on another train, hung up in a drift in Brookfield, Connecticut, was not quite so sweet. There a brave stationmaster forged his way through the raging storm loaded down with all the eggs and bread he could handle, plus a gallon of brandy. This sorted out to one egg and two slices of bread for each famished passenger to keep them going another 24 hours until help arrived.

There were recollections chronicled by a group called the Blizzard Men of '88. All of them had lived through the storm, and they got together for years afterward to share their memories. Here is one that Judd found: "By night the drift had reached the second-story windowsill. When we were ready to depart at 6 o'clock, we found a solid wall of snow as the lower door was opened. . . . We did have two shovels. It was necessary to tunnel through for about 15 feet, carrying snow upstairs and throwing it out the back windows. Making an exit . . . our combined strength weathered the gale in an almost exhausted condition." The accounts were numerous and tragic as well as bizarre, such as the story of the woman in Hartford who had taken a dozen strangers, trapped by the storm, into her home. Food

Below: *A society called "The Blizzard Men and Ladies" started up quite informally in 1929, when two men got to talking about their experiences in the 1888 Blizzard. By 1938, the fiftieth anniversary of the Great Storm, the group had grown so large that their reunion filled the ballroom in New York City's Hotel Pennsylvania. The society continued to meet annually until the early 1970s.* **Opposite page:** *Outside a hotel in downtown Hartford, local wags hung John Whitaker Watson in effigy. Watson was the author of a popular poem entitled "Beautiful Snow."*

ran out quickly, but under her back porch she discovered another group of refugees—a flock of perhaps a hundred sparrows. She gathered them up and served the hungry strangers sparrow pie.

Working at a frantic pace, 16 hours a day, 7 days a week for almost a year, Judd collected these tales and wove them into a text that went along with the more than 300 illustrations he chose for the book. It was not always easy—he remembers spending one entire day in Concord, New Hampshire, sorting through mountains of pictures and finding not a single one of the blizzard.

And he worked hard to find someone who had lived through the storm. He thought it was possible—the person would have to be about 106, with a clear memory, but he figured there are such people, so he put ads in some of the newspapers. He got no response. He did find a woman in Hopkinton, New Hampshire, who was known as the Blizzard Lady, reputedly because she was born on the day of the blizzard. She would not, of course, *remember* the storm, but it was the closest he had come, so he and Wayne drove up to Hopkinton and spent the day with the woman, whom he found to be very sharp. Wayne took a lot of pictures. "She was over a hundred years old, still drove her own car, owned her own home, and had her own garden," Judd said. "We had a wonderful day with her, but it turned out she was born on March 31. Everyone in town thought she was born on the day of the blizzard, but that would have been March 12. She did know when her birthday was, but there was another blizzard on the thirty-first. So I couldn't use it in the book. That was a big disappointment because I was going to dedicate the book to her."

At a certain point he had to stop and turn to the business of producing the book. He found a printer in Michigan. Of course, there are printers closer, but this was the one he liked the best, and that involved a lot of travel and phone calls. In the end, the book came out late, a little over two weeks before Christmas, which was a disappointment because Judd more or less missed the pre-Christmas sales. The books were delivered to his house, where he handles all the mail orders. Five thousand books on skids arrived one morning in a tractor trailer from Michigan. There was a total weight of 15,000 pounds to be unloaded. He was afraid the foundation would crack if they unloaded the books all in one place, so he spread the weight around—2,000 pounds here, 2,000 pounds there, 6,000 pounds in the basement next to his roomful of old phonograph records.

Orders started to come in, and the burden began to lift. On the weekend of the anniversary of the storm, March 11, 12, and 13, Judd found himself involved in a blitz of radio and television interviews, which was

To Know Snow

☞ For every inch of snow, on average, each square foot weighs approximately 0.6 pound.

On average, an inch of rain equals ten inches of snow.

Street scene in Springfield, Massachusetts, after the Blizzard of 1888.

something of a surprise to him. When the weekend ended and the centennial of the storm had crested and waned, he went home and slept, for days it seemed.

After that the orders continued to come in, slow but sure, to the storm-swept rooms of Judd's house. He still has not paid back his mortgage, but he thinks he will eventually break even. He did not, as he had hoped, make a bundle. He has been thinking lately of other projects that might be more lucrative. He thought about capitalizing on the fluctuating foreign exchange rates by importing things from Europe. He looked into importing chocolate and traveled to Switzerland to arrange to buy a bulk load of it. "But they wanted me to

buy 100,000 pounds at a time, and I realized that chocolate, if you don't get rid of it real quick, spoils. So that was out." A couple of other things didn't pan out. He keeps going back to the storms. When last we talked, he was getting together all his material collected over the years on the Hurricane of 1938. September 1988 was the fiftieth anniversary of that storm, and he thought there might be something in that.   ∞

Editor's Note: Blizzard! The Great Storm of '88 *is available for $24.95, plus $2 for shipping, from VeRo Publishing Co., P.O. Box 1888, Vernon, CT 06066-1888.*

Following are two different perspectives, published in *Yankee* a decade apart, on the mystery of the steamer *Portland*'s last hours during the great storm of November 1898, which ever since has borne the name of that unlucky ship.

The Day the Weather Bureau Was Right

BY E.B. RIDEOUT

In the early years of this century, I first heard the facts that led to the sinking of the steamer *Portland*. The *Portland* had left her berth at Boston, Massachusetts, and steamed down the harbor in the early darkness of Saturday, November 26, 1898. Portland, Maine, was her destination, but she never arrived there. As she turned her course northeastward toward Maine, she plowed into the teeth of one of New England's heaviest November snowstorms on record. Never before or since has so much snow fallen in the Boston area in one November storm, which packed terrific 60- to 80-mile-an-hour winds. This memorable storm has since become known as the "*Portland* Storm." Of the nearly 200 passengers and crew aboard, not a single soul survived. In that same storm, about 140 other craft were either blown ashore or sunk off the New England coast.

For a great many years after, three questions were topics of endless discussion: (1) Why did Captain Blanchard sail in view of the ominous weather reports or not turn back when he first ran into the fury of the storm, or why didn't he turn in toward Gloucester? (2) Just where did the steamer go down? (3) Could she have collided with another ship?

Captain Blanchard had the reputation of being a reliable man with experience on side-wheelers. Before the turn of the century, there were few propellers. Side wheels were the means of propulsion for ships in those days, except on riverboats, where paddle wheels extended the full width of the broad stern of the boat. These steamships had big paddle wheels enclosed in fancy paddle boxes on each side of the ship and were not seaworthy in rough weather. Captain Blanchard knew this. Realizing his responsibility to his passengers, he became a staunch friend of those at the U.S. Weather Bureau in Boston and abided by their advice before sailing.

About 1908, when I was not yet 20 years old, I became acquainted with three Weather Bureau men who had known Captain Blanchard. My greatest interest then was the weather, so I located the Weather Bureau in Boston and introduced myself to the first man I met. He gave his name as Mr. Crosby, and he was then the oldest employee in the Boston office.

We had a very nice chat, and quite naturally our conversation drifted to the *Portland* tragedy, which had occurred but ten years before. Mr. Crosby was the first to tell me why Captain Blanchard had sailed, and he made my visit so pleasant that it wasn't long before I became a daily caller during my lunch hour. Then I met John W. Smith, who had been the official-in-charge at the Boston office for about 30 of his more than 40 years

Top: *The steamer* Portland *under construction at the New England Company shipyard in Bath, Maine.* **Above:** *The* Portland *was a smart-looking side-wheeler, but her sleek design made her unseaworthy in heavy swells.*

with the service. He told me the same story about Captain Blanchard that Mr. Crosby had, and this was later corroborated by Mark T. Nesmith.

The *Portland,* which ran her maiden trip in 1889, was considered a very fine ship of its kind, with all the latest furnishings, including electric lighting. Captain Blanchard appreciated the gracefulness and fanciful beauty of his ship, but, more seriously, he felt a responsibility to his passengers and freight. Several years before the disaster the captain began making calls to the U.S. Weather Bureau in Boston. He became very friendly with the entire force, and John Smith would explain the morning weather map to him. The captain became familiar with the map and, through Mr. Smith's instructions, was able to draw his own conclusions as to whether it would become rough and the winds would be unfavorable for sailing. He learned much from the map concerning the direction of the wind and what its strength would be for his evening trip to Portland. If the wind, according to the barometric pressure lines and gradient, would be too strong from abeam, then he would not risk the trip. He knew there was a danger of getting into the trough of a sea, which was always a very weak point in the navigation of a side-wheeler. Because of his familiarity with the daily weather map and the advice of the men at the Weather Bureau, as well as his knowledge of the *Portland*'s weaknesses, Captain Blanchard earned the reputation of being a cautious man.

There came a day, however, when Captain Blanchard was called on the carpet and told that he was being *too* cautious in view of the fact that the alternate and competitive route would be by rail. He would henceforth sail on company's orders. Blanchard felt that, sooner or later, these orders could well go against his better judgment. He told his friends at the Weather Bureau about this meeting but continued to make his daily trip to the bureau before sailing.

On this Saturday after Thanksgiving, there were a great many passengers in Boston anxious to get back home to Maine before Sunday. The morning of that terrible night dawned with sunshine, except for some very thin cirrus clouds that caused a faint ring around the sun. It was a quiet morning with little wind. At the Weather Bureau, the captain recalled that he had seen a slight disturbance in the eastern Great Lakes region the previous morning, but it had moved east-southeastward with a very rapidly increasing secondary development by Saturday morning.

"It looks bad," Mr. Smith said when he finished drawing his map. Captain Blanchard was solemn, but he told them he was following orders. He went out the door, saying he hoped the storm would go off the coast and that he would get his passengers home safely. Warnings had already been issued at Washington for a northeaster along the New England coast. That morning special observations were ordered. Before noon, additional warnings for the increasing severity of the storm were telegraphed from Washington. Immediately Mr. Crosby called Captain Blanchard by phone at the wharf. When he received the information from Mr. Crosby, he thanked him and said, "I am going." Obviously he had been ordered to sail.

Other than a slowly disappearing sun behind steadily thickening clouds, the day remained quiet. Evening settled in. The *Portland* left the wharf at seven o'clock. A very light, gentle snow began, which blurred her rows of deck lights from those remaining at the wharf.

The Storm That Changed Provincetown

It's unlikely that many of Provincetown's contemporary inhabitants, an imported crazy quilt of artists, nature lovers, and refugees from the city, have even heard of the *Portland* gale. Yet it was the November 1898 storm that opened, or perhaps more accurately blew down, the door through which these offbeat new settlers have streamed.

According to historians, the *Portland* gale put an abrupt and untimely end to Provincetown's reign as New England's major commercial fishing port. The storm devoured so many of the town's working wharves, and the boats associated with them, that the fishermen and boatmen, with no capital to rebuild, were forced to turn away from the sea for their living. The scenic waterfront, newly vacated, beckoned to artists and writers. With improvements in transportation, the tourists and summer folk followed.

At the time of the *Portland* gale, Provincetown's year-round population was 5,000—1,000 more than it is today. The town boasted no fewer than 52 wharves and a fishing fleet of more than 700 vessels. Today, the town's modest fleet of 28 draggers huddles around MacMillan Wharf, the single municipal pier.

— *Susan V. Seligson*

She soon disappeared from view as the snow began to thicken. Within an hour after the handful of onlookers had seen the *Portland* disappear, the snow began swirling with an increasing wind. The storm continued to increase, as thick snow and a lashing gale suddenly swooped down along the entire Massachusetts Bay and coastal areas. Soon it reached hurricane proportions.

Very few knew that there was a steamship with nearly 200 people aboard just off the coast in that death-dealing storm, for there was no wireless or radio in those days. In the late evening, William J. Hackett, living in Gloucester at the time, was one of several who heard repeated blasts of a steamship whistle. Many times after I was married to his daughter Laura he told me that he recognized the whistle as that of the steamer *Portland,* as she used to salute the Thacher's Island twin lights on clear nights on her way to Portland. On the night of the storm, he knew that her whistling repeatedly meant she was in distress. It finally became fainter and then died away. No sound but the roar of the storm shrieking outside was heard thereafter.

The constant whistle blasts of the only steamer out that night indicated that Captain Blanchard was calling for help. In those moments he must have reached a point of desperation. What was in his mind? He must act quickly by first calling for help, but where would it come from in an increasing hurricane wind? Further progress into such a blast would put great pressure on his paddle-wheel shafts, which would render his ship wholly at the mercy of the storm if they should break. Therefore, he had to abandon hope of getting his passengers home for Sunday. He must have known it would be disastrous to turn his ship toward rockbound Gloucester and get into the trough with the wind hitting his ship broadside. The only thing that remained, which involved an equally great risk, was to turn around and head for the end of Cape Cod, with the wind astern as much as he could keep her that way, thereby taking off much of the strain on her engines and paddle shafts. Then, if he had to, wouldn't it be better to beach her,

since her chances of rescue would be better? Was that his final thought in those whistle-blasting moments of desperation off Gloucester?

The second and third questions mentioned at the beginning of this piece were answered some years ago when divers discovered the hull of the *Portland* with a hole in her side. A sworn statement by the diver says that the *Portland* lies four and a half miles from Pilgrim Monument and four and a half miles out to sea from Highland Light, and that she collided with a granite ship seen during a lull in the storm by a man at Highland Light.

The discovery of the *Portland* beneath the sea off Truro makes it seem likely that Captain Blanchard did head for Cape Cod, crossing Massachusetts Bay in the process. What a night of horror it must have been aboard that ship! How did she make it that far? How much of the way was she aided by the terrifying gale from astern? Did her engines fail her at any time? How much coal was still available in her bunkers to keep up steam? Captain Blanchard must have been tortured by these grim questions during every moment of guiding his ship toward what evidence indicates must have been his destination.

Piecing together an account of what Captain Blanchard did and what he may have intended to do is indeed difficult, but to me one thing is certain: Captain Blanchard was a courageous man, and his success in getting his ship so near to a beach was little short of a miracle. I feel he might have been successful in beaching her and rescuing those aboard, for, like other side-wheelers, the *Portland* was a wide-bottom ship with paddle wheels on both sides and probably would not have listed much once she was driven well onto a beach. Unfortunately, a little more than 24 hours after the *Portland* left India Wharf in Boston against—as we now know—the better judgment of Captain Blanchard, she was struck by another ship, which tore a big hole in her side and landed her beneath the waters off Cape Cod, where she still lies after more than 90 years. ∞

The Truth about the *Portland*

BY EDWARD ROWE SNOW

At exactly seven o'clock on the night of Saturday, November 26, 1898, a deep-throated whistle split the chill night air of Atlantic Avenue on Boston's waterfront. It was the steamer *Portland*, announcing her departure on schedule from famed India Wharf for her regular down-east run from Boston to Portland, Maine. Although none could possibly realize it, that whistle was the last Captain Blanchard of the *Portland* would ever sound at India Wharf. Eternity was waiting for all hands aboard the vessel, an eternity that would catch up with them 26 hours later.

Although more than 90 years have passed since that beautiful side-wheeler sailed out to meet the hurricane that still bears her name, the average New Englander has a false impression of what actually happened. It is erroneously believed in many Yankee circles that the *Portland* not only disappeared completely after leaving Boston Harbor, but that no wreckage from her ever came ashore anywhere. Both beliefs are wrong.

The Saturday night when the *Portland* sailed fell two days after Thanksgiving, and because of those returning from the holiday, more passengers than usual were anxious to make the homeward passage on the *Portland* to the city of the same name.

There has been considerable discussion through the years as to what transpired between the *Portland*'s captain, Hollis H. Blanchard, and the company officials of the line up to the moment of the departure. Captain Blanchard's son, who went aboard the *Portland* just before she left the pier, later stated that his father had been ordered to sail, and sail he did. Thus he followed orders and did not sail on his own responsibility.

The *Portland*, contrary to popular belief, was sighted several times before she disappeared forever. Captain Charles T. Martell of Medford was but one of a dozen sailing masters out in the storm that night, and his statement of more than 50 years later follows:

"I was steering the tugboat *Channing* in a southeasterly direction, and the weather began to spit snow about eight o'clock. We were off Nahant. The weather was not bad at the time, but I knew a serious storm was coming.

"There were ten or 12 young men gathered on the topside of the *Portland* just forward and aft of the paddle wheel box. When one of the young bloods on the *Portland* shouted across to me to get my old scow out of the way, I shouted back at him, 'You'd better stop that hollering, because I don't think you'll be this smart tomorrow morning.'

"By this time I was less than 20 feet from the

61

Portland, and could easily make out the features of the young men sailing to their death. I gave three blasts of the *Channing*'s whistle, and Captain Blanchard, whom I could easily recognize in the wheel house, answered them promptly.

"I was the last person to speak to anyone aboard the *Portland,* and even after 50 years it makes me feel queer whenever I think of it."

The great side-wheeler had proceeded down Boston Harbor on schedule. She met spitting snow off Deer Island Light and, without anything unusual taking place, had proceeded across from Boston Harbor to a point near Thacher's Island.

By nine-thirty, however, when the steamer was still off Thacher's, the storm smashed into the area with great fury. Captain Frank Scripture, ashore at Cape Ann, later stated that the advance fingers of the storm struck with such force that long rows of trees were knocked down by the miniature tornadoes. For years thereafter the evidence was still present in the Cape Ann forests.

Conjecture is aided by facts concerning the storm fingers. It was about eleven o'clock that night when the *Portland* was sighted off Thacher's Island by Captain Reuben Cameron aboard his schooner *Grayling,* only this time she appeared battered and bruised from her encounter with the gale. The side-wheeler was then rolling and pitching badly, but was evidently trying to keep headed toward the open sea.

Fifteen minutes after Cameron sighted the *Portland,* Captain Frank Stream of the *Florence E. Stream* passed the side-wheeler, and at 11:45 P.M. Captain D.J. Pellier of the *Edgar Randall* narrowly escaped a collision with the *Portland.* At the time it appeared that the superstructure of the steamer had been damaged.

The *Portland* was unreported from 11:45 P.M. until 5:45 the following morning, but Captain Blanchard probably continued his efforts to stay out on the open sea, for his next known position was entirely across Massachusetts Bay, down off the shore of Cape Cod!

On Sunday, between 9:00 and 10:30 A.M., the eye of the great hurricane, then sweeping New England, passed directly over Cape Cod. In the partial clearing that developed, the *Portland* was sighted out to sea in company with the freighter *Pentagoet* and the granite schooner *Addie E. Snow.* Not a single person from any of these vessels lived through the storm to tell his story.

It was Patrolman John L. Johnson of Race Point who made the first awesome discovery. At 7:20 that bitter evening, wending his way from the Half Way House, Johnson noticed something out in the surf, something white in color. At that moment a wave, greater than the others, caught the small white object in its relentless grasp, pushed it high on the sloping shore, and then retreated seaward.

Down the slope Johnson plunged and snatched the object from the sand. Clutching it to his breast, the lifesaver staggered up the cliff to climb over the edge of the bank to safety. As the snow and sand bit into his face, Johnson lighted a Coston flare to examine his find. It was a life jacket, and by the flickering light he read the words on the jacket, *Steamer Portland.*

Actually, the *Portland,* although in serious trouble some distance offshore, had not as yet gone to the bottom, and it was several hours before masses of wreckage from her stricken hull began to come up on the beach.

The lifesavers were still hopeful of finding someone still alive in the wreckage, but this was not to be. Every single soul of the 190 who had sailed with the *Portland* went down with her.

The bodies began to come ashore shortly afterward, and several of those that were clothed had watches, each of which had stopped between 9:15 and 9:28. Thus, we can estimate fairly accurately that if the *Portland* was seen afloat as late as ten-thirty that Sunday morning, she could not have gone down until about nine-fifteen or so Sunday evening, because of the time on the victims' watches.

Today nearly every cottage or residence in the vicinity has some memento of the side-wheeler. Stateroom door numbers, doors, cabin posts, stanchions, and other souvenirs are often on exhibit, and Yankee residents of the Cape still cling tenaciously to the valuable relics of the disaster, handing them down from generation to generation.

Many years after its sinking, the *Portland* was located on the bottom by Captain Charles Carver of Rockland, Maine. In 1945 I visited Captain Carver at his home. He told me how his scallop drag had caught

Opposite page, top: *This photo of the* Portland's *crew was taken on land, not long before the ship went down with all hands.* **Opposite page, right:** *Some of the wreckage that washed ashore included stateroom doors, deck chairs, and rowing oars.*

The salvaged wheel of the ill-fated steamer Portland.

on the *Portland,* which he accurately identified by the Portland Steam Packet design on a doorknob that his drags had brought to the surface. Taking me into his chart room, he gave me the identical chart he had used over the wreck, with the *Portland'*s position marked.

On July 1, 1945, under my direction, diver Al George went down to the bottom to find the *Portland* and the granite schooner *Addie E. Snow* relatively close together on the bottom about six miles out to sea from Highland Light. It was evident that the two ships had collided and gone to the bottom. George brought to the surface debris that included a stateroom key marked *Portland* and other wreckage indicating that the hull of the steamer he visited in 144 feet of water was without question the famous Bath-built side-wheeler.

Some time after the disaster, the relatives and friends of those who were drowned on the *Portland* decided to meet together on the anniversary of the loss of the steamer and drop flowers into the sea in memory of those they loved. This practice became an annual custom, which culminated in 1948, the fiftieth anniversary of the sinking. At that time the Portland Associates, as the group had become known, decided to disband, as most of the members had reached old age. To mark the occasion, John A. Thornquist, president of the associates, unveiled a tablet at Highland Light, Cape Cod, commemorating the loss of the ship. Later, the sons and daughters of those same friends and relatives agreed to revive the group under the name Sons and Daughters of the Portland Associates, and they continued to drop flowers in the sea on the anniversary of the *Portland's* sinking.

On November 27, 1956, the Sons and Daughters of the Portland Associates made the long journey from all over New England to a wintry Cape Cod, where at the Race Point Coast Guard Station a tablet with a list of all the victims of the disaster was unveiled.

The unusual significance of this unveiling is that not until one month before the dedication could the list be completed, for when the *Portland* sailed from India Wharf that memorable night, she took with her the only list of crew and passengers in existence, and it was only after years of research that the list of 190 persons could be assembled again. Those who gathered on that November eve at Race Point, Cape Cod, took part in what was probably the last historical act connected in any way with the saga of the *Portland's* sinking, an event that was truly one of New England's greatest sea dramas.

∞

Adrift
in a Blizzard

BY Charles Wesley Greenleaf,
as told to Patricia Kettner Greenleaf

I never met my grandfather, but he had great influence on my life—mostly because we shared the same experience. Seventy-odd years apart, we shared the miracle of survival in a blizzard, all night, at sea.

It was twelve noon, Monday, February 6, 1978. I packed my gear, knowing there would be no more work that day. The island marina was closing early because a blizzard was due by nightfall. There was no need to be careless; we'd all get home well ahead of this kind of storm.

Home lay seven miles of sound away, but I was well used to making the crossing in all kinds of inhospitable weather. Commuting to an island job in my 17-foot Boston whaler had long been my routine.

My coworker, Lance, was bundling up to go with me. He had come across from the mainland with me that day, and now he, too, wanted to play it safe and get across early.

The crossing we'd make would be a bit exposed but short, 15 minutes at most. Fishers Island, part of Suffolk County, New York, but located just off the southeastern Connecticut shore, creates its own sound out of the larger Long Island Sound. This first small and fairly protected body was the one we were preparing to cross.

We listened to the marine weather station report. A storm warning was in effect with high winds and heavy seas due in our area at about 3:00 P.M. We computed course corrections for existing wind and tide. Usually I'd take a compass reading and head out, but since I had a passenger today, I thought I'd better be more cautious.

The wind had reached about 20 knots. We were accustomed to anything up to 30 knots. Many times we had had to turn around because of gusting or high seas, and today we would use that option if necessary. We would know better when we got to the head of West Harbor on the island, where we'd have a good look at things.

"Now, if we don't get a phone call from you guys by 12:55, we'll pick you up in the Sea Stretcher," said Peter Sanger, marina owner and lifelong island resident. Also aware of the risk that accompanies any winter crossing, Peter helped us make emergency plans. He and a crew of volunteers would come after us with the island's hospital emergency boat if necessary.

As we rounded the head of Pirate's Cove and en-

Four Days in the Rigging

BY BARBARA TALLMAN

My great-great-uncle was Charles Tallman of Osterville, Massachusetts, a mate on the two-masted schooner *Christina*. On January 7, during the storm that would become known as the Great Blizzard of 1866, the *Christina,* laden with cement, was off Martha's Vineyard. She was captained by a Mr. Leach and carried Mate Tallman and a crew of four.

When they were off Cape Poge on Chappaquiddick, which is on the east coast of Martha's Vineyard, a northeast gale arose with such rapidity and of so great an intensity that those aboard feared for their lives. Helplessly they watched as the *Christina* went aground on Hawes Shoal, a few miles east of the light.

Uncle Charley believed in preparing himself as well as he could and, while the other men hoped the storm would abate or chose to take their chances if it did not, he pulled on all the clothing his body would support, including extra sets of underwear and trousers, and covered all with a rubber coat—which may have saved his life.

The sea was breaking mast-high in below-zero weather, and the men were being lashed with icy water, battered with cold wind. Captain Leach, Charles, and the four other men climbed up into the rigging, above high water, and lashed themselves there; then began the slow tragedy. Uncle Charley watched as, one by one, his five shipmates froze to death, their bodies assuming grotesque postures silhouetted against the swaying masts.

Although the schooner could be spotted from the Vineyard, no boat could battle the angry sea to attempt a rescue. The hours became days; the days seemed like years. To keep his arms from freezing and to encourage the circulation in his stiffening body, Uncle Charley had to thrash his hands and arms, although his fingers were now becoming frozen solid. So were his toes. On the third night, he was the only man still alive.

The fourth day he was nearly without hope. If help did

tered West Harbor, we set the compass for 30 degrees northeast. That would put us at Noank and Singer's Boatyard on the mainland. The edge of a cold, northeast wind stung our eyes. It would be a push to get across into the wind, but she seemed a steady wind in direction and speed; we'd only have to adjust our time a bit.

We pounded some. The icy spray showered over the port and glazed our foul-weather gear, but home and warmth were closer with each lurch, and that gave us reason enough to endure. I ran my 65-horsepower Johnson at a safe two-thirds throttle. Snow had been falling for a few hours, but the visibility was still fair—about one and a half miles—enough to see the coastal markers that would direct us to the channel buoy and safe harbor.

As the channel marker slipped astern, I checked our time. Just past 12:30 and right into the harbor! I had just glimpsed the familiar Mystic spindle when the engine quit.

Damn! Of all the darned, cold spots to fool with the engine. I carried my tools on board, of course, and every now and then I had to use them, but of all the rotten luck.

We had a full tank of gas and six gallons in reserve, so the problem was in the engine. Most likely an electrical failure, we agreed. I put my gloves down on the deck and checked the ignition system first, where I found the beginning of the problem. I disconnected a ground wire to the power pack, and the engine turned over. We regained some of the distance we had lost drifting, but the engine quit again. I dreaded the thought of more engine work. My hands were already red and numb, and the storm wasn't getting any nicer.

In fact, something was very wrong here. This storm was getting really nasty in a short time—nastier than the weather station had predicted. Growing gusts of wind churned the water, making our little boat pitch so wildly that I could barely steady myself, let alone examine the silent engine. Waves smacking us hard in succession showered us with ice water. I was making no time, and time was the key to regaining our rapidly diminishing headway. By now we had drifted yards from the channel marker.

I made several attempts to restart the engine, but it would only sputter and quickly die. Only days later would we discover that a tiny spring in the ignition had fallen out of place and shorted everything. Our breakdown hadn't been caused by the weather or by routine engine failure. A rare, unforeseeable accident had been our undoing.

Finally, a fuse blew. I had no fuses on board that

day, so I put a penny in the bypass, but it didn't do the trick. The engine, opened all the time I worked, was soaked, as we were drifting with our stern facing into the still rising waves, which by now were large enough to break against or slightly over the low transom. There was no juice left. The battery was dead, and we had to start bailing.

We both knew our situation then. Without words, Lance and I both knew the graveness of our predicament. We were both suddenly, unexpectedly sick.

"We're overdue by nearly an hour now. Peter and the Sea Stretcher crew must be out here, too," I reasoned. We strained to separate the sound of boat engines from the din of howling wind and crashing waves.

We discussed dropping anchor because we were probably in the path of any rescue attempt. We decided to drift to maintain better control over the boat. By drifting, the drag of the engine would keep the bow from pointing into the driving wind, which was easily strong enough to scoop the boat up and flip it. We'd lose control over our direction by drifting, but our first objective had to be to keep the boat afloat.

"I can't believe we haven't crossed paths with the Sea Stretcher by now. This wind should be shoving us right back to the island."

Winter scene, Old Lyme, Connecticut.

not arrive before sundown, he knew that he, too, would surely die. The only solace he found was to look through the "hole in the wall" and see, rising above the horizon, the steeple of the Osterville church. The coast along Wianno was heavy with pine groves, but opposite Eel River, for 100 yards or less, there is an open space, and the church spire could be seen from the ocean through this so-called hole in the wall.

What did Charles think about, swaying alone above an angry sea, his eyes on the church steeple? God? And the measure of his gratitude if he survived? God was ever present to the men of Uncle Charley's generation—and to be depended on.

On that fourth day, when the weather had cleared and the seas calmed somewhat, a longboat put out to rescue any survivors on the *Christina,* although it was believed there could be none. In the longboat were Captain Thomas Dunham, James Fisher, George Fisher, Charles Fisher, Edward Luce, and Eugene Wilber. My uncle, Joseph Tallman, Jr., of Osterville, has a picture, beautifully sketched by one B. Russell of New Bedford, showing the longboat alongside the schooner.

As Uncle Charley told it, his heart rose when he saw, at long last, help approaching. But, to his great despair, the boat circled the schooner twice, and the rescuers decided that all hands on board must have perished, that no one could have lived through such an ordeal. Those remaining in the rigging were dangling like wooden puppets with broken strings.

The rescuers had started to row back toward Chappaquiddick when they heard a feeble voice. It was ghostlike—supernatural—that sounds should be coming from the throats of dead men. But Uncle Charley said that his words, no matter how they sounded on the winter air, were, "Come back, you landlubbers, and cut us down!"

Of course they did, and Charles was taken to Edgartown, where the natives cared for him until he was removed to Holmes Hole (now Vineyard Haven). His feet had been so severely frozen that it was necessary to remove them to the ankles; it also was necessary to remove his fingers. In February he was able to leave for home.

In *Martha's Vineyard, 1835–1935,* Henry Beetle Hough writes of Uncle Charley, "The *Vineyard Gazette* referred to him as 'one of nature's noblemen' and, in the summer of 1874, the Oak Bluffs Land and Wharf Co., through the Hon. E.P. Carpenter, presented him with a small octagonal building not far from the Sea View Hotel."

Each summer thereafter, Charles Tallman occupied his small octagon, where he sold simple refreshments (including 85 bushels of peanuts in 1877), souvenirs, and pictures of himself with an account of his survival . . . a survival made possible by a Cape Codder's determination and a rubber coat. ∞

"Hope we land close enough to hike to a warm house for a late lunch. Hay Harbor, Silver Eel Pond, or Race Point is my guess."

With no fix on a land mass for a compass reading, we could only guess at our heading. Dead reckoning works only as long as the wind and the current don't shift. The swirling snow and water that enveloped everything were moving so crazily that we could only pray that land would soon appear. Any land with a place for shelter would do. Because the area was full of coastal inlets on both shores and numerous little islands between, we felt we'd be on land in no more than two hours.

Hope of sighting or being sighted by Peter's vessel diminished steadily as the minutes passed. As we bailed, we listened. Working against the rising water was the only way to save our hands from frostbite and our minds from panic.

Then in the midst of the deafening racket of wind came the piercing blare of a horn. Another blast and our hearts froze as we recognized the sound of the New London light that marks the mouth of the Thames River. The wind must have veered to the east, taking us far from our hoped-for course toward land or rescue.

We dropped anchor, but the whaler began taking on too much water. We would surely be spending the night in the boat now, and any water in our clothes or shoes would only increase the danger of hypothermia.

So again we drifted slightly southwest, straight toward the treacherous waters of The Race and beyond. These waters would take us 40 or more miles to Long Island at best or to infinite miles of open ocean at worst. In either case, we would be exposed to the potentially fatal chill of wind and water.

The Coast Guard was certainly out there by now. We knew that they were risking their own lives for the sake of saving ours. We hoped our friends had returned to safe harbor, but our senses strained for any sign of rescue. We knew that our chances were lessening with each minute away from the sound of the New London light.

We bailed together, and I prayed silently, tensing every muscle against the cruel exposure. Our legs and arms, already stiff from the cold, cramped quarters, had to be kept in constant motion. Lance used the battery cover as a makeshift bailer, while I used the hand pump. Pretty soon I had to stop. Without gloves, I couldn't bear the pain of prying my frozen fingers from the pump every few minutes. My worst fear now was the dread of frostbite. I exercised constantly—deep knee bends and arm flexes to keep active and stay awake. Lance bailed continuously. I cursed the clothing

I hadn't worn, the gloves that lay soaked beneath the ice-encrusted deck.

Through layers of sleet we glimpsed our last readings of time and direction before being swallowed up by total darkness. Though only a few feet apart, neither of us would see the other for the rest of the long night. We were completely cut off in this madness. The dead battery left us with no hope of any light until dawn. There would be no way of knowing for hours how much time we had spent or what direction we had taken. The only contact we could make would be to shout periodically to each other to startle and reassure—certainly to make sure the other was still on board.

No one could have found us in that raging darkness. The odds against our survival were frighteningly high. The waves, driven by 70-mile-per-hour gusts, were relentless, pouring over us in rapid succession, a big one and several smaller. Three successive big ones would have capsized us. The boat rose to frightening heights, then pitched wildly into the trough between the two mountains of water. Would the next trough be filled with rocks that would dash our small whaler to pieces? Would we be effortlessly flipped by one of the endless cresting breakers that we could hear on every side? The water was heaving over the gunwales so rapidly that Lance had just enough time between hits to bail the ice water to a safe level.

I had to keep exercising to keep my mind and body under control. My gloveless hands wanted to stop moving. I sat with my back to the wind, my arms wrapped around the railing to keep from pitching out. I knew the seat of my pants had long since frozen to the gas can. When I tensed and relaxed my muscles I felt the pull and the creeping numbness. I responded to Lance's shouts, but the urge was growing to give in to the fatigue, to just lie down, forget the endless nightmare, sleep. I knew there was no hope of rescue. We had reached the limit of our endurance. We would die in this hurricane.

I couldn't grasp anything real. I just fell in and out of a deep, sleepless trance. Sometimes I saw strange things like lights. Sometimes I would forget where I was for a moment. I shook myself, and the splintering sound of cracking ice falling from my shoulders roused me.

I shouted to Lance. I wanted to tell him that I had been dreaming of one of my favorite family stories, which related how my grandfather and his crew survived on their wrecked schooner by lashing themselves to the rigging overnight through a raging blizzard. By some miracle they had endured the storm, and although there might not be a miracle out there for us, it had

It was a full two weeks after his harrowing experience before Wes Greenleaf could return for his boat, which he and his passenger had abandoned when they washed up at Mattituck on the North Fork of Long Island. But it was a full two years before he could reveal to his wife just how close he had come to death that night in the Blizzard of '78.

happened before, and I felt somewhat reassured. I had prayed so much that night, and this time I gave thanks—thanks for the glimmer of hope to hold on to.

I was not afraid to die, though. That surprised me. The sorrow was in the fear of leaving my family. My little girl was only two and had so many years, so many needs, and I hated to think I wouldn't be around.

As I thought of her, I noticed several clear, bright lights in the swirling darkness. They were stars. There was a break in the storm. Soon the entire night sky was visible. Brilliant, naked stars shone all around. The first light in hours was welcome, but the clearing brought with it an almost instant temperature drop. I could feel the change through water-soaked layers of rain gear, snorkel coat, woolen sweater, flannel shirt, and under-wear. Water had been running down my neck all night, and now I began to shiver uncontrollably. I think Lance thought I was freezing to death. He huddled beside me under the protection of a frozen tarp to create what little warmth he could. We drained the accumulating water from our boots as we had been doing all night, and we

thought of the grim prospects of hypothermia. I warmed my hands as best I could by tucking them inside my coat against my skin or under my arms. When my exposed skin became too chilled, I would warm one finger at a time in my mouth.

During the clearing, we saw that the whaler had turned into a misshapen iceberg. Ice humps had formed on the console and motor. I tried to kick a wind-formed icicle off the side of the motor, but my leg felt like a lifeless stump. The extra weight of all that ice wasn't going to help us any, but there was nothing we could do about it.

Even though the skies cleared, the seas were un-relenting. Waves crested around and over us in an end-less barrage. The unabating wind chilled our bodies. There could be nothing worse for me. Even as the eye of the storm passed and the heavy clouds and darkness returned, a determination came with it. Dawn was ap-proaching. The longest night I had ever known was coming to an end.

We felt dawn before we saw it. Its full light

seemed infinitely long in arriving. Lance was the first to spot land.

"Mattituck!" He recognized the snow-covered bluffs of Long Island's North Fork and Mattituck Inlet. We had drifted nearly 50 miles from our intended port.

But the joy of sighting land was quickly tempered by the knowledge of the severity of the seas before us. The wind was still high, too, though nowhere near the heights of the past night. We put the helm hard to port and began to drift slowly toward shore.

While we drifted, we listened for the approach of rescue copters. Only later would we know that the severity of the blizzard on land had grounded all the helicopters. An hour passed, then two. We could see the dangerous, breaking surf between us and the shore. We shivered and steered. It was 5:00 A.M.

We knew we could never ride the boat ashore, but thinking about an arctic swim was frightening. How could we move our frozen limbs? Wouldn't we sink helplessly? But then, what choice did we have? To surf on those gigantic breakers in a small fiberglass boat would mean risking serious injury. We could not take that chance.

We steered toward the nearest sandy section. We'd try to get as close as possible. Neither of us could survive the cold water for more than a few minutes. As we closed in on the surf, a wave caught us. Lance was swept out. I held on a little distance and stuffed an emergency blowtorch and flint igniter into my coat before I followed him into the foaming waves. I hit bottom, then surfaced. The terrible shock we'd expected from midwinter water hadn't come. The ocean felt warm as waves lifted us toward shore.

Tossed onto the snow-drifted beach close to each other, we both tried to stand and fell. My hands felt better now after my swim. Wanting to start a fire with gas from a tank that drifted alongside us, I reached for the torch and found it was gone, lost in the surf.

We didn't have an hour left. We had to move, to make our blood circulate.

"We've gotta run," I said, breaking into what I thought was a strong sprint. But as I looked at Lance walking slowly beside me, I realized that I could barely move. We had to find shelter quickly.

I settled into a stiff shuffle in ankle-deep, icy water. The entire beach was covered with deep drifted snow. We walked in the water for about half a mile. As far as we could see in either direction were the snow-covered beaches and sheer bluffs of Jamesport. We had begun walking east because of large rocks that blocked

our way to the west. But which way meant shelter? People?

Then about 30 yards away we spotted a set of old summer sea stairs that led up the bluffs. We could only pray that up there we would find more signs of civilization. We had to crawl carefully up the drifted, ice-slick steps. Several rotten steps gave way under the combined weight of ice and water-soaked bodies.

At the top we saw some deserted-looking beach cottages, welcome shelter even without people. Four hundred yards of drifts lay between us and the first cottage. We took turns falling into the drifts. One of us first got the foothold and made the trough. The other followed.

We knew we'd make it now. Nothing could stop us. The crisis had passed. On the beach we could have wandered too long and frozen to death. But here by the cottages we could laugh. For the first time I noticed that the pitching and tossing of the last 18 hours were over.

We shuffled up the steps to the cottage door. I was all for breaking down the door and burning the whole place for warmth. We pounded on the wooden door instead, because we noticed a half-buried car parked next to the porch. We really didn't expect to find anyone at home. The door gave way to our pounding fists, and we fell inside just as a couple, who turned out to be John and Mary Taber, were rounding the corner of their living room to see what the commotion was about. They saw us shivering on the floor and thought we were stranded motorists. We told them we were shipwrecked.

We were warmed and fed. We spoke to our families, the Coast Guard, and local authorities. Friends were already on their way in snowmobiles to transfer us to Central Suffolk Hospital. They had been searching for us on land and on the water all night. My best friend, Alan Chaplaski, a commercial fisherman out of Stonington, Connecticut, had gone after us in his 52-foot commercial fishing vessel, *The Black Whale*. He had followed us into the heart of the storm, then he had cut his engines off Noank and let his boat drift for half an hour. Then, with the power on, he had followed our course as far toward Long Island as possible. He had missed us by minutes, risking his own life. When warned to return to port at 10:00 P.M., he had shut down the radio and gone on until he was satisfied that he had covered all the possibilities.

We were unspeakably grateful to everyone, and I could only marvel at the miracle of it all.   ∞

We Survived (in Comfort) the Blizzard of '78

BY LEIGH MONTVILLE

A t the time I was living in a small house on a small street in a western suburb of Boston. The snow began on a Monday—February 6, 1978. A warm air stream met a cold air mass, and you know what *that* means. The television weathermen gleefully told those of us who didn't. Snow. Followed by more snow. Followed by even more snow.

The remnants from a record 21.6-inch storm were still on the ground, so this was not exactly a welcome prediction. The new snow landed on top of the old snow. They formed a happy snow marriage. There was no place to push the new snow in a hurry because of the old snow. There was no way to keep up. The new snow arrived too fast, covering everything, stopping everything, putting normal day-to-day living into a freezer chest for the next workweek.

I was at home. The Blizzard of '78 began on my day off.

"I should be working," I told my wife as the implications of this snow became evident. "This is news. I am a newspaperman. I should be covering the biggest storm of my lifetime."

"You're a sportswriter," my wife said. "You don't cover news."

"I would for this," I said. "This is one of those situations when everyone covers everything. All hands on deck. At the very least, I should be stranded at Boston Garden."

In 24 hours, 23.6 inches of snow fell. In 32 hours, a record 27.1 inches fell. Tides rose 16 feet above normal due to a full moon in the middle of the storm.

Winds reached 69 miles per hour in Boston and 92 miles per hour in other parts of the state. Fifty-four people died in New England, 29 of them in Massachusetts. More than 10,000 people had to be evacuated due to flooding along the coast. The governor, Michael Dukakis—working in a crew-neck sweater—declared the entire state a disaster area and mobilized more than 5,000 National Guardsmen.

"If I were still in the National Guard, I'd be out there," I told my wife. "I'd be in the middle of this."

"I thought you said the happiest day of your life was when you *left* the National Guard," my wife said. "Or do I have that wrong? Didn't we go out to dinner to celebrate?"

The television brought constant reports. The storm was a curiosity outside the windows of our house, the snow getting deeper and deeper, so deep the door wouldn't open and the steps were obscured and bushes and boundaries disappeared. The storm was a terror on television.

Each report was more unbelievable than the last. Homes were swept into the sea. Homeless were rescued from rooftops. Sandbags were piled next to seawalls that were under attack. The *Peter Stuyvesant* sank in Boston Harbor. The most-painted shed in America, "Motif Number One," was destroyed in Rockport. The amusement pier at Old Orchard Beach in Maine collapsed. These were all places we knew. Didn't we wait for our reservations at Anthony's Pier 4 on the *Stuyvesant?* Hadn't my mother painted Motif Number One? The picture hung in our basement. Hadn't we ridden the rides at Old Orchard?

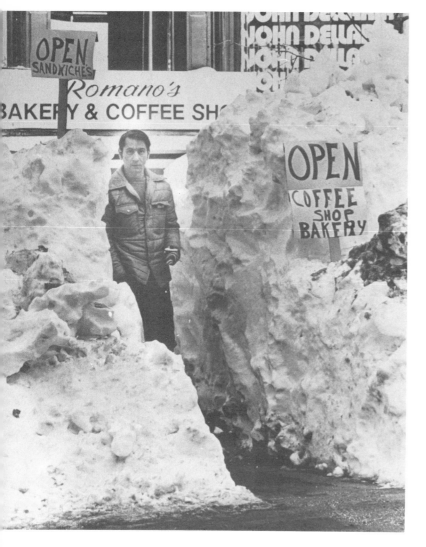

Above: *Reminiscent of scenes from 1888, some Boston-area merchants used the towering snowbanks left by the Blizzard of '78 for some free advertising.*

One of the biggest stories was the string of stalled and abandoned cars on Route 128. As many as 10,000 cars were stuck in the snow, as few as 3,000. No one could say for sure, adding to the strangeness of the situation. Many of the drivers had decided to stay with their cars. Many had left and were finding shelter or trying to walk home. The television pictures simply showed a long line of white bumps along the road. The scene was a twentieth-century nightmare, as inconceivable as a fire in a concrete skyscraper. How could all

these cars be stalled like this? Unbelievable. The highway was no more than five miles from my house.

"Do you know how easy it would have been for me to be stalled on that road?" I asked my wife. "Do you know how easy it would have been for you to be stalled? We use that road every day of our lives. These pictures are weird. You keep thinking you're seeing some disaster in the middle of Kansas. Then you catch a peek at the Muzi Ford sign, where you usually turn."

"You're lucky that you were off," my wife said.

If I had been working, I would have covered the Beanpot college hockey tournament that Monday night at the Boston Garden. The games did go on; I would have gone. Will McDonough, the other sports columnist for the *Globe,* went. He did not get home for three days.

"I took my son and two of his high-school friends with me to the game," McDonough said. "I never thought the snow was going to be as bad as it was. The one smart thing I did was to park underneath one of those bridges behind the Garden so I was able to drive the car after the games.

"All night there were announcements that people should leave and go home on the T. I stayed. I wrote my story. I picked up the kids and we got in the car, and that's when we knew we had trouble. The snow was a lot deeper than I'd thought. Luckily, we got out onto Causeway Street and three snowplows came past and turned onto the Expressway. We got behind them. It was like magic. We followed them and had no idea what we would do when they got off the road.

"Luckily, they got off the road at Morrissey Boulevard, and we were able to follow them all the way to the *Globe.* Magic. I parked the car and that was where we stayed. I knew we weren't going any farther."

I called in to the *Globe* every day. I got reports. There was a core of people—as I had expected—who had landed at the office and were putting out the newspaper. McDonough was one of them. The first edition, printed Monday night, went no farther than nearby Koziuszko Circle, the trucks stalled in the snow. This was the first time in 106 years that the *Globe* was unable to deliver its papers. The afternoon *Globe* did publish, and each of the subsequent editions on following days went farther and farther into the circulation area.

The people at the newspaper were sleeping on desks and eating every bit of food available in the cafeteria. When the plows arrived, management rented some rooms at the Howard Johnson's Motor Lodge on the Southeast Expressway. One shift of workers would replace another in the rooms without the linens being changed. The people were transported in the backs of delivery trucks, the canvas on the back pulled tight to keep out the cold. The motor inn had lost its power. People were constantly moving through the gloom and the cold. Dorchester resembled London during the blitz.

"Are you sure you don't want me to come in?" I asked as I heard these stories every day. "I could start walking. I don't live any more than ten miles from the office. I could walk there in half a day. . . . "

"Don't be silly," my editor said. "We have everything under control here. There are enough people here to handle what we have to do."

What could I do? Helpless, I surrendered. I handled the domestic scene. The power never quit. The phone never stopped working. My children were three and five years old, and the snow was an excitement ordered off the menu at an ice cream shop. So I joined them in their fun.

On the afternoon of the second day, we made the first move outside. I climbed out the first-floor window and sank into the snow as if it were the shallow end of a swimming pool. I waded to the front steps, where I cleverly had left the family snow shovel. I waded back to the window. I cleared a spot underneath. My five-year-old was lowered into the spot. The snow on either side was as tall as he was. What must that be like? Snow as tall as you are? I almost knew. The drifts against certain trees were as tall as I was.

I spent most of the afternoon shoveling a path to the street. No plows had arrived on our street, but I could see they had moved down the larger street at the corner. I shoveled. I talked with my neighbors. When my path was large enough, I took my son on an expedi-

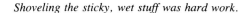

Shoveling the sticky, wet stuff was hard work.

Shoveling Out in '78

BY JOSEPH PARZYCH

Forty hours is a long time to go without sleep, but somehow I managed. Massachusetts was desperate for heavy-equipment operators to pitch in and remove the aftermath of the Blizzard of '78. So I got in my truck with the tag-along trailer and drove the 90 miles from my home in Gill, Massachusetts, to Route 128, where the snow had stopped everyone in their treads.

If the situation hadn't been so serious, it would have been funny. The military brought in these huge machines that were operated, I suspect, by folks from down South who had never seen snow before. The oversized military payloaders had these teeth on the buckets, which were useless for removing snow. I mean, they just couldn't scrape the ground clean. One operator found an unintentional use for the teeth: In attempting to resurrect a station wagon, he punctured the gas tank. The result was better than any Fourth of July. I remember that one career soldier told me that the publicity generated by the whole operation would be a great recruitment aid. I didn't think so; after all this was over, I thought for sure they'd have to bring back the draft.

We worked practically around the clock. I felt as though the payloader were part of me; I responded quite naturally to the sway of the machine. Sweep left, scoop, raise, dump, and flip to reverse—all in one motion. Hour after hour. One night we had a brief rest at 3:00 A.M. when a policeman drove us to an emergency shelter at Canton High School. Volunteers fed us some soup and coffee. That soup went straight to my feet—a quick thaw.

After 20 hours or so, my speech started to slur. My head was killing me; it felt as if it had been split open. The coffee I kept drinking started taking its toll—I started feeling sick and had the jitters. I had begun Thursday evening and had gone practically nonstop to Saturday. By Saturday afternoon the sun seemed to sear my eyes every time I looked out of the cab.

Finally I could stand it no longer—my head was throbbing as I climbed down from the cab and shuffled over to one of the folks standing by. I tried to buy his sunglasses . . . no dice. "There aren't any stores open, so if I sell you mine, I won't be able to buy a replacement."

I went back to the cab. A few minutes later the fellow with the sunglasses came up to the loader, took off his specs, and handed them to me. I tried to pay him. He refused. I guess when he changed his mind he changed his priorities. I welcomed the windfall.

Perhaps the nicest part of receiving this unexpected gift was that it gave me something tangible to remember the storm by—and an excuse to share examples of the kindness I had seen and experienced. Bleary-eyed, I went home that Saturday and was greeted by one of my kids. "Hey, Dad, where'd you get the sunglasses?"

"Long story . . . " ∞

Opposite page, top: *Days after the '78 Blizzard, crews were still working to clear Route 128, digging out cars abandoned in the storm.* **Above:** *Chaos also reigned on residential streets, as the storm paralyzed eastern Massachusetts and other parts of the Northeast.*

tion. (My daughter, alas, was not allowed out of the house. The snow was too deep for her until further shoveling was done.) We walked to the village, five blocks away, and bought a pizza.

All the other stores, except for a small variety store, were closed. I have no idea why the pizzeria was still open, except that it was doing business as if it were the last pizzeria left on earth. I bought a large pepperoni. My son and I returned home, frontiersmen who had trapped and killed the family meal. No pizza ever tasted more exotic.

"Tomorrow," I said, "I will go out and kill some hamburger. I will trap the buns."

"Take the sled," my wife said. "Go to the A&P. It'll be a lot easier. We can use some milk and things, too, if they're available."

The days followed this pleasant pace. My kids dug tunnels and made snowmen. I shoveled and talked, shoveled and talked. Marie Clancy, who lived across the street, had been stranded at her job as a nurse at Boston City Hospital. One day. Two days. Three days. Her husband, Joe, took care of their two kids. We shoveled and talked. He described the meals he was cooking every night. He seemed to be enjoying himself.

"Marie calls every night," he said. "She's worried about how we're making out. I tell her we're doing great."

I met neighbors I had never seen before. It was as if we now had something we could say to each other. There was a meaningful subject for discussion. People came past on cross-country skis. People dragged sleds everywhere. People rang the doorbell to say they were going to the store and wanted to know if they could buy anything for us. A week earlier they wouldn't have said hello on the street, driving past in their cars. I drank beer on a Wednesday afternoon with a couple from the next street over. There was no rush, no obligation. None of us had to work.

"We should do this more often," I said.

"We *should* do this more often," the neighbors agreed.

We all knew this would never happen.

The reports on the news gradually became more optimistic. The work on the stalled cars on 128 proceeded slowly. Police theorized that cars had become stuck on the exits during the heaviest snows and that this had caused cars to become stuck on the highway. A couple of tractor trailers had jackknifed to complete the mess. Drivers had found refuge in industrial plants and in homes along the road. More than 2,000 drivers had landed at St. Bartholomew's church hall in Needham. First the northbound side of the road was cleared, from Canton to Route 9 in Newton. Then work began on the southbound side.

In Scituate, Hull, Revere, and dozens of other shoreline towns, the damage estimates were enormous—the mayor of Hull said he thought 80 percent of the residences in the town had received at least some damage from the high tides—but the cleanup and legal work began. Who would pay? Where would displaced

Snow: Artificial snow from a natural cloud was produced November 13, 1946, by Vincent Schaefer. General Electric had Schaefer fly in a plane over Mount Greylock, Massachusetts, dispensing dry-ice pellets over an area three miles long.

LOTS OF SNOW, ENJOY THE SHOW

☞ Blizzard of 1978: Eight hundred folks were trapped for three days at the Showcase Cinema in Dedham, Massachusetts. According to then assistant manager Rob Laird, "Yeah, we ran the movies—people saw a lot of Henry Winkler in *The One and Only*."

"Where did you come from? Well, let's see . . . it was February of '78 and a great blizzard had inundated the Northeast. Your Daddy and I were stalled in the break-down lane of 95 northbound near the Jefferson Blvd. exit . . . There we were, stuck in a '72 Matador with lots of time on our hands . . ."

people live? Would they be able to rebuild where they had lived? Logan Airport, closed except to emergency military flights, reopened on Friday. The MBTA gradually reopened public transit lines. More and more people moved onto the roads.

Will McDonough went home on Thursday. Marie Clancy went home on Friday.

"You couldn't drive—only emergency vehicles were allowed—but a roof collapsed at Jordan Marsh at the South Shore Plaza," McDonough said. "One of the editors said, 'Look, why don't you drive out there and see what happened? Then phone in the story from home. If anyone says anything, you're on the job.' That's what I did. I got the kids, who had been working as copyboys for three days, and we drove home. There was nobody else on the road. It was eerie."

"A guy drove me home from the hospital in some kind of jeep," Marie Clancy said. "He was a deaf-mute and had no idea where he was going. I tugged at him to show which direction we were supposed to turn. All we saw were other emergency vehicles. I came home for the night, then went back to the hospital. The same guy gave me a ride."

I did none of this. I was home already.

The plow arrived on Thursday night on my street, greeted as if it were the liberation army hitting Paris, but I didn't drive anywhere until Saturday. I didn't go back to work until Sunday. By that time, there were no problems. The streets were clear, and the Massachusetts Turnpike was shoveled down to the pavement. Driving was legal. The adventure was over.

A snowboarder takes the easy way down Boston's snow-clogged Beacon Hill.

I was one of those people who went through the Blizzard of '78 as if it were a quiet, different vacation. I read that there were outdoor parties on streets in Wellesley, dinner served on picnic tables that featured place settings and candelabra. More parties at the local colleges. More parties on Beacon Hill. I read dozens of quotes from people who enjoyed the camaraderie of the storm, the coziness, the isolation. I suppose I would have said the same thing if asked.

"I enjoyed this," I told my wife at the end. "I feel guilty saying it, but this was pleasant. I never knew I could sit still this long."

"I never knew you could either," she said.   ∞

A Message in the Wind

BY PETER LA ROCHE

Blizzards and below-zero temperatures are not out of the ordinary in a New Hampshire winter. I've seen it as low as 42 below, and I've seen 20 inches of snow over a period of 24 hours come driving in before a gale straight from the top of Mount Washington. Such a storm, with the thermometer standing at 18 degrees below zero, caught me on a day in January 1934—a day I shall never forget.

Since 1932 I had been caretaker on Governor's Island on Lake Winnipesaukee in New Hampshire. After the summer homes were closed for the season, my sole duty was to patrol once a day to see that all was well. As the heavy snows came, we dug in, and it didn't matter if we did not get to Laconia for a week or more. Both my wife, Edna, and I are natives of New Hampshire and, not given to caring much for bright lights, didn't mind the isolation. Our only child, Beverly, was then only 20 months old, so there was no school problem.

The large farmhouse where we lived on the island stood about two-thirds of a mile from the highway. (The island is joined to the mainland by a long causeway broken by a high bridge to allow for boat traffic underneath.) As the island was private property, we had no plow service, but this did not matter much because most of my travel about the island was on snowshoes or skis. And when we had to go to Laconia, I had plenty of time to break out a passage for my little roadster.

But January 1934 was not just another winter month. That was the month our second child was supposed to be born. Beverly had given my wife quite a rough time before and during birth, and the doctor was not sure when our new child would be born. As soon as it became evident that the time was drawing near, we were to come immediately to the hospital. "Take no chances this time," Dr. Armand Normandin warned us. "It will be best to come a week or so ahead of time, just to make sure."

We knew the good doctor had our best interests at heart, but those were the Depression years, and $5 had to go a whole week for food. An extra week at the hospital could really hurt. So we watched the weather and kept everything prepared to make a run for it. Snow was light, days were fine, and we hung on.

Then it struck!

In the middle of the night the wind came lashing at the house sitting on top of the hill. I jumped out of bed and looked out the window. It was only the wind, no snow, except for what was being blown about. With a sigh of relief I climbed back into bed and fell asleep.

About seven o'clock in the morning my wife woke me up to tell me the pains had started. The wind was still battering at the house as I hurriedly dressed, stoked up the fire, and put on the coffee. Then I looked outside, and I'm sure my heart skipped a beat. Sometime during the night it had started snowing and had turned into a blizzard. It was impossible to see more than a few yards, and the snow was already piled well over a foot deep, where it hadn't drifted to twice that depth.

I grabbed the phone and started to call the doctor. I jiggled the hook, banged the phone, and pounded on the box, but it was no use . . . the phone was dead.

Thirty minutes later, dressed as warmly as possible and having had a quick breakfast, we climbed into the roadster, roared out of the barn, and started for the highway. Two hundred feet from the barn I realized I was going to have a battle on my hands. When the car bogged down, the snow was even with the top of the radiator. I opened the trunk, took out my big snow shovel, and cleared a spot in front of the car. Then I hopped back in the car, reversed as far as I could go, and, with the car in low gear and the motor roaring, slammed ahead into the ever-mounting snow. I gained about 25 feet.

For the next hour I worked like a man possessed. Icicles formed on my face as I jumped out of the car and shoveled with all my might, then jumped back in, reversed, and slammed the little car ahead. My wife sat huddled in the seat with Beverly wrapped close to her in a blanket. The car had no heater, and the snow came in through the flimsy side curtains. I was mighty scared and tried to hide it in the loud voice I usually used when denouncing the weather and the state of New Hampshire in winter. But outside, while I shoveled, I prayed to God for help.

At the end of an hour I was less than halfway across, and I knew then that I'd never make it. My lungs ached with a burning pain, and I could hardly lift my arms. There was only one thing to do—go back to the house.

Then I found that the car would never take us back, for the road was drifted in solid behind us. And, in my exhausted state, I could never carry the two of them up that hill through those drifts. And to leave one behind . . .

I opened the door, climbed into the car, and looked over at my wife. "How . . . how is the pain?"

"Not too bad. I think I can wait. You'd better rest a little while."

I didn't know what to say. I just nodded, then looked away. I don't know why I looked away. There was no longer anything to hide. Little Beverly started to cry.

I thought of trying to get across the lake to Harold Mitchell's farm and have him come over with his team of horses to pull us out, but I knew I could never get back in time to find my wife and child alive. At 18 below nothing lives long.

Then my wife said, "Why don't you try shouting? Someone might hear you."

Suddenly I felt like laughing. Shouting in a blizzard! Even inside the car we had to speak loudly to hear ourselves. She insisted that I try, so I stepped out and started shouting as loud as I could. Every time I did, it brought on a coughing spell, and after a few tries I had to stop.

Feeling a bit rested, I decided we might as well die trying, so I resumed shoveling, but was making no headway as a languorous feeling started to come over me. I rested against the car.

Then I saw him, and I jumped in astonishment. Out of the blizzard he came—a big man dressed in a heavy mackinaw and a fur cap. He came on strongly through the drifted snow and stopped before me. I peered at him to see if it was someone I knew who might have guessed my predicament, but this was a stranger.

"Why th' devil are you out here in a car?" he shouted.

In my joy at seeing him, my words tumbled one over the other as I told him I was trying to get my wife to the hospital. He grabbed the shovel and began clearing snow like a plow. I continued to ram ahead to gain every foot. When we hit the causeway where the road was elevated and the wind kept most of the snow blown away, my helper rode the back bumper to give me traction, and we managed to get all the way across the causeway without shoveling.

From the end of the causeway to the highway this man must have shoveled tons of snow. When I tried to relieve him, he'd wave me back into the car, shouting that this was just exercise for him.

Two or three times I looked at my wife and knew by the whiteness of her face and the tightly pressed lips that the cold was getting to her and the pain was increasing. I was badly frightened, and my nerves were jangled to the extent that my foot bounced up and down on the accelerator.

I prayed to God that the big figure ahead of the car who shoveled snow like a madman would hold out. And hold out he did. Two and a half hours after leaving the house, the little car broke through onto the partly cleared highway, and we were on our way.

When I made as if to stop, our benefactor waved us on, and in the rearview mirror I saw him standing in a drift at the roadside—a big figure encased in a mantle of snow. He waved once more before the blizzard shut off the view between us.

At two o'clock the next morning, in the warm safety of the hospital, our daughter Norma was born. Then I began the search to find the big man who had come to us in our greatest hour of need. For days I snowshoed from one bobhouse (a little hut or cabin put on the lake for ice fishing) to another asking anyone I could find about the man.

At first I was confident I would find him close in along the channel by the causeway, but after I had eliminated the few bobhouses that were there, I began to range farther out. It was ridiculous to think that

"I looked outside, and my heart skipped a beat. Sometime during the night it had started snowing and had turned into a blizzard. It was impossible to see more than a few yards, and the snow was already piled well over a foot, where it hadn't drifted to twice that depth."

Tragedy on "Cold Friday"

BY BONNIE SIMPSON

AUTHOR'S INTRODUCTION: *When my sister and I were small and living near Laconia, New Hampshire, our parents often took us for Sunday afternoon hikes. One place in Sanbornton I remember them taking us to several times was "where the Ellsworth place used to be." My father would tell us the tragic story connected with it, and we would never fail to be impressed and saddened by it. In these days of affluence and, for the most part, luxury and comfort, it is perhaps worthwhile to remember that it was not always so.*

January 19, 1810, was "Cold Friday" and "a memorable day throughout New England. From the mild temperature of 43 degrees above zero at sunset the evening before, the mercury sank to 25 degrees below zero in 16 hours. This change was attended by a violent, piercing wind, prostrating trees and overturning buildings. Young cattle and wild animals were frozen, and many a stage-driver and school-boy received ear-marks which they wore through life."[1] Thus was occasioned the death of the Ellsworth children, the most tragic event that has ever occurred in Sanbornton, New Hampshire. We offer this account, taken, with slight amendments, from the Boston *Journal* of March 18, 1869:

"The farm-house of their father, Jeremiah Ellsworth, on the old New Hampton road, gave way to the violence of the gale, half an hour before sunrise, the windows being blown in, exposing the whole building to destruction. Mrs. Ellsworth and her youngest child took refuge in the cellar. Mr. Ellsworth covered his two other children in bed and started for his nearest neighbor's, David Brown's, reaching there at sunrise, and though but a hundred rods distant, yet with feet and face badly frozen and himself unable to stand. Mr. Brown hastened to the house with his horse and sleigh, and found the inmates as left by the father, except that the wind had blown off the clothes from the oldest children. He loaded mother and children in the sleigh, covered them with the bedding, and started for his house. Twice the sleigh was overturned by violent gusts of wind. The first time Mr. Brown urged the mother to try to reach his house immediately, as her limbs were beginning to fail. She did so, crawling much of the way on her hands and knees; while he, having a second time loaded the half-dressed children, soon found them again scattered upon the frozen snow, with his sleigh broken. Covering the youngest under a log, he started with the two oldest on foot towards his house. Their cries stimulated him to intense exertion; but before he reached the house they were frozen stiff, so as to die in a few minutes after. Other neighbors came to the rescue, and the body of the remaining child was soon returned. Mr. Brown was blind the rest of his life, in consequence of this exposure, and the children's parents suffered long and severely from their injuries."

[1]*Rev. M.T. Runnels.* History of Sanbornton, New Hampshire, *vol. 1 of 2 vols. Alfred Mudge and Son, Printers, 34 School Street, Boston, Mass., 1882.*

anyone that far away could have heard me shouting. But then, it was ridiculous to think that anyone 500 feet away could have heard me calling. Maybe he had been caught out on the lake and was trying to make his way to our house on the hill. This seemed the only logical answer.

Four days later, I found him in a bobhouse by Eagle Island, about a mile and a half from where he had come looming out of the blizzard. It was an unusually large house, and I figured whoever owned it must have equipped it for long fishing sessions. I was right. I banged on the door, and in a moment it opened, and there he stood. He looked at me quizzically for a moment, then smiled.

"What was it, a boy or a girl?" he boomed.

I told him it was a girl, over eight pounds, and that my wife and daughter were doing well. He invited me in, and I shook off my snowshoes and stepped inside. The hut was fitted out like the cabin on a cruiser, with a little galley, bunks, and a drop table that made into a dinette.

My first question, after my profound thanks, which he waved away, was how he had come to be near us.

"Well, it's a funny thing," he said. "I've been fishing here in the channel by Eagle Island for about eight years. Now, here about ten days ago, I got the idea I could do better if I set my house in the channel north of the causeway bridge. So, I drugged it over there and, would you know it, I never caught a fish! So, day or two after the blizzard let up, I drugged it back. I'm doin' all right here. Averagin' two, three a day."

He stuck out his hand. "Oh, by the way, the name's Schrader. Nick Schrader. Pavin' contractor in the summer, fisherman in the winter."

I introduced myself and shook hands. Then I asked what had been in my mind for the past week. "Mr. Schrader, what brought you out of your bobhouse at the height of the blizzard?"

A surprised expression came across his face. "Why, I heard you shout."

"You heard me shout over a quarter of a mile away in a roaring blizzard, and you inside your bobhouse?"

"As plain as I'm hearin' you now."

In a moment of silence it became evident to Mr. Schrader that what he had said was physically impossible. He cleared his throat and looked away. Then said, "It . . . it must have carried on the wind, eh?"

"It must have," I agreed. ∞

Other "Cold Fridays"

Throughout the written history of New England—from the earliest colonial farmers, professors, and other weather observers to modern times, when we calculate wind-chill factors and heating degree days—one would think that there would be enough cold weather to spread evenly around the week.

Yet for some odd reason, Friday bears the singular distinction of having the greatest number of days that have rated a "Cold" designation in the annals of New England weather history. Oh, sure, there were two Cold Tuesdays (in 1788 and 1855) and even a Cold Sabbath in 1773. And we suspect that, once this book appears, we'll be getting letters lobbying for Cold Mondays, Wednesdays, Thursdays, and Saturdays. Why Friday should be so favored (or slandered) by history remains something of a mystery.

Weather historian David Ludlum mentions no fewer than three Cold Fridays in his various works, including the first official Cold Friday of 1810. The other two notable days were:

☞ **Cold Friday II (January 23, 1857):** Unlike the Cold Friday of 1810, which occurred in the middle of one of the mildest winters on record, Cold Friday II fell in the coldest month of the nineteenth century. The cold snap followed a big snowstorm on January 18–19, and strong northwest gales made the cold even crueler. Bath, Maine, registered a low temperature of −52°F., while Craftsbury, Vermont, experienced the coldest day ever recorded in the Northeast, with a mean temperature for 24 hours of −28°F.

☞ **Cold Friday III (February 9, 1934):** February 1934 was the coldest month on record since January 1857, and southern New England was particularly affected, with new low temperatures set in many southern cities on Cold Friday III. Boston registered −18°F., Providence −17°F., and New Haven −15°F. Folks in northern New England were not exactly in their shirtsleeves, either. Bloomfield, Vermont, recorded a low temperature of −41°F., and Burlington, Vermont's *high* for the day was a bracing −9°F.

A Cruel Beauty

BY DAVID M. LUDLUM

The most spectacular ice storm I ever witnessed occurred during a January just after we had moved into a new house with three young boys. An overnight storm, silently at first, had spread an icy sheath on trees, shrubs, and power lines. The line along the street in front of our house became so encrusted with ice that the wires actually sagged down to the ground. We clustered at the window staring at the glittering beauty while wondering when our power would go off, leaving us with only Sterno to cook with and a fireplace for heating. But it didn't. A utility inspector came along later and told me that the power company was using a new type of wire that had great resilience to stress. Once the icy burden was removed, it returned to a normal position between the poles.

Ice storms have always been part of our winter life. An early reference was made by Judge Samuel Sewall, the eminent colonial jurist and diarist of Boston: "Fifth-day, Nov the last 1699. The Rain freezes upon the branches of the Trees to that thickness and weight, that great havock is thereby made of the Wood and Timber. . . . "

Fortunately, the occurrence of a damaging ice storm is a relatively rare event in most northern climes. Only about once every ten years, when the atmospheric layers are properly stratified—a warm stratum of air aloft, a deep layer of below-freezing air below—does a sufficient coating of ice develop on outdoor objects to cause serious damage. Probably the eeriest night I ever spent came just after the big snowstorm in the New York suburban area in December 1947. The next storm on New Year's night started as snow, but soon changed to a glaze storm that coated all the trees with a half inch to an inch of ice. It was accompanied by strong northeast winds. First one heard the creaking of the branches as they swayed up and down under their icy load. Then came resounding crashes as the burden became too much to bear. Eventually, with thunderous noise, whole limbs split from the main trunks of large trees. The fallen timber formed obstacles the next morning astride the deep snowbanks on either side of the streets. It required a full week for workers to clear the streets enough to allow for normal traffic movement.

An ice storm is essentially freezing rain that starts its fall from the clouds in liquid form and ends as an icy coating of glaze. Meteorologists use the term *glaze* to differentiate freezing rain from what is popularly known as sleet. The latter consists of little round balls of opaque ice, which usually bounce on hitting a hard surface. The official name for these is ice pellets. Unless accompanied by alternate rain or wet snow, they do not cling to wires or vertical surfaces and do not pose the menace to orderly living that glaze does.

A typical scenario for a widespread ice storm occurs over New York and New England when a winter storm center is moving from southwest to northeast. Rain may fall in a zone extending 50 to 100 miles to the northwest of the storm track since temperatures are above freezing. Farther northwest, in a contiguous zone of about a hundred miles' width, freezing rain may occur, and beyond that a zone of either ice pellets or

snow. One traveling northwest from a storm center would experience alternate periods of rain, freezing rain, ice pellets, and finally snow. The great post-Christmas storm of 1969 demonstrated the varied forms of winter weather possible in a single storm through a zone of Maine, New Hampshire, and Vermont.

The worst New England ice storm of the present century affected a strip from northern Connecticut, through central Massachusetts, and into southern Maine on November 26 to 29, 1921. After a day and a half of alternate snow, ice pellets, and rain, the latter continued to fall in liquid form even though the thermometer at the surface slumped to 25°F. Freezing rain took over the precipitation process, and glaze ice formed on all exposed objects. Electric wires sported icy sheaths three inches in diameter that weighed nearly a pound per foot.

Professor Charles F. Brooks, the founder of the American Meteorological Society, described the impact that the storm had in the area around his home in Worcester, Massachusetts:

At night it began to rain steadily and ice as steadily to form. Morning saw an inch-thick armor of ice over everything out-of-doors, and still it rained and froze, while the northeast wind increased to a gale. By afternoon city streets were dangerous. Everywhere branches and trees and electric wires and poles were falling. A wild and terrible night followed. Electric lights were extinguished, and cities and towns lay in blackness, trolley cars ceased running, telegraph and telephone service was gone, streets were impassable to vehicles, some of them to pedestrians. The climax was a thunderstorm, the thunder crashing to the accompaniment of falling trees.

In late December 1969 rain fell on the villages and

Opposite page: *Trees sheathed with ice, looking down Washington Street in Hartford during the 1880s.* **Above:** *An elm tree after a January 1891 ice storm, on Farmington Avenue in Hartford.*

Right: *A World War II corvette lying at anchor, encrusted with ice.* **Bottom:** *Icicles hang from wires near tobacco barns in Sunderland, Massachusetts.*

towns along the upper Connecticut River, but the surrounding hills experienced a severe ice storm that continued for as long as 48 hours. Devastation of forests and utility lines was described as "havoc unbelievable." To the west, along the crest of the Green Mountains, one of the heaviest snowfalls of modern times occurred. Vermont governor Dean C. Davis declared a state of emergency. The accumulation of thick ice on a previous snow cover in the Northeast Kingdom ruined skiing for the rest of the winter.

Connecticut endured a severe icing siege in December 1973 when a coastal storm moved over eastern Long Island and southeastern New England. Trees in the Nutmeg State were said to have experienced more damage than during the Hurricane of '38. More than 250,000 customers were without electric power, and in some cases the outages continued for more than a week.

What should you do about an ice storm? Common-sense precautions—working flashlights, a ready non-electric heat source, a battery-operated radio—will pay off when one of the loveliest yet most destructive of storms menaces our orderly life indoors. The best thing I know to do is to relax and enjoy nature's quirk. Put film in your camera and catch both the beauty brought and the destruction wrought by the ice. Then one day you can show your children and grandchildren how rugged life was back in the 1990s.   ∞

DON'T EVER DO THIS

☞ It's against the law in Woonsocket, Rhode Island, to remove icicles by shooting at them with a rifle.

Left: *Dark tree limbs outlined against glittering icy branches, Litchfield, Connecticut.*

The Diary of Boston's Big Freeze

Boston Harbor does not freeze over very often—at least not anymore. Today, big iron-hulled ships can break up newly formed ice, and powerful icebreakers are on call. Also, some theorize that there's less fresh water and ice flowing into the harbor from the now extensively dammed Mystic and Charles rivers. For the really big freeze-ups, then, one must go back to the last century—back to 1817, 1821, 1832, 1835, 1844, 1856, 1857, 1869, and other years listed in *The Old Farmer's Almanac*'s records. In 1856, for example, Boston Harbor was frozen to the extent that sleighs were driven from City Point in South Boston across the bay to Thompson Island and right to the door of the main building of The Farm School.

In the early 1840s, the first transatlantic steamers were beginning their regular schedules, and in January 1844, the first Cunarder in the Boston–Liverpool service arrived in Boston Harbor. That year turned out to be one of the most formidable nineteenth-century winters in New England, and once the *Britannia* was safely berthed, the harbor commenced to freeze over solid from the wharves

right out to the lighthouse. Even Long Island Sound was frozen over during this period, as was just about every harbor from Connecticut to Maine.

As the *Britannia*'s sailing day, February 1, approached, a meeting of Boston merchants was called to consider the situation. The mayor, Martin Brimmer, presided, and after some discussion it was decided that the steamer should be cut out without expense to her owners and sent to sea as near the advertised time of her departure as possible. This unique project began on Thursday, February 1, 1844, and was recorded in the old *Boston Post* as follows:

Thursday, 1 February 1844

"The pilots and about 140 laborers proceeded down the harbor yesterday, and commenced cutting a ship-channel in the ice, but ere they had been at work an hour, the cold was so intense, that many of the laborers were more or less frost-bitten; and the pilots, finding that their forces would be unable to hold out, and that the openings froze up almost as quick as made, were compelled to abandon the enterprise for the present.

"No sooner was it known by the committee, appointed at the meeting which was held on Tuesday, that the first effort to open the harbor had failed, than they at once determined to make another effort, upon a more extended scale. Accordingly, they contracted with Messrs. Gage, Hittinger & Co., and Mr. John Hill, gentlemen connected with the Fresh Pond and West Cambridge ice companies, to open the harbor within a given time. The services, too, of our pilots have again been secured. Indeed, without their superintendence, the proper track for a ship-channel could not very well be opened. They are worthy of praise for the exertions which they made yesterday, and no doubt, to-day, they will be the last to abandon the enterprise. The ice companies, we understand, will open a track with ice-ploughs, drawn by horses, and, should the ice be found too weak to bear horses, men will be substituted. They will have 250 men from the country, besides perhaps as many from the city, employed. To guard against being frost-bitten, it is contemplated either to have a tent on the ice, or a steamer in attendance, where the men when benumbed can at once receive shelter and suitable refreshment.

"We understand that the gentlemen who have contracted to open the harbor, are sanguine that they will be able to open a channel by to-morrow night sufficiently large to admit the departure of the steamer *Britannia*."

Friday, 2 February 1844

"Yesterday morning the gentlemen who had contracted to open the harbor, commenced operations. They had a force of about three hundred men and six horses, and ice implements of all shapes and sizes, among which, the most effective were ice-ploughs. The forces were divided into two parties, one of whom commenced at the open sea below, and the other at East Boston, in the vicinity of the Cunard wharf. Four furrows were cut, about 25 feet apart, thus making a channel 75 feet wide, sufficient space to admit of the departure of the steamer

Britannia. The ice between the two southern furrows, 25 feet wide, as soon as cut, was broken up and hauled under the ice by means of ropes and grapnels. Last evening, about sunset, a channel 25 feet wide and five miles long had been opened by the party who commenced at East Boston. The party below, at the same time, had cut an opening two miles in length and 75 feet wide. When the two parties meet, the remaining ice, which is cut into two furrows above, will be broken up and floated out with the ebb tide, thus leaving an open channel 75 feet wide, from East Boston to the southern outlet of the harbor, which is entirely clear of ice. The party who commenced at East Boston used horses to drag the ice-ploughs, but below it was found impracticable, and men had to perform that labor.

"A horse and sled and two men, while driving over the ice below, fell through, and were rescued with much difficulty. This is the only accident, so far, that has occurred. The weather was remarkably mild during the day, and large numbers of people were on the ice, including several ladies, witnessing with apparent glee the opening of the harbor.

"Last night the weather continued so mild that the contractors continued their exertions, intending to continue them through the night until they have completed a channel sufficiently wide to admit the steamer *Britannia* to depart to-day. They have tents and fires on the ice, and suitable refreshments for their forces."

Saturday, 3 February 1844

"The ship passage through the ice was finished yesterday at dark—the channel is now entirely clear.

"The *Britannia* went to sea in gallant style on Saturday morning at about 11 o'clock. A passage of one hundred and fifty feet wide was opened for her through the ice. For a couple of miles she was accompanied by a multitude of citizens, on the ice, cheering her most vehemently. The *Britannia* takes out a large complement of passengers, for the season, her number being fifty-four, and forty berths reserved for Halifax."   ∞

What's the Coldest It's Ever Been In:

State	Temperature (degrees Fahrenheit)	
Connecticut	−32	(Falls Village, February 16, 1943)
Maine	−48	(Van Buren, January 19, 1925)
Massachusetts	−40	(Chester, January 22, 1984)
New Hampshire	−46	(Pittsburg, January 28, 1925)
Rhode Island	−23	(Kingston, January 11, 1942)
Vermont	−50	(Bloomfield, December 30, 1933)

The Great Christmas Storm of 1778

BY GAIL M. POTTER

From time immemorial, superstitious Yankee seamen have considered Friday an ill-omened day on which to set sail. Nevertheless, it was on a Friday morning, the twenty-fifth day of December in the year 1778, that Doctor Herbert Mann stowed his medical kit and surgical equipment on board the brig *General Arnold*. Later the same day, Captain Magee gave orders to weigh anchor, hoist sail, and clear Boston Harbor.

The *General Arnold*'s destination was the southern coast of the United States. Her orders were to harass the British ships then trying to cut off the southern states from the North.

A week later, on New Year's Day, the body of young Mann was back in his hometown of North Attleboro, Massachusetts. His sea voyage had been a short one. The reason for its brevity is stated on a slab of slate:

In Memory of Doctor Herbert Mann Who with 119 sailors with Capt. James Magee, Master, went on board the Brig General Arnold in Boston harbour Dec. 25th 1778, hoisted sail and made for the sea and were immediately overtaken by the most tremendous snow storm with cold that was ever known in the memory of man and unhappily parted their Cable in Plymouth harbor in a place called the cow-yard and he with about 100 others were frozen to Death, 66 of which

were buried in one grave. He was in the 21st Year of his Age. And now Lord God Almighty, just and true are all thy ways, but who can stand before thy cold?

By nightfall on Christmas Day, a northeast gale had forced Captain Magee to anchor his pilotless vessel off Gurnet on the outer arm of Plymouth Harbor. During a temporary lull in the storm, 16 of the brig's 20 guns were hastily secured below decks, her sails securely furled, and her anchor cable given a wide scope.

Minute by minute, through the night, the blizzard increased in its ferocity, and the cable parted. Off a lee shore, the *General Arnold* was soon grounded on the sand flats by the furious winds and the terrific battering of mountainous seas. Her seams were pounded open. The entering trickle of seawater soon swelled to a flood that filled the hold of the ship. The slaughterous billows, smashing over the main deck, forced the crew of 105 men and boys to seek the wave-drenched and snow-blanketed quarterdeck.

The coming of dawn on Saturday, December 26, found the gale continuing in its intensity and adding blinding snow to its ferocity. As the day wore on, the tempest increased its fury. The sky, wrathfully shedding its burden of snow, became darker. The sea, cladding the men in icy shrouds, persisted in its crusade of extermination.

Late in the afternoon the tide turned, giving the

crew renewed heart to fight on for existence through the coming night. But even by that time, death had mercifully spared a frozen score the need to further face the wind, which, at midnight, veered to the northwest and rose to mortally stiffen another score of seamen.

When the blackness and horror of Saturday night had ended, the men of Plymouth rallied to the dread cry of "Ship ashore and all hands perishing." They labored in vain throughout the Sabbath to reach the icebound vessel. Abandoning a futile effort to approach the *General Arnold* in boats, when high seas threatened to crush their small dories, the men began building a causeway over the ice floes. By nightfall, however, they were reluctantly forced by the cold and biting winds to give up and return to their snug homes. The men on board the ship faced another frightful night.

The below-zero weather and the driving winds soon compelled the survivors on the ship to take desperate measures in an effort to withstand the cold. More than half the original complement were dead. Their frozen corpses were piled high into a protective windbreak. Behind this, the remainder of the men huddled together, desperately holding on to life through the seemingly endless night.

At dawn, under a cloudless sky, the men of Plymouth resumed their efforts. By noon the construction of the causeway was completed, and they went on deck.

The *General Arnold* was embedded ten feet in the sandbar. Her main deck, which had been swept for more than 36 hours by murderous seas, looked like a museum of horrors. The dead, frozen into grotesque caricatures, remained in the same postures in which they had perished. Some stood erect. Others were sitting with their heads resting on their knees, huddled close beside a gelid fellow seaman. A few had faced eternity with arms outstretched or clasped around the shrouds and spars.

The task of separating the quick and the dead was made more difficult by the fact that many of the living were so nearly dead. It was only by rolling his eyes that one lad was able to indicate he was still among the living. Hearing himself referred to as one of the dead, Barnabas Downes, who could neither move nor speak, managed with superhuman effort to move his eyes. Luckily, one of the Plymouth rescuers noticed this and had him sent ashore to be placed in one of the tanks of cold water that were waiting to thaw out any of the frozen survivors.

With the return of circulation to his legs, the pain was more excruciating than that which he had already suffered on board ship. In his own words, the return of feeling was "attended with the most exquisite pain." Barnabas lost both feet as a result of his ordeal. In spite of this disability, he married and sired five children in his hometown of Barnstable, Massachusetts, where he continued to live for 40 years after the catastrophe.

Another survivor, Cornelius Marchant, had to live the rest of his life with crippled feet. He later wrote his memoirs of the shipwreck and gratefully paid tribute to the courage and good management of the *Arnold*'s officers. The last survivor of the disaster, Marchant died in 1838.

Captain Magee attributed his being alive to the fact that he had followed his own advice to his men: to pour their allotments of rum into their boots instead of drinking it.

By late afternoon on December 28, the living and the dead had been transported over the ice on sleds and boards to shore. The living were sheltered in village homes, and the dead were piled on the courthouse floor.

During the next two days, burial services were conducted in Plymouth for those of the 74 whose bodies were not to be returned to their homes. Attempts were made to thaw out the corpses so that they might be made to conform to the shape of the coffins. Some of the caskets had to receive two bodies, however, since it was found impossible to separate those who had been too closely locked together. Captain John Russell and Lieutenant David Hall, for instance, were placed in one grave. A huge pit was dug on the southwest side of Burial Hill, and into this single, unmarked grave the men of Plymouth laid the bodies of more than 60 of the *General Arnold*'s crew.

It has been said that the Reverend Chandler Robbins, pastor of the Plymouth church, fainted during the funeral ceremonies he was called upon to perform. No doubt one of the most tragic entries in the church records he had to make during his pastorate of 39 years was the one he penned on December 30, 1778. It reads: "74 Persons froze to Death. Cast away in ye Harbor in a Privateer brig. Capt. Mcgee."

Nine others died during the following week. Only 15 of the entire crew recovered completely from their horrible experience.

More than 80 years after the tragedy, Stephen Gale of Portland, Maine, intrigued by the story of the wreck of the *General Arnold,* determined to provide a just memorial to these Revolutionary War marines. Accordingly, in 1862, he erected an engraved marble obelisk over these Yankee mariners "Who perished in their strife with the storm." It remains to this day—a reminder of that great and tragic Christmas storm of 1778.   ∞

In a letter to Dr. John Woodward dated December 10, 1717, Cotton Mather recounted the details of what may well have been the worst blizzard to hit colonial New England.

The Great Snow of 1717

On the twentieth of last February, there came on a snow which being added unto what had covered the ground a few days before, made a thicker mantle for our mother [the earth] than what was usual; and the storm with it was for the following day so violent, as to make all communication between the neighbors everywhere to cease. People for some hours could not pass from one side of a street unto another, and the poor women who happened at this critical time to fall into travail, were put unto hardships which anon produced many odd stories for us. But on the twenty-fourth day of the month comes Pelion upon Ossa. Another snow came on which almost buried the memory of the former, with a storm so furious that Heaven laid an interdict on the religious assemblies throughout the country on this Lord's-day, the like whereunto had never been seen before. The Indians near a hundred years old affirm that their fathers never told them of anything that equalled it. Vast numbers of cattle were destroyed in this calamity, whereof some that were of the stronger sort were found standing dead on their legs, as if they had been alive, many weeks after, when the snow melted away; and others had their eyes glazed over with ice at such a rate, that being not far from the sea, their mistake of their way drowned them there.

One gentleman, on whose farms there were now lost above eleven hundred sheep, which with other cattle were interred (shall I say, or inniced) in the snow, writes me that there were two sheep very singularly circumstanced. For no less than eight and twenty days after the storm, the people pulling out the ruins of above a hundred sheep, out of a snow bank which lay sixteen foot high drifted over them, there were two found alive, which had been there all this time, and kept themselves alive by eating the wool of their dead companions. When they were taken out, they shed their own fleeces, but soon got into good case again.

The Light That Was "Perfectly Safe"

BY T.M. PRUDDEN

inot's Ledge, off Cohasset, Massachusetts, lies in a particularly dangerous position. It is so situated that vessels entering Boston Harbor, especially those from the northeast, could run afoul of it, and they frequently did when the weather was thick and Boston Light could not be seen. So the government decided to mark these ledges with a lighthouse, the first one being completed in November 1848.

It was a spidery-looking structure, consisting of eight iron legs plus a central iron core, two stories of living quarters, and the light on top. It was common sense that such an open-work design would offer less resistance to huge waves than would a solid masonry construction. But evidently the power of such waves was underestimated. Those officials who visited the finished light could do so only on fairly calm days, and therefore they did not have the chance to observe the shocking power of a great storm.

Within a year the light had shown a tendency to whip back and forth in a storm, so much so as to frighten the first keeper, a Mr. Dunham of West Bridgewater, Massachusetts. In an interview given by Mr. Dunham to the *Boston Journal* on April 18, 1851 (the day after the light fell), the paper states: "He [Dunham] set forth his views and opinions as to the security of the structure in a communication to the proper authorities in May of last year after witnessing the effects of the several storms of the preceding 4 or 5 months. He, at the same time, gave notice that he should resign his post the following October unless measures were adopted for the better security of the structure. His suggestions

for the better protection of the work were not complied with and he was taken at his word, and is now in retirement."

Other whispers of the weakness of the light were the occasional reports of failure of the tie-rods diagonally bracing the iron legs. Apparently these tie-rods were all too frequently dismounted and sent ashore for straightening and welding. An editorial in the *Boston Evening Transcript* of April 17, 1851, says: "A visitor who was present during the great gale of last December wrote, 'Of the Lighthouse I was coolly told that it was very doubtful if it stood through this winter, as one of the iron supporters had split the rock.' "

At the time of the disaster, and for some time previously, the keepers were a Mr. Bennett (salary $1,000 per year) and two young assistants, Joseph Wilson and Joseph Antonio (salary $550 per year each).

It is of the greatest interest that these same two assistant keepers were alone in the light just a month before its overturning and lived through a storm of almost equal intensity. Bennett was ashore on official business during both storms. After the first storm, one of these two assistants came into the office of the *Boston Daily Journal* and told of his experiences. Thus he reported firsthand the horrors and fears that were repeated a month later when the light fell.

The interview was printed March 22, 1851: "The following facts gathered from one of the assistant keepers of the Lighthouse on Minot's Ledge have thrilling interest. It is well known that this Light is constructed with a light iron frame, the posts being set in the rocks, drilled for that purpose at low water, the ledge being 3 miles distant from the shore. The late storm commenced on Sunday morning about 2 o'clock, the wind blowing from the northeast, accompanied with heavy snow and preventing objects from a distance of ½ mile being seen. During the day the storm increased, and on Monday morning the oscillation of the Lighthouse became so great from the action of the sea, that the inmates could with difficulty keep upon their feet and indeed were frequently knocked down. They were finally obliged to retreat to the store room, the next below, their cooking utensils having been broken, and it being impossible to remain where they were. Here they remained for 4 days without sleep and compelled to live on dry bread and uncooked meat. The [lamp] chimneys in the Light were continually being thrown out and, of course, broken, and the difficulty of ascending to replace them may be inferred from the fact the person who was compelled to perform this hazardous duty was several times thrown from the ladder in consequence of the vibration of the building, caused by the storm. The spray ascended to the receiving deck, a distance of some 50 feet, and thoroughly soaked the provisions and everything contained in that division—making it necessary to secure or remove them to the store room above.

"Thus for 4 days and nights the persons in charge of this Light were not only in imminent danger of losing their lives but subjected to hardships that would have discouraged most men.

"On Thursday morning the storm abated, and the wind changing to the north broke the sea.

"The only danger to this novel Light is by storms from the east-south-east. No protection is afforded in that quarter, being a free and unobstructed opening from the sea. From other points comparative protection is afforded by the shore and rocks."

On April 17, 1851, the light overturned. The tragedy was reported in the *Boston Courier* of April 18: "Minot's Light was regarded as a structure of great strength but it could not withstand the fury of the elements on Wednesday night; although unharmed, it had sustained the shock of many severe gales. The structure was composed of iron throughout—whole height from the Ledge 75 feet. Diameter of lantern 11½ feet and it contained 15 reflectors of 21 inches each.

"The last time the Light was seen standing was about half past 3 o'clock on Wednesday afternoon, and the Light was not seen burning that night.

"About 4 o'clock yesterday [Thursday] morning,

A contemporary depiction of the toppling of Minot's Ledge Light on April 17, 1851.
Residents of Glades heard the furious ringing of the tower's bell . . . then silence.

The present stone lighthouse, seen on a calm day.

Mr. Bennett the Keeper, was on the beach and discovered strewn all around, fragments of the building. Parts of the residence room and of the lantern itself were on the beach, and also portions of the bedding, Mr. Bennett's clothes, etc. One of Mr. Bennett's life buoys came up on the shore having the appearance of having been used by one of the unfortunate men who were in the Lighthouse.

"The Keeper himself was not on the Light at the time of the disaster. One of his boats was swept off in the last storm, and he came up to purchase another, under the direction of the collector, and not returning soon enough to enable a boat safely to convey him from the shore to the Ledge, he providentially escaped.

"The two who were lost were Joseph Wilson and Joseph Antonio (a Portuguese). Wilson we learn was about 20 years of age; Antonio was 25 and formerly kept a boarding house at Cohasset. They were both true and faithful men.

"It is but a few weeks since, when the public was much excited in relation to the safety of this structure, that the engineer under whose superintendence the lighthouse was built, in a long communication published in the *Advertiser,* demonstrated on scientific principles that the building was perfectly safe. The communication contained a most ungenerous sneer at the fears which had been expressed by Mr. Bennett.

"We were confirmed in our opinion as to its insecurity by the testimony of pilots, fishermen and other nautical men who were aware of the dangers to which it was exposed, and of the fearful force of the waves by which it was washed, so that it oscillated at least 12 inches each way in a gale. It now appears by the testimony of Mr. Bennett that where strength was most

An artist's rendering of a storm on Minot's Ledge, off Cohasset, Massachusetts. Vessels frequently ran afoul of the shoals in heavy weather.

Other Fallout from the Minot's Light Storm

In addition to toppling the Minot's Ledge Light, the fierce storm of April 1851 caused some severe damage on the mainland of coastal New England. At Cohasset, Massachusetts, several houses were swept away, and a large three-story hotel was floated off its underpinnings and destroyed just after its guests had been evacuated.

Boston was isolated, as the extraordinarily high seas cut off the Neck, and the city's downtown was flooded. East Boston's new Episcopal church was moved from its foundation on Tuesday night and destroyed the following day. Waves swept away the new seawall on Deer Island, carrying three island buildings out to sea. And at New Castle, New Hampshire, residents of Jaffrey Point reportedly thought that the Second Deluge had arrived, having been surrounded (though only temporarily) by the rising waters.

required the braces were of cast iron." [**Note:** This cannot have been so; the braces must have been wrought iron.]

"A few days after the great gale of March last, young Wilson—a modest and unassuming young man—called at our office, and gave us an account of the fearful and appalling scenes through which he passed during the 4 or 5 days which the gale lasted. We remarked to him that probably it would be difficult to keep the Light if Mr. Bennett should leave it. 'Yes, sir,' said the brave fellow, 'I shall stay as long as Mr. Bennett does, and when we leave the Light it will be dangerous for any others to take it.' "

One eyewitness report tells of seeing the light tilted over 30 degrees before a succeeding wave smashed it down. This seems unlikely, since the consensus was that the light fell during the night—a very dark and stormy night—and the light was three miles offshore. Residents of Glades, however, reported that they heard the furious ringing of the tower's bell during the night and that the ringing suddenly ceased just before one o'clock on the morning of April 17.

The body of one of the keepers was found in a cleft on a tiny rocky islet outside Cohasset Harbor. It is reported that the position of the body indicated that the man was alive when cast ashore, and he died from injury and exposure.

The two keepers wrote out a message on a piece of paper and signed it with both of their initials:

Wednesday night April 16
The lighthouse wont stand over tonight—
she shakes 2 feet each way now. JW & JA

This was put in a bottle and tossed overboard. Some fluke of the tide and wind washed it into Hingham Harbor (some say it was picked up in Massachusetts Bay). It is now a prized possession of the Hingham Historical Society. Its existence seems to be largely unknown except by a few history enthusiasts.

Shortly after the overturning of the light, the underwriters decided to send the steam towboat *R. B. Forbes* to Minot's Ledge to remain until a permanent lightship could be provided.

Four years after this tragedy the construction of a second light of stone was started, the new iron framework being inserted in the holes left by the wrecked tower. After one season of work "a fearful gale obscured the Ledge, and when the seas moderated it was seen that the work had shared the fate of the first tower."

Two drawings depicting the new Minot's Ledge Light (**top**) *and the old light* (**above**). *The old light was "a spidery-looking structure" that perched on eight iron legs; the theory was that the open design could better withstand violent wave action.*

The present-day light was finally completed and illumination first poured forth on August 22, 1860. It has withstood everything Mother Nature has had to offer—including giant seas that have, on occasion, swept clear over the top of the 97-foot structure.

On May 1, 1894, a new lantern was installed with a one-four-three flash—which romantic souls have decoded as representing "I love you." Since then, Minot's Ledge Light has been known as "Lover's Light" along the Cohasset shore. ∞

CHAPTER THREE

Tornadoes

Tornado!

BY EVAN MCLEOD WYLIE

ven though Wednesday, October 3, 1979, dawned gray and gloomy, it could not dim the glory of another autumn in the valley of the Connecticut River. In Colonial Village, a thickly wooded development in the Poquonock section of North Windsor, Connecticut, the autumn-tinted leaves fluttered down to dapple backyard swimming pools, patios, and carefully tended green lawns. With its trim ranch and split-level homes set amidst groves of oaks and birches, the village was a picture-book scene of suburban America. A striking aspect of the development was a steeply walled ravine through which Hollow Brook flowed down into the Farmington River.

On Pioneer Drive, Pat Levesque, mother of three children, was busy in her kitchen preparing the crab-meat canapés and nut cake she had promised to bring to a guild meeting at Poquonock's St. Joseph's Church that evening. It was only early afternoon, and she still had the house to herself. Her youngest daughter, Neysa-Ellen, 6, was attending a Brownie troop meeting that was just getting under way at the Poquonock Elementary School. Her son, Michael, 13, would not be getting off the bus from Sage Park Junior High School until close to 3:00 P.M. Her other daughter, Michelle, 10, had arrived home at 1:30 but had gone over to play with a neighborhood chum, Andrea Spadafora.

"Be sure you stay inside," Mrs. Levesque had cautioned her. "It looks as if it's going to be a wet afternoon."

She finished her trays of canapés and stacked them in the refrigerator. By 2:30 P.M., when she put the nut cake in the oven and set the timer, it was raining heavily, and from the south came a distant roll of thunder. Shadow, the family German shepherd, immediately departed for his usual sanctuary in the bathroom.

What no one had any way of knowing was that in the darkening sky over Windsor turbulent weather conditions were transforming the thunderstorm into something far more menacing. The mass of dry, cold air from the west was sweeping in beneath the rain-laden tropical clouds, pushing the moist air upward. At the same time, a narrow band of strong westerly winds above the storm clouds was creating a sudden updraft with a counterclockwise spin. The result was the spawning of a tornado.

In Windsor, just north of Interstate 91 and south of the Farmington River, concealed in a great black cloud, the swiftly rotating mass was forming into a funnel. Initially the wall was composed of nothing but water vapor, but as the circulation of the wind reached toward the ground, it picked up dust and debris. As it crossed the Farmington River into the Poquonock section of North Windsor, a finger of the funnel reached down to earth and sought out the deep cleft of the Hollow Brook ravine and followed it up into Colonial Village.

On nearby Hollowbrook Road, close to where the ravine in Colonial Village descended toward the Farmington River, Mrs. Candace Fatemi had been playing with her two children, Kiam, 3, and Melanie, 1, in the living room as she watched television. Soon after 2:30 P.M. she kept losing the picture in sudden blurs of static.

All her life Mrs. Fatemi had been frightened of

summer storms, especially tornadoes. She had been brought up in Illinois by parents who had been raised in Kansas, and her mother particularly had a phobia about them.

"To me tornadoes had always been a symbol of terror and tremendous danger, and I had had my share of bad dreams about them," she recalls. "But living in Connecticut I had thought much less of them."

Now, as the thunder boomed closer, she glanced out the window and saw a sight that she will never forget. "The sky was turning green and black. It was horribly menacing. Then the lights in the house blinked, and my ears popped. All my life I had been taught that when your ears pop and you're not moving, it can mean only one thing: tornado!"

Sweeping up Melanie and grabbing Kiam by the hand, Mrs. Fatemi made a dash for the stairs to her basement. Behind her came a deafening roar "like the sound of a huge jet plane."

The walls of the living room and kitchen were crashing down. She was only four steps down the basement stairs when she fell in a heap, clutching the children, blinded by clouds of dust, glass, and fiberglass insulation. Above their heads the house was being torn to pieces.

At the Spadafora home on adjacent Pioneer Drive, Arline Spadafora, mother of six, by profession an operating room nurse, also had been viewing the heavily falling rain with increasing concern. Her daughter, Andrea, 8, and Michelle Levesque were safe at home, playing together in the downstairs family room. Upstairs her eldest daughter, Christine, 16, was in her room doing her homework while she listened to the radio. Her son, David, 6, also was safely under cover, across the street at the Cirillo house. But her two older sons and her daughter, Tracy, 12, were due to be getting off the Sage Park Junior High School bus over on nearby Poquonock Avenue at 2:50 P.M. and would be soaked to the skin by the time they reached home.

"Christine," she called upstairs, "I'm going over to meet the bus. Keep an eye on Andrea and Michelle."

Flinging on a coat, she jumped into the family station wagon and drove over to the bus stop on the corner of Poquonock Avenue and Meakin Drive. There was a line of other cars driven by other mothers who had come to pick up their children. The bus pulled up,

and she saw Tracy making a dash for the car.

"Where are Brian and Tony?" she asked.

"They stayed at school for band rehearsal," Tracy said breathlessly.

"All right," Arline said, "we'll pick up David."

Arline swung into the Cirillo driveway and tooted her horn—the signal for David to come out. There was a delay as Mrs. Cirillo searched for a raincoat for David, and Arline was aware that the storm was much worse. Gusts of wind shook the car. The sky was black. Arline wanted to get home quickly.

"Hurry up!" she cried, honking her horn impatiently. David emerged running, but now the wind was so strong the little boy could hardly reach the car. Just as Tracy leaned out and pulled him in, a wall of rain and wind struck with terrible fury.

"Get down!" she screamed to her two children. "Get down and cover your heads!"

David, in the seat behind her, was still popping up to peer around. Just as the car was enveloped in inky darkness, Arline reached back and pulled him into the front seat and thrust him down to the floor next to Tracy, doing her best to shelter both of them with her own body.

A bombardment of heavy objects was pounding the sides and roof of the car. The station wagon was shuddering and rocking. Fighting a force that seemed to be lifting the car into the air, Arline clung grimly to the steering wheel and pressed with all her might on the foot brake. Suddenly the car windows burst, and a blinding deluge of rain, glass, and debris poured in on them.

"It's the end for all of us" was the thought that flashed through Arline Spadafora's mind.

In the Spadafora home across the street, Christine Spadafora had been studying when her sister, Andrea, and Michelle Levesque came knocking on her door.

"Let us in with you!" they cried. "We're afraid of the lightning and thunder!"

Christine had taken them in, but the storm outside was mounting in fury. Suddenly the lights went out, and she saw trees flying past her bedroom window. There was a hideous crack of lightning and then a shattering "Boom!" The roof of the house split open, and the walls were tumbling. Christine pulled the two terrified younger children closer to her next to the bunk bed. Debris was showering down upon them, and then came a terrible suction. Christine tried desperately to cling to the girls and the bed, but she felt herself being carried away and lost consciousness. In an instant the three girls had been swept upward into an engulfing, roaring darkness.

A jumble of wreckage—walls, furniture, appliances, and phonograph records—lies in the wake of the tornado that tore through Windsor, Connecticut, on October 3, 1979.

In her kitchen Pat Levesque waited for the bell to signal that it was time to take her nut cake out of the oven. It was 2:50 P.M., and her son, Michael, should be getting off the junior high school bus over on the corner of Meakin Drive and Poquonock Avenue. Pat Levesque could picture him sprinting home through the downpour, and she would be relieved to see him coming through the door. Suddenly a bolt of lightning seemed to stab right through the kitchen, and the whole house was shaken by a stupendous crash of thunder. Shadow bolted out of the bathroom and hid under the kitchen table, whimpering in terror.

Rushing to the living room window, Pat saw the boys from the school bus dashing past her house, and she ran to the front door to ask them if they had seen her son. To her bewilderment she found that there was a strange suction holding the door shut. She could not open it. The house lights went out, and from the window Mrs. Levesque glimpsed a low-lying mass of black clouds swirling around her house.

Into her mind flashed the word: "Tornado!" She turned and flung herself into a storage closet in the family room. Then came the sound. "It was like the roar of an approaching train," she remembers, "getting louder and louder."

Crouching in pitch blackness on the floor of the closet, Pat Levesque felt an invisible force reaching into the closet, searching for her like a great beast. She clung to the doorknob, screaming, fighting to hold it shut. Her feet were braced against the floor. Her wrists locked around the doorknob. Her long hair streamed away from her face. It was being sucked out through cracks in the door.

"Oh, my God!" she cried. "I can't hold on!"

A stunned child, injured in the tornado, sits in the wreckage that once was home.

Nearby on Settler Circle overlooking Hollow Brook Ravine, Dennis Cahill, 28, was about to take a shower before dressing and departing for work on the evening shift at the telephone company. His brother, Jeff, also working a night shift, was asleep in his room, and Chris, 21, was sitting at the dining room table working on a college term paper.

In his bedroom, Dennis was pulling on a bathrobe when he was drawn to a rear window by a furious gust of wind and rain. In disbelief he saw the huge trees that filled the ravine behind the house being torn to pieces and the roof lifting off a neighbor's home.

"Chris!" he cried. "What's happening?"

From the dining room Chris shouted, "I don't know, but our back deck is going!"

The entire house trembled, and then there was a hideous roar as the floor gave way and Dennis and Chris found themselves falling into the garage below.

"I remember hitting a canoe that we had stored there," Dennis recalls, "and then a tremendous force seized me as if I were a speck of dust and flung me into the air. I grabbed a piece of furniture and flew out across the lawn. I saw our microwave oven bouncing like a basketball."

As Dennis landed on the lawn of the house across the street, the smashed wreckage of the Cahills' Buick

Opel hurtled out of the sky and plowed into the ground a few feet away. Heavy debris showered down all around him, and he thought, "This is the end for me!"

Veering away from Colonial Village, the tornado moved northwestward up Poquonock Avenue. As it swept through St. Joseph's Cemetery, marble and granite grave monuments, anchored in concrete, were tossed and tumbled and carried off into nearby woods. A thick-walled brick mausoleum, once used to store coffins during severe winters, was pounded into a heap of rubble.

Just north of the cemetery, a local branch of the Hartford National Bank was nearing the end of another business day. The last customer had left the lobby. Tellers were closing their drawers and counting their money. By television camera, one teller was cashing a check for a person in a car that had pulled up at the drive-in window.

Manager Thomas Bourque and his assistant, Eve Campanelli, were locking the front door of the bank when Bourque heard a hissing, screaming roar. The outside door blew away, and insulation tiles in the vestibule were sucked right off the ceiling.

"Get down!" Bourque yelled. "Everybody take cover!"

Behind him heavy cement blocks and bricks were crashing through the window. The tellers were huddling under their counters. Customer representative John Powers made a dash for an inside conference room. As he threw himself on the floor, he glimpsed Tom Bourque on the floor, trying to squirm into the room. Within the bank the air pressure suddenly was so great that Powers felt as if his head were in a vise and might burst at any moment. Then the entire building blew apart. Furniture and file cabinets were tumbling. On the floor, jammed up against a desk, Tom Bourque thought to himself, "This is it. This is the end." As the roof came down upon him, he lost consciousness.

Across the street from the bank, Irving Hartmann, a foreman with the Farmington River Power Company, had just pulled up at Dale's Drugstore in his yellow ladder truck. Leaving his dog, Thumper, in the front seat of the truck, Hartmann went inside the store for a cup of coffee. It was raining harder, and construction workers Michael Vendette and William Kowalsky, who had been enlarging the parking lot, sought shelter inside their truck. A curtain of wind and torrential rain enveloped the drugstore and the parking lot. The windows

Above: *The tornado ripped through the Bradley Air Museum, mangling beyond recognition many of the priceless vintage planes stored there. This used to be a Corvair T-29.* **Left:** *The twister lifted the roof of this hangar at the museum and pulverized it into a shower of debris.*

blew out. As he lay on the floor, Irv Hartmann heard the wall of the store being peeled away and the roof of the apartment overhead being torn off. Out in the parking lot, his yellow truck was being rolled over and over. An immense piece of timber flew like a javelin through the windshield of the truck in which Kowalsky and Vendette were sitting.

In the sky above Bradley International Airport, United Airlines Flight 220 was coming in for a landing after a nonstop flight from Chicago. In command of the Boeing 727, which carried 114 passengers and a crew of six, was Captain George Deihs, a veteran airline pilot with 23 years of experience at United and previous flying time with the military. As the big airliner dropped down through ominously swirling clouds, it encountered increasing turbulence. Stewardesses strapped themselves into their seats, and passengers eyed each other apprehensively as the plane was rocked by gusts of wind and lashed by heavy rain. Darkness blotted out all visibility. The plane's crew was forced to fly entirely on instruments.

"I knew that it was going to be an approach that would require some effort," Deihs would later say. The plane's flaps were down. The landing gear was in place, but there was no sign of the ground. At just above 200 feet, the Boeing broke out of the murk at the north end of the airport, but the crew could barely see the runway, and the plane was slightly off to one side.

Suddenly there was a brilliant flash of lightning and a roar of thunder, and the lights in the plane flickered out. In the cockpit, Captain Deihs, making a split-second decision to break off the landing, slammed his throttles wide open. There was a tremendous roar and surge of power as the Boeing 727 streaked across the airport with its three jet engines screaming.

Only 400 yards to the east, the tornado was tearing apart buildings and aircraft on the ground. On the west side of the airport, bordering Route 75, was the Bradley Air Museum, containing one of the largest collections of historic aircraft in the world. In the museum's outdoor exhibit, spread over four and a half acres, were famed World War II bombers and fighter planes, amphibious patrol craft, helicopters, and huge cargo and passenger planes that had been collected from all over the United States. In a nearby hangar named Museum Hall were 30 aircraft that had flown the skies since the earliest days of aviation.

Open year-round, the museum was usually filled with visitors, but the driving rain had emptied the outdoor exhibit, and at 2:45 P.M. Carol Symack, stationed at the admissions booth, decided that it was a good time to take a short break. She locked up the booth and drove over to Museum Hall. Philip O'Keefe, the museum's director, had been working in his office and came out to chat with Carol and with Carl Prince and Robert Horner, who were talking in the gift shop.

Wondering if any break in the weather might be in sight, O'Keefe stepped outside. He saw a massive low black cloud rushing up from the south. The nearby trees began to bend and blow wildly. Branches were breaking off. As O'Keefe jumped back in the hangar and slammed the door, a window blew out next to a display case, and a piece of wood shot in and speared the wall.

"Take cover quick!" he cried.

The people in the museum huddled together on the floor next to the admission counter. Above their heads they heard rending, cracking sounds and glimpsed the roof of the huge hangar, 24,000 square feet of asphalt, wood, and stone, being lifted up into the sky as a blizzard of rain, glass, and gravel engulfed them.

At 2:30 P.M. Deputy Chief Kenneth Smith, responding to a report that lightning had struck a utility pole, had taken the Poquonock Fire Department's Engine 4 south on Route 75. On the way he had run into the heaviest rain he had ever encountered. When he jumped off the fire truck to check the utility pole, the wind was blowing so hard it nearly swept him off his feet. On the radio another alarm was coming in: a roof collapse in an auto plant on Tunxis Road on the south side of the Farmington River. When Smith arrived at the plant, he found that four workers had been injured. While he was helping free a man trapped beneath a steel beam, the radio reported that a senior citizen bus had been overturned in Colonial Village.

Speeding north again on Poquonock Avenue and still believing that he was answering the kind of calls that might be expected during any heavy thunderstorm, Smith reached the bridge across the Farmington River and found it blocked by trees and power lines draped across it in a crazy pattern that seemed to extend all the way up Poquonock Avenue. He dispatched his firemen on Engine 4 on a roundabout route to another bridge across the river. Climbing over, under, and around the tangled wires, he crossed the bridge and began running hard up Poquonock Avenue. Terrified, a woman was calling to him from a car festooned with wires and broken tree branches. He yanked open the door and pulled her out.

He saw that the roof and steeple of the Poquonock

The tornado was cruelly fickle in its choice of targets. This stack of smashed cars and debris marks the site of one home, while across the street a neighbor's house was left relatively unscathed.

Congregational Church were gone. Then, looking toward Colonial Village, he found nothing but a jumbled mass of flattened wreckage.

On his hand-held radio Smith gasped, *"To all units . . . Disaster! . . . Disaster! . . . Notify all emergency services! Notify the governor!"*

In her home on Hollowbrook Road, Candace Fatemi was crawling up the basement stairs amidst a suffocating cloud of dust and particles of fiberglass insulation. Melanie clung to her with a vise-like grip. Kiam was shaking and crying. Reaching the kitchen, Mrs. Fatemi found that the walls had collapsed. Rain was pouring in through jagged holes in the wreckage, but there was no way out.

Sitting on the floor, she began to sing "Row, row, row your boat" to soothe the children.

A block away Arline Spadafora raised herself from the floor of her station wagon and peered out through its smashed windows. The wind was gone, but it was raining heavily. The Cirillos' home lay in rubble around her. She turned and looked across the street and saw her own home roofless.

"Then I had a terrible fear," she says. "I thought, my God, the girls, I left them at home! What's happened to the kids?"

She jumped from the car and ran across the street. Her first thought was that they might have hidden in the family room, but there was no sign of them in that part of the house. She began tearing at a heap of broken wall and tumbled plaster screaming, "Christine! Andrea! Michelle! Are you in there? Can you hear me?"

There was no answer. In the midst of the torrential rain, Arline heard a horn blowing. Someone was calling out to her from a car in the road, "They're here! They're with us!" Mrs. Spadafora ran to the car and found the three girls.

"My God," she cried. "How did you get here?"

The girls had been swept out of Christine's bedroom, carried over the roof of the house and over a tall spruce tree in the front yard, and then dropped in a corner of the front yard about 80 feet away. Dazed and hurt, they had crawled across the lawn to the car of Mrs. John Cosgrove of Hollowbrook Road. Their faces were blank with shock. Their skin and hair were embedded with glass, dirt, and sand. Christine had a badly injured leg. Andrea was pale and vomiting. Michelle was battered and bleeding.

Arline gathered Andrea in her arms and took Christine by the hand. She led them back to her station wagon, where Tracy and David were still hiding. A young man with a dangling arm came down the street. It was David Walsh, driver of a senior citizen minibus that lay on its side on a nearby lawn, its windows smashed. Walsh had been sucked out of the bus, and in addition to the broken arm, he had suffered crushed vertebrae in his back.

"I need help," he said. "I need somebody to help me get some elderly people out of my bus."

"I can't come now," Arline said. "But when you get them out, you can put them in with us."

Down the street, Pat Levesque was crawling out of her closet. Instead of the familiar family room, she saw sky and falling rain. The roof of her home was gone. Running through water, splintered timbers, and shards of broken glass, she went looking for her daughter. Her heart nearly stopped when she saw that the Spadafora home was destroyed, but then she was reunited with Michelle in the Cosgrove car. On the way back to her house, she found the Cahill brothers.

When Dennis Cahill regained consciousness, he found himself lying in the pouring rain, naked and bleeding. He raised his head and saw in front of him a row of shrubs that he recognized as the ones that grew around the house across the street. But that house was gone. Only the shrubs and the foundation were left.

He turned slowly and saw that the Cahill home had been torn to pieces. Painfully he got to his feet. He had landed with legs doubled under him, and one leg was injured. He saw a pair of strange trousers and sandals in the debris in the road and pulled them on. He found his brother Chris mumbling incoherently, lying on the ground on the other side of the Buick Opel. The car had fallen between them. He saw his other brother Jeff clinging to a utility pole.

With Pat Levesque's help, Dennis got his brothers off the ground and took them over to what was left of the Levesque family room. There were six inches of water on the floor, but they found some chairs intact and put Chris in one of them.

"Did anyone see my son, Michael?" Mrs. Levesque kept asking distractedly. "He was supposed to be on the school bus. Did anyone see him?"

At the Hartford National Bank, John Powers was dragging himself out of the wreckage of the meeting room. The bank tellers who had taken shelter beneath their counters were stumbling across the street to Dale's Drugstore. Eve Campanelli lay pinned by an air conditioner, and Powers hobbled over to his car to get an automobile jack to lift the cabinet off her. Manager Tom Bourque lay buried out of sight, beneath the fallen roof. Someone was blowing a horn, and Powers discovered that the car that had pulled up at the bank's drive-in window was completely buried under a mountain of rubble.

Men were coming out of the wreckage of Dale's Drugstore, and Irving Hartmann of the Farmington River Power Company was calling on his radio for an emergency truck with hydraulic jacks.

Deputy Chief Smith had run the rest of the way up Poquonock Avenue. He looked in the construction truck that had been parked at the drugstore. The timber that had crashed through its windshield had killed one of the men, and the other was severely injured.

In the group from the power company that responded to Irving Hartmann's radio call were John Grakowsky, Jim Griskewicz, and Dave Hayden, all volunteer members of the Poquonock Fire Department. As Deputy Chief Smith joined them, they began to jack up the roof of the Hartford bank and used chain saws to cut timbers to brace a tunnel into the debris to reach Tom Bourque. Bourque, lying in four inches of water with his leg crushed beneath a desk, took heart when he heard their voices. "I may lose my leg," he thought, "but at least I'm alive. Maybe I'll make it."

At the Bradley Air Museum, Philip O'Keefe was staring in numb disbelief. The 55-ton Douglas C-133, the largest plane in the museum's collection, lay on its back, nose and tail sections ripped off. In similar condition were a Constellation airliner, a Fairchild C-119, and a Navy fighter plane. One of the rarest aircraft in the collection, a Douglas World War II fighter, was so crumpled that it could be recognized only by the color of its fuselage. Helicopters were smashed. In all, 16 aircraft representing high moments in aviation history had been destroyed. The admissions booth in which Carol Symack had been sitting until moments before the tornado struck was demolished.

For many families in the area of devastation, the first act of recovery was the defiant display of the American flag. In a sense, they were nailing their colors to the mast, refusing to surrender.

To the bewildered victims on the ground, signs of a rescue effort seemed slow in coming. Telephones were not working, and when they turned on the radios in their wrecked automobiles, afternoon disc jockeys were playing music and chatting away as if nothing had happened.

After nearly an hour, a construction worker freed Candace Fatemi from the wreckage of her kitchen. Two nurses from another street in Colonial Village that had been spared were caring for the injured Cahill brothers. Arline Spadafora had regained some of her strength and ran across the street to drag coats and blankets out of a cedar chest in the splintered remains of her house. She used them to cover the soaked and shivering children and the elderly women from the van who had been placed in her station wagon.

Wandering through the eerily silent, devastated, and deserted streets, Pat Levesque finally found a telephone that was working. She dialed the junior high school and with a trembling voice asked, "My son, Michael, have you seen him?"

"Yes," someone replied, "he's right here. He's all right."

Mrs. Levesque put down the telephone and began to sob hysterically.

An ambulance transported the Cahill brothers to a Springfield, Massachusetts, hospital. Jeff, his back broken, was placed in a cast. Dennis, with head, back, and leg injuries, spent the rest of October in the hospital and a year later still wore a brace on his leg. Chris suffered a concussion.

By mid-afternoon on Wednesday a massive rescue effort was under way. Teams of fire, police, and con-

Before and after: *A survivor shows a photograph of a neat, comfortable suburban home, reduced in seconds to a heap of splintered rubble in a desolate no-man's-land.*

struction workers cut away dangling wires and chopped and sawed through fallen trees, while bulldozers cleared a path for the ambulances that poured into the area to pick up scores of injured. Hospitals from Hartford to Springfield treated a steady stream of victims and admitted many for surgery and medical assistance. A command post was set up at the Poquonock Fire Department, and doctors and nurses treated casualties awaiting trips to the hospital, while volunteers brought cots and blankets to provide a dormitory for the homeless. Victims and rescuers were served hot meals throughout the night by a Salvation Army mobile canteen. Vocational students at Bloomfield High School in Windsor baked and shipped 400 loaves of bread to the firehouse, and a Hartford restaurant sent in buckets of chicken. Throughout the night, searchlights lit the sky as firemen and state police combed the wreckage for more trapped victims. Infantry companies of the National Guard, Army Reserves, and a U.S. Navy unit rolled into the stricken area.

As Thursday dawned, hundreds straggled back to their crushed and battered homes and businesses. Some sat down and stared in paralyzed disbelief. Others sifted haphazardly through mountains of sodden debris searching for cherished possessions.

Canceled checks, family photographs, and ticket stubs from the Bradley Air Museum fluttered to earth 50 miles away in the Berkshire Hills. Tracy Spadafora's birth certificate was found in Westfield, Massachusetts, and returned with a check and a note that said, "We thought that the enclosed might help out a bit."

On Thursday afternoon, the body of Mrs. Carol Dembrowski, 42, who had been at home alone on Settler Circle during the tornado, was found in the backyard of the Cahill property, 110 feet away from the ruins of her colonial house. State police with bloodhounds searched for more victims. In the days that followed, volunteers came from as far away as Pennsylvania to help out in the stricken towns.

Taking stock, officials estimated that within 15 minutes the tornado had done $215 million in damage, caused 3 deaths, hospitalized 143 persons, and injured 350 others.

In Windsor alone, 69 homes were destroyed. Damage to civilian and military facilities at Bradley International Airport amounted to $65 million. In Windsor Locks, damage estimated at more than $100 million was done to commercial buildings.

The tragedy could have been much worse. If the Poquonock Elementary School had not closed at noon for a teachers' meeting, more than 300 young children would have been out on the streets, afoot and in buses, when the tornado struck a few minutes before 3:00 P.M. The main terminal at Bradley International Airport, filled with hundreds of people, was spared by less than 300 yards.

President Carter soon declared the towns a major disaster area and the devastated region became eligible for federal aid. On October 8 the *Windsor Phoenix,* a newsletter printed daily by the town of Windsor to provide information to tornado victims, reported that the first of the furnished mobile homes that would provide temporary shelter for the homeless were on their way from a government storage facility in Kentucky.

One night in early December, Pat and Tom Levesque and their children moved into the trailer that had been set up on their property to be their home throughout the winter.

"I'll never forget that trailer arriving," says Pat Levesque. "When we walked in and knew it was ours, that was the most beautiful sight I have ever seen. As it got dark that evening, I looked out, and up and down the street the lights were twinkling in other trailers. It was spellbinding. We were all back together again. We were home!"   ∞

For some Windsor residents, the fierce passage of the tornado left little behind worth saving. Others were luckier; although their homes had been seriously damaged or destroyed, they managed to salvage a few cherished possessions.

Tornado Tips

Despite the general impression that tornadoes occur only in the Midwest and plains states, New England has had its share of severe twisters, particularly over interior sections. Here are five basic tips (mostly of the common-sense variety) to remember the next time you hear a tornado warning:

☞ Opening some windows in the house may help, but be sure to stand clear of the windows once you've opened them.

☞ Head for the basement of your house immediately and try to take cover under heavy furniture.

☞ If your house doesn't have a basement, take cover near the center of the house on the first floor, preferably in a small space such as a closet or bathroom. Never take shelter in a large enclosed space such as an auditorium or shopping mall.

☞ Mobile homes are particularly threatened by tornadoes and should be evacuated during a tornado warning.

☞ If you should be caught out in the open, move away from the tornado (as quickly as possible) at a right angle to the tornado's path.

Totally demolished in the Worcester Tornado of 1953 was Assumption College, a local school administered by a religious order. Here, vestments lie in the foreground of what had been the major college complex.

"Heavy Squall and That's Not All"

The Worcester County Tornado of 1953

BY TOM KOCH

t was June 1953, and summer was on its way in New England as usual—a cool spring growing warm with the first late May/early June heat; occasional showers with a few nights of lightning to brighten the hushed, late spring nights.

In Worcester, Massachusetts, the weather was seasonal and pleasant following a wet early spring. Occasional thundershowers cleansed the air, and the night breeze caressed young leaves into vibrancy. Tired of winter, residents lounged on their front porches, enjoying the warm night air.

Early June meant commencement time in Worcester, a college town. The daily newspaper solemnly reported a commencement speaker's urging the graduating class of Holy Cross College to "walk in truth," that "they might be an honor to their teachers."

That was June 7, a Sunday.

In Arcadia, Nebraska, on that same day, a tornado killed ten people as they sat down to a family reunion dinner in the farmhouse that was their ancestral home. It, too, was destroyed by the storm. The story was a small item in the news across the nation.

But that, of course, was Nebraska, not New England, where residents of the six states congratulated themselves over toast and morning coffee for living in a sensible climate, where things like that didn't happen.

That misconception was laid to rest on Tuesday, June 9, when at 5:08 P.M., the world came to an end for many Worcester residents. For others, the tornado that struck put an end to lifelong hopes and plans. Some lost their life savings, their homes, or their shops or other livelihood.

Born in the Midwest of unsettled air, the tornado had attacked Nebraska in its adolescence. Unsated, it left the earth and, growing greater still, moved east, touching Flint, Michigan, before disappearing into the upper reaches of the atmosphere until it was ready to descend and strike again.

With more power than any creation or dream of man, the furious funnel of swirling wind set down where its kind had never been seen before, first in Petersham, Massachusetts, and then at the Quabbin Reservoir in central Massachusetts, where it excavated a crater 100 feet in diameter. Fully grown and unreasoning, it then moved southeast toward Worcester.

The large, black funnel, shaped like an ice cream cone carved of granite, fell on Holden, a town next to Worcester, bulldozing a path of destruction through what had been quiet residential streets. Now at the height of its fury, the tornado fell on northern Worcester, demolishing a machine shop before sweeping east to the Worcester Poor Farm. It crushed Assumption

College, decimated three churches, then moved into Shrewsbury and towns eastward. Finally, all its fury spent, it left the earth and died.

That day, June 9, James P. Abdella and Melvin G. Johnson, construction workers, were driving home from work to Shrewsbury. "All of a sudden," Abdella said later, "I saw a chimney flop over." Then a roof sailed above his truck, and he saw row after row of Maple Street homes topple like card houses upset by the kick of a naughty child. "And that's when my stomach came to my mouth," he said.

A few minutes earlier, workers from local factories had begun to go home. The nine-to-five shift at the Norton Company was punching time clocks on the rim of the machine shop. J. Roy Erikson of the purchasing department had left work a few minutes early.

"It was hailing and a few minutes to five, so I decided to go home," he said. "Traffic was backed up on Brook Street, below the plant. The sky was dark, and I thought, maybe it's another hurricane like 1938's, or more probably just another summer thunderstorm. I was going to get out of my car and walk up the road to see what the tie-up was but decided not to."

It was a good thing he didn't. Glass from a broken greenhouse was whipping through the air. He still thought it was "just a bad storm, because who the hell ever heard of a tornado around here."

Turning around, he looked for another route home. Nearing his house later, he found branches down and some homes collapsed, though his was still intact. His wife told him she thought that an unscheduled freight train had passed on the tracks near their house and that maybe there had been an accident.

"It sounded like a train's roar," she said, "and there were all these cars with their lights on, beeping horns, so I thought there had been an accident."

There were no trains passing the house at 5:08 P.M. that day. The roar she had heard was the tornado sweeping through.

Erikson's brother Harold was putting his car in the garage near Roy's home when the tornado struck, dropping the roof on him. He was pinned inside until neighbors freed him and took him to a hospital.

When Roy heard the news, he and his older brother, Andrew, an ex-Navy medical corpsman, began to tour the city's hospitals, looking for Harold.

"There was no time to fill out admittance forms," Roy recalled. "Bodies were just put wherever there was room, and doctors looked after them when they had a chance." At City Hospital, the third or fourth one they had visited, Andrew stopped looking to lend a hand in preparing blood for the injured, while Roy continued the search. Around midnight, the two brothers got together again, having looked through all the hospital wards. An undertaker they met suggested they look in the morgue.

"It wasn't like a morgue on TV. It was just an area, the only open one around, with bodies laid out wherever there was room, like a field station after a rout," Erikson said. Harold Erikson was there, one of the 90 people killed that day in June.

Others were luckier. When the storm struck, Hilding H. Anderson's family was in the den of their Holden, Massachusetts, house. Hilding, a Norton employee, was working late when the storm struck. It was an hour before he knew that anything unusual had happened. The building he worked in was on the other side of the plant from the decimated machine shop. It was hours more before he knew that his home had been destroyed.

Preceding the tornado had been a milder storm of rain, hail, and wind. As it grew worse, Mrs. Anderson had contemplated going to the cellar for refuge, but her teenage daughter said, "Naw, Mom, it's just a storm." When the tornado hit the home, it tore the chimney cap from its foundation, dropping it through the roof, a half foot from Mrs. Anderson's head.

The house was a total ruin, yet only three-quarters of a mile away, Anderson's parents' home had suffered no damage. "It was no worse than a windstorm there," Anderson said.

Anderson's seven-year-old son was playing with a friend at a house nearby when the storm dropped on residential Holden. The boys, alone in the house, were scared by the darkening sky and overturned a sofa to crouch underneath it. The tornado shattered windows and hurtled glass through the room, cutting the sofa but not the boys.

"I'll never understand how they knew to do that," Anderson said. "But it saved their lives."

In the Andersons' garage stood a power lawnmower and a 12-cubic-foot refrigerator. The mower never moved, but the storm picked up the refrigerator, which was never seen again.

Although his house was totally destroyed, its cupola, hand-carved by Anderson's father, was found intact the next day. It was 100 yards away, lying in the woods. A canceled check from Anderson's records, stored in the house's attic, was later found 65 miles away in Southwick. It came to rest, ironically, on the lawn of a bank president, who returned it to Anderson

A woman sits in stunned disbelief amidst the wreckage of her home.

via a Worcester acquaintance. Anderson kept it as a souvenir.

Not only roofs but people were carried away by the storm. One mother and child were reportedly carried yards through the air to a safe landing, only to have the baby snatched from its mother and hurtled another hundred yards to its death.

The night of the storm, there was widespread pillage. The National Guard was called out to control looting and assist the injured. "I can't believe, I never could, the looting that went on after the storm; but I know that, if I could have laid my hands on a gun, I would have shot the guys who looted my house," Anderson said.

In the weeks that followed, as the hospitals emptied, reconstruction began. It took Erikson a week to decide to rebuild because "at first, all we wanted to do was move. It was as if we would never feel safe there again." Some people did move, but most, like the Erik-

sons, rebuilt because "where can you go and be safe, at least safer than we were? Nowhere. It was a freak of nature, and there was no place we could think of that was safer than Holden; so we rebuilt, and so did most of our neighbors."

Federal and state aid poured in. Private companies such as Norton donated transportation, building materials, technical assistance, and financial aid to the stricken. Spokespersons for the company say it gave more than a million dollars in disaster relief in the weeks immediately after the tornado struck.

Two days after the storm, Worcester police stamped out what they described as an illegal lottery to benefit tornado victims. On June 11, members of the Worcester police vice squad seized 125 books of lottery tickets that were being sold at five cents a ticket. The drawing was for a $50 bond; the seller was to receive, all told, a profit of $625.

Three Stages of a Tornado

For those people unfortunate enough to be caught in the storm track of a tornado, the seemingly impossible suddenly becomes real. In the short time it takes a typically fast-moving tornado to wreak its havoc on a particular spot, the world as we know it seems to be subverted by an invisible force—incredibly destructive, incredibly strong, yet at times almost playful in its disregard for "normal" physical laws.

The passage of a tornado occurs in three main stages:

☞ **Stage 1:** High-velocity winds blow windward windows of houses *in* and leeward windows *out.* In a large, severe storm the size of the Worcester tornado, winds of several hundred miles per hour swirl around the outer ring of the funnel cloud's vortex. These initial storm winds pose a threat mainly to people who are out-of-doors.

Outside of the storm track, just a short distance away, conditions are drastically different. One nineteenth-century anecdote describes a tree on the fringe of a tornado track. After the storm, observers noticed that on one side of the tree the leaves were scorched and killed, while on the other side (the side outside the storm track) the same tree's leaves were completely unaffected by the tornado.

☞ **Stage 2:** The "vacuum cap" of the tornado vortex passes over the area, causing an instantaneous and drastic drop in air pressure. In the Worcester storm track, it was estimated that air pressure dropped about two pounds per square inch.

The air inside houses and other structures tries to force its way out in an attempt to balance the sudden pressure drop. Buildings slowly explode, seeming to dissolve away, as roofs lift up and walls push outward.

Some witnesses have seen lighter objects "float" in the air and even heavy objects move across floors. One young survivor of the Worcester tornado remembers watching baked potatoes sitting in the open oven suddenly fly across the room and strike her father in the head!

☞ **Stage 3:** The "back wall" of the tornado again brings high wind velocities following the passage of the vortex. These winds can be far more deadly than the initial blasts, since many people are caught in the open amidst the rubble after their houses have collapsed around them. Still, there are numerous stories of tornado survivors who have been picked up by the wind, carried a considerable distance, and set down gently and uninjured.

Another gruesome aspect of the winds is that airborne mud, dirt, wood splinters, and other trash often plasters the survivors, increasing the risk of infected wounds. In overcrowded Worcester hospitals, some wounds were closed without thorough cleaning, which resulted in bacterial infections and sepsis, or blood poisoning.

A tornado is one of nature's most powerful and, climatologically, unique contributions to the misery of mankind. Most storms, from rainy downpours to devastating hurricanes, are broad-based furies that sweep across the land in a moderately predictable fashion. But a tornado is different. It is not earthborn, but a creature of the atmosphere—a funnel of swirling wind bouncing across the country, touching down only at certain points. Its fury is contained in a narrow band of power less than a mile across, and it is difficult to plot, predict, and prepare for. The revolving mass of air and vapor, preceded and followed by ferociously strong winds, is a vacuum. The destruction comes not so much from the fury of the winds as from the power of this vacuum.

When a tornado hits a building, the pressure in the storm center is lower than in the building. In an attempt

to equalize inside and outside air pressure, the building collapses "like a house of cards." The closest analogy is when a paper bag filled with air is clapped between two hands. It explodes, not just because you are strong, but also because the compression creates a higher air pressure inside the bag that must escape. The "pop" when the bag bursts is caused by the air pressures equalizing. It is the same with a tornado. The pressure inside a house, office, or shop is higher than the pressure in the storm outside. In attempting to equalize the air pressure, the atmosphere forces the building out. On June 9, 1953, within half an hour, Worcester barometers fell an unprecedented one-half inch.

Soon after this storm, meteorologists instituted a "tornado watch" to give area residents time to prepare in case another blow appears. The chances of that happening, however, are very slim. Weather bureaus with new, sophisticated systems are prepared for such storms and can give people warning. Yet despite these early warning systems and the more than 35 years that have passed since the tornado struck, some Worcester area residents still wait in fear when a thunderstorm brings night hours early and winds whip the trees. Survivors of the 1953 tornado, like Mrs. Anderson and the Eriksons, head for their cellars and wait out the storm.

There are some things that, never experienced, can never be understood and, once known, can never be forgotten. Among these are love and close brushes with death—and tornadoes seen from the inside. ∞

In the wake of the tornado Worcester's streets became a bedlam of cars and pedestrians, picking their way through the aftermath of the storm.

One of the worst tornadoes in New England's history struck Wallingford, Connecticut, on August 9, 1878. It killed 31 people and destroyed 30 homes, a church, and a school.

Addicted
to Tornadoes

BY BOB TREBILCOCK

"The winds picked up about three o'clock in the after-noon when the western sky turned absolutely black. The farmer and his wife watched the funnel form in the tumult above and hurried their five children into the storm cellar. They had seen tornadoes before—as had anyone who lived on the Kansas plains—but somehow they misjudged this one. When the funnel struck, the house exploded with the farmer and his wife still inside. She was killed instantly. The debris landed a hundred yards away in a field across the state line in Nebraska. When the children finally came up from the cellar, they ran to the nearest neighbor for help a half-mile away. Hail the size of baseballs followed in the twister's wake, and the children were bloodied and bruised by the time they reached safety. The farmer died in the hailstorm."

That tornado struck more than 50 years ago. As he reads the newspaper accounts from his study in North Danville, Vermont, Tom Grazulis can picture the splintered timbers and hear the howling wind. He is a tall, lanky 46-year-old tornado detective, searching for the details buried in the copy from which he will recon-struct the storm.

"They knew it was coming," Tom says. "Other-wise they wouldn't have gotten all the kids into the cellar. The funnel would've looked like an elephant's trunk, this ropelike thing whipping back and forth. For some reason they misjudged it—with tragic results."

Judging by the extent of the damage, Tom esti-mates the funnel was rotating in excess of 150 miles per hour. He is uncertain about where to place the father's death, since the house exploded in Kansas but he was found in a field in Nebraska. In his notes he reduces the twister to the facts pertinent to a scientific readership studying the possible link between tornadoes and land-scape. At the end he adds a few poignant sentences about the life and death of a family on the plains. "This is not human interest work," Tom says of a study that has occupied the past 18 years of his life. "But in some cases you cannot ignore the human interest."

Considering who he is and where he lives, torna-does are an odd choice of study for Tom Grazulis. Most weather research is conducted by Ph.D.s in laborato-ries chock-full of scientific equipment and cadres of graduate students.

Tom, on the other hand, is a former weather fore-caster, high-school science teacher, and environmental filmmaker with a bachelor's degree in meteorology. He works on a home computer in a cramped office while his wife, Doris, helps with the typing. He has never actually seen a tornado except on film. Nor is North Danville a hot spot for severe storm activity: The last twister to threaten the community touched down on May 10, 1880, in Island Pond, about 35 miles to the northeast. Slow Clearing Farm, the Grazulises' 50 acres of woods, trees, and hills, sits on the other side of a homemade suspension bridge at the end of a 300-foot-long wooden walkway. "Lamb's wool products and disaster research" is the working motto.

As improbable as it seems, Tom is an authority on the history of severe storms. Over the years he has logged 100,000 miles through 33 states and threaded 25,000 reels of microfilm. In the process he has reviewed 35,000 storms. Since 1984, when the National Science Foundation (NSF) awarded him a five-year grant, Tom has been writing the definitive work on the granddaddies of windswept mayhem: a one-volume analysis of the 12,000 most severe storms to strike the United States between 1880 and 1988. (The book was published in 1989.)

The purpose of this massive undertaking is to aid researchers trying to determine whether topography plays a role in tornado formation. Scientists understand how tornadoes form; they don't understand why they strike where they do. Why, for instance, is Dallas battered by destructive twisters more often than beans are served in Boston, while nearby Fort Worth sees very few severe tornadoes?

"We don't know," Tom says. "What you do is document this over time and wait to see what happens next." His was a project only talked about for years because no one was willing to sort through the archives until Tom volunteered. "I'm like a sieve through which everything passes," he says. "I don't mind the tedium involved."

Given the unpredictability of tornadoes, the loca-

tion of Slow Clearing Farm is possibly a benefit. A twister forms in an instant and strikes like a band of Hell's Angels crashing a debutante ball. In a matter of minutes it is just an ugly memory. "The only way to study a thing so fleeting is to do it indirectly," Tom says. "Tornadoes are probably the last major meteorological event you can significantly study from a farmhouse in Vermont."

If you factor in the overhead, Slow Clearing Farm even has a competitive advantage as the ideal spot from which to launch a major research effort. "I cut my own firewood," says Tom. "We're cost-effective."

Bottom: *Tom Grazulis, tornado aficionado.* **Above, right:** *As a boy, Grazulis spent his allowance on film to take pictures of clouds.*

Tom Grazulis has been fascinated by the weather since he was a boy. His first recollections are of the camera his father gave him and how he spent all his allowance buying film to take pictures of clouds. He was 11 and watching "Howdy Doody" on television at home on June 9, 1953, when a tornado struck Worcester, Massachusetts. The storm killed 90 and left thousands homeless. By the time he was 13, Tom was regularly riding the bus out to the Worcester airport to draw weather maps while his friends were studying box scores.

"It was like an addiction to weather," Tom says now. "It wasn't until I went to college that I discovered there were other kids out there like me. It was like that scene in *Close Encounters of the Third Kind,* when all those people were drawn to Devil's Mountain. There are weather buffs out there. I get letters from them all the time."

"The irony is, I didn't choose this," he adds. "It chose me. It is a malady that I don't understand. I must have some inner frustration to be afflicted by a preoccupation with the atmosphere. How many kids do you know who were handed a basketball and reached for an anemometer?"

For Tom, the fascination isn't just with tornadoes but with weather in general. "I'm intrigued by things out of control," he says. "The weather is this one thing you can't control, and it develops all these fascinating aberrations. A tornado is the most out-of-control of them all."

Moving through the countryside with the deliberateness of a runaway train, a tornado is the most violent and unpredictable storm produced by nature. Tornadoes generally form late in the afternoon after several hours of warm, humid weather. Dry air from the west collides at ground level with warm, moist air from the south. The lighter moist air cools and condenses as it rises, releasing heat. If it bumps into a wind shear blowing in the opposite direction, the clouds dance around one another, and the sky darkens as if a pot of ink had just been spilled. Hail, rain, and violent lightning often accompany the theatrics. It is a random confluence of elements generally present in the atmosphere. When the conditions are right, says Tom, "it just goes berserk."

There is no average tornado. Funnel clouds range from one yard to two miles wide and travel along paths as short as a few feet or as long as 100 miles. While there is a tornado season that lasts from March through October, and a Tornado Alley that extends from the Texas panhandle to northern Wisconsin, twisters have struck in every state, in every month, and at all times of the day and night. "A tornado is a rogue," says Tom, "a bothersome thing with a mind of its own."

"Tornado prediction" is almost a contradiction in terms. Ripe conditions can be spotted up to 48 hours in advance, but guessing exactly where and when a twister might strike is no more precise than guessing the correct time and place at which a random murder might occur. The state of the art in tornado prediction can narrow the watch box down to an area of 20,000 square miles— roughly the equivalent of telling everyone in New Hampshire, Vermont, and western Massachusetts to duck. The chances of a tornado striking any one particular spot are about once in every 5,000 years.

Once it touches down, a tornado rarely follows a straight course. Some tornadoes have been known to make U-turns, stops and starts, and even complete circles. They have a logic of their own that is apparent only after the storm is complete.

Tom Grazulis followed a similarly erratic path. After college he worked for two days as a weather forecaster in Hartford, Connecticut, before deciding that the job wasn't for him. Later he taught school in Monmouth, New Jersey, and in northern Vermont. He went into the environmental film business during the summers. In 1969 he produced a 20-minute documentary about the New Jersey shoreline. Two years later he completed a movie about tornadoes, *Approaching the Unapproachable*. As unconnected as that all seems to the work of a tornado detective, it eventually served as the vehicle for Tom's return to meteorology.

After *Approaching the Unapproachable,* he was inundated with requests for more information about tornadoes. Between 1972 and 1979 he spent his summers producing posters and filmstrips that focused on tornado history in individual states. Since official storm records have been kept only as far back as 1950, Tom scoured the newspaper files at Dartmouth College and Harvard University for information.

Those files had their limitations. For instance, on the day in 1945 when Franklin Roosevelt died, there was an inordinate number of severe storms. The death of the president, however, completely overshadowed an important atmospheric event in the metropolitan papers. To do really significant work, Tom felt he needed the time and money to visit state historical libraries with large collections of local papers.

About that time the Nuclear Regulatory Commission (NRC) was funding two independent projects to study the question of why tornadoes strike where they do. The two groups were working from the same records and arriving at different conclusions. Tom thought he knew the reason why. "The scope of the research was limited to the official records maintained from 1950 to the present," he says. "That isn't a long enough period of time to determine where tornadoes hit and where they don't."

Tom presented his findings to the NRC, and in 1980 he received a grant to conduct his own study of tornado history. He still recalls walking into the first library in Illinois, where 60,000 reels of small-town newspapers were stored on microfilm. "For me," he says, "it was like walking on hallowed ground. Here I was, and there were all those reels waiting to be put in front of me."

His theory was proved one day while he was working in a library in Texas. He came across a reference to a 1916 tornado in Davis, Oklahoma. It turned out to be a significant storm that killed eight people and destroyed property in a path nearly a mile wide. Yet the storm was barely reported even in the metropolitan papers in Oklahoma. For all practical scientific purposes, it didn't exist until Tom dug it up.

In 1984 *Violent Tornado Climatology 1880 to 1982,* a 200-page catalog of 969 killer tornadoes, was published by the NRC. With that book, and his anecdote about the Oklahoma tornado, Grazulis approached the NSF and proposed a definitive study of all the tornadoes with wind speeds over 120 miles an hour to have struck the United States since 1880. Though he was one man working from a humble farm in northern Vermont, the NSF awarded him a grant.

"Twelve thousand tornadoes is about as far as I can go," he says now. "After that we run out of source records." Spring is the start of the tornado season, and as this article is written [1988], the first rumblings have already been heard from down south. Two people died in a small tornado outside of Omaha, Nebraska, but the storm wasn't significant enough to look into. A Florida tornado that left four dead will undoubtedly be included in the book.

After 18 years Tom sometimes interprets the world through tornadoes. He once won $20 in the lottery playing 3-18-25-6-5-16, a number that combines the dates of his two favorite storms: the 1925 Tri-State Tornado, the most violent tornado ever to strike the United States, which smashed 200 miles through Missouri, Illinois, and Indiana, killing 600 people; and the day in 1916 when 45 twisters, 20 of them killers, touched down in Arkansas.

He can recite the odd fact and intriguing anecdote: Thirty chickens are found sitting in a Lansing, Michigan, henhouse, stripped entirely of their feathers; a passenger train traveling 60 miles an hour barrels straight into a twister that lifts five coach cars weighing 70 tons each off the tracks—one car lands in a ditch 80 feet away. As Tom says, "Nothing is common in a tornado."

He also has collected eloquent accounts of storm victims. After the Easter Sunday tornado that struck Omaha on March 23, 1913, a newspaper editor wrote that he looked up "into what appeared to be an enormous hollow cylinder, bright inside with lightning flashes, but black as the blackest night all around. The noise was like ten million bees, plus a roar that beggars description."

"Most of us live such mundane lives that an event like this brings out the poet in us all," Tom says. The event no longer frightens him, but he understands why twisters loom so large in our imaginations. "It's the incredible illogic," he says. "Anything that strikes at random is abhorrent. This thing violates your house, like terrorism. Tornadoes are the terrorists of the atmosphere."

Tom also has taken note of social changes reflected in the public response to tornadoes. He recalls the story he once read in a small-town Mississippi newspaper. Much of the report was devoted to the suffering of a white woman who had injured her arm. In an aside near the end of the piece, it was noted that ten Negroes also were killed. Afterward, Tom suggested to a friend that the progress of the civil rights movement could be tracked by the date when southern newspapers began to list all victims of a tornado in alphabetical order, regardless of their race.

Despite the publication of his book, Tom will never know whether it has practical value. Climatology takes a long view, and a century may pass before his work will be validated or repudiated. He accepts this as part of the bargain of science. "I can only look back over time and try to make judgments on what I think happened," he says. "One hundred years from now, if the same concentration shows up, then we've got something. Then again, in a hundred years this may all be a coincidence. But I'll never know if it's a major work."

"It's a major amount of work," Doris adds.

The tornado that crumpled these houses in Lawrence, Massachusetts, on July 26, 1890 was the only major New England twister to strike in the morning.

New England's Ten Worst Killers

Here's the good news: While tornadoes are a potential threat to the life and limb of anyone living east of the Rockies, they are a rarity in New England. Topography may be one of the reasons why—it's thought that mountains break up the wind currents. Still, there is a theory that the Connecticut River Valley is a microcosm of Tornado Alley. Cold, dry air sweeps down from the Adirondacks and bumps into warm, moist air from the Atlantic. It's not exactly a tornado-producing factory, but according to Tom Grazulis, there has been a fair number of killer tornadoes in the recorded history of New England. (To qualify for this list of the ten worst, more than two people had to have died of other than natural causes.)

☞ **August 15, 1787** (Connecticut): The main funnel touched down in Wethersfield, but severe storms also were reported in New Hampshire, Massachusetts, and Rhode Island. A woman and her son were caught in the open and killed. Clothes from their house were carried three miles.

☞ **September 9, 1821** (New Hampshire): Known today as the Sunday Tornado and the Great New Hampshire Whirlwind, this twister stands with the 1953 Worcester tornado as the most violent in New England history. At least five persons were killed as the storm moved southeast across the rugged terrain from Cornish to 12 miles northwest of Concord. Had it hit a densely populated area, it might have produced a huge death toll. As it happened, most of the damage was to forests.

☞ **September 9, 1821** (Massachusetts): Later that same day, another funnel struck about 50 miles to the south of the New Hampshire twister. The storm killed two and moved east-southeast from one mile south of Northfield to Warwick, Orange, and Royalston. The account book of a tavern was carried aloft for 45 miles.

☞ **August 9, 1878** (Connecticut): A twister passed along the north side of Wallingford, killing 31 persons and destroying 30 homes, a church, and a schoolhouse.

☞ **July 16, 1879** (Massachusetts): At least seven tornadoes hit eastern New York and western New England on this date. The funnel first touched down at Pittsfield, damaging the whole region and leaving three persons dead.

☞ **July 26, 1890** (Massachusetts): The tornado struck at 9:15 A.M. just north of Lawrence. Twenty-five houses were destroyed, 500 people were left homeless, and eight people died. It is the only killer tornado in New England history that occurred in the morning.

☞ **June 9, 1953** (Massachusetts): The Worcester County Tornado equaled in size and intensity the most powerful storms seen in the western United States. Winds estimated at 250 miles per hour rampaged along a discontinuous path for 46 miles, from Rutland through Holden, Worcester, Shrewsbury, Westborough, and Southborough. Ninety people were killed, 1,200 were injured, and 10,000 were left homeless; damage was estimated at $52 million. A piece of a frozen mattress fell from the sky into Boston Harbor, 40 miles to the east. Though the 90 deaths are often assumed to have occurred in Worcester, they were actually spread over all six communities.

☞ **August 28, 1973** (Massachusetts): Six houses were destroyed and four people killed when a funnel touched down at Canaan, New York, then roared through West Stockbridge. Three of the deaths were at a truck stop in West Stockbridge, the other in one of the homes.

☞ **August 10, 1979** (Massachusetts): Two boys were killed by falling trees at different locations in a Boy Scout camp at Paxton. This was probably the least violent of all the tornadoes on the list, with wind speeds of around 100 miles per hour.

☞ **October 3, 1979** (Connecticut): One hundred buildings were destroyed and three persons were killed in Windsor Locks. Several historic aircraft stored at an air museum also were ripped apart by the storm.

What keeps him at the microfilm reader is the satisfaction of trying to rein in something over which he has little control. There is also a certain fragrance of immortality to the job. He knows that a century from now scientists will glance through his book, even if it's just to study the mistakes of the past.

With the completion of the tornado project, Tom has received a new assignment, also funded by the NSF: the study of floods. Like his tornado research, it involves the kind of tedious record-combing that no one except a guy living in an isolated farmhouse in northern Vermont is willing to undertake. When that's through, he may actually have the time to see a twister.

"I'd really love to spend a month in the Texas panhandle chasing tornadoes," he says. "But that's way down the line. That's for retirement." ∞

CHAPTER FOUR

Floods

Top and right: *Two views of a house on Main Street in Unionville, Connecticut, following the Farmington River flood of 1955.* **Previous pages:** *A locomotive churns through rising floodwaters.*

The Nightmare That Was True

BY DOROTHEA JACKSON CRANDALL

It was raining at three o'clock on the morning of August 19, 1955. The sudden roar of a truck in front of the house jarred me awake. I plunged my head deeper into the pillow to smother the sound, but the roaring and grinding got louder. Exasperated, I pounded to the window. What I saw, I did not believe. There was water in the street—everywhere—as far as the eye could see.

The truck I had heard was a car. The grinding quit, and a man jumped out, not bothering to close the door. He swept his small son up into his arms, grabbed his wife, and the three, clad in nightclothes, started up the street in water above their knees.

Through the night came the cries of women and children and terse, barked commands from anxious men. The Farmington River was flooding.

My mother came into my room. "I can't believe it. What are we going to do? We can't walk out into that." Even as she spoke, I could see the river rising. Already two feet high in the street, the black, fearsome water began to course briskly as it swelled. The streetlights barely illuminated the odd collection of objects tumbling along with the current. The rain kept falling.

At 3:30, a fire alarm blared and a fire truck swam down our street almost to our house. A voice shouted through a megaphone: "There's 27 feet of water coming! The dam's broken. Get ready to leave immediately. We'll send a boat to pick you up." The truck churned slowly back up the street.

It never occurred to us that 27 feet of water would swallow our house. The imminence of such a wall of water seemed unreal. Yet, stunned as we were, we knew the trouble was real. It is a paradox that strength and calm can sit upon fear in time of crisis. That strange acceptance of our peril came to us.

Doing something is better than waiting. Up the attic stairs went clothing, scrapbooks, picture albums, jewelry, canned goods—in case the boat didn't come after all. The attic became the place of refuge. Once I pictured the two of us standing in the attic with water up to our necks while all around the steadfast house the waters raged.

The apartment where my mother and I lived was on the second floor of a large white frame house with a double front porch. As its former inhabitants grew in number, the house had grown too, mushrooming out in two rear annexes on the first-story level. Around these sections of the house and the shed beyond, the climbing water now swirled.

An hour passed. Still no boat. I picked up the phone and called a friend who lived on a hill in another part of town. In minutes I had cleared her head of sleep. She at once offered her home to us. Encouraged by her voice, I hung up and continued to watch for the boat.

Daylight came, blurred by the wind and rain. But the dark at the bottom of the stairs was deepening. The water was stealing steadily up. Soon the front door would be hidden. And then? I turned from the hallway.

6:30. If only the boat would come!

"Here it is!" I shouted. My mother and I ran to the living room. An aluminum tank of bottled gas hissed as it floated past, a few feet below our upstairs front porch. Then a real boat did go by—a shining new motorboat, captured by the runaway waters.

We existed in a vacuum. We couldn't talk. We tried not to think about the boat.

8:30. We heard it. Stepping through the living room door onto the front porch, I began to yell and wave frantically at the amphibious craft touring the area not a hundred yards away from us. My mother called. Her voice grew hoarse. The wind grabbed the words from our mouths. My throat stung; my heart pounded. We were neither seen nor heard. The wind, the rushing water, and the thick foliage of the elm-lined street silenced and obscured our presence. The rain beat down.

From our kitchen window, we had an unhampered view of the river, until now hidden by the shed, catalpa trees, and weeping willows that had stood a hundred years. They were all gone. Ferocious, boiling waves raced eastward. Bits of chairs, beds, roofs, and whole washing machines charged along with the current. All the time the rain came down, a hazy curtain of water billowing with the wind.

As we stood in the old-fashioned kitchen, with its towering old gray oil stove and slightly sloping floor, we looked out on the river. It had been just a creek, gliding unobtrusively through towns and valleys. Although it threaded its way right through the center of Unionville, Connecticut, it never interrupted life. Bridges tied the town together, and you almost were able to ignore the river, if you chose.

Suddenly, from our kitchen watch, we saw the downstairs left wing of the house rise up, turn slightly on its side, splinter, and sink away into the boiling confusion. Then there was a shudder, a wrench, and our bathroom and the annex below were gone. A doorless sill now afforded a still more panoramic view of the river.

We went into the living room on the street side of the house. A corner room, it, too, permitted a good view of the moving spectacle outside, but here the "street" water, slowed by houses and trees still standing, did not look quite so ominous. It was misleading.

Curled up tightly in a chair by the window, I stared hypnotically at the debris clinging to trees. Then terror such as I had never before known gripped me. Soundlessly, a house up the street suddenly splintered and fell away to nothing. For a second it made one last attempt to survive, seeming to clutch at its telephone wires as if they were lifelines. They, too, went down.

When the water began to rise from the living-room floor, we went up to the attic. Piled on the table, chests, and boxes were many things that recalled other days. But we had little chance to think of those days. The time had come. There was a tremor, a chilling shudder of the old house, and we were sinking into the murky black depths.

The next thing we knew, we were still sitting on the bed by the attic wall. Although slumped to one side,

A man surveys the broken ruins of the Unionville Dam, which gave way in the flood of August 1955.

The Great Flood of 1955

BY RUTH SCANLON

In August 1955, 13 inches of rain sent the Farmington River over its banks in one of the worst floods in the history of Connecticut. When we heard that the water over in Simsbury was still rising, we decided to try to get over there to see how my 90-year-old uncle was faring.

We got to within half a mile of my uncle's house before being stopped by the water. There were six or eight people standing around sightseeing. Then one of them yelled, "There's a woman in the water!" My husband jumped in and pulled her out. She had managed to make her way from one of the flooded homes. She said her mother was still in the house in an upstairs room. The first floor was completely flooded.

My husband volunteered to try and make his way to the house. The water was up to his armpits as he approached the front door. Just then, a man's voice came from an upstairs window.

"If you take one more step on my property, I'll shoot you!"

My husband said that he just wanted to know if there were any women in the house. The voice said, "Get the hell off my land!" There was a good five feet of water covering his land!

Then a woman's voice came from the window. "David, I have lived with you for 40 years, and if I want to leave this house, I'm going to!" By that time, another man had joined my husband, and the two of them carried the woman to safety. The man with the gun refused to leave.

the room was still in one piece. Flat against the attic window was the roof of the house next door. We sat still and waited.

After awhile we groped our way down the stairs, now tilted back at an almost impossible angle. Chinks of plaster had fallen in the living room, leaving gaping, jagged holes in the walls. The water was about 12 inches deep in the room. It was brown and felt cold as we stepped into it.

Leaning through the doorway to the porch, I saw that the other side of the house had sunk several feet. Our side still seemed almost upright. The big house on the right had moved into ours, causing ours to leave its foundation and move into the one on our left.

At last the rain stopped. Whenever the wind caught its breath, we became aware of the whir of helicopters overhead. Were they photographing the disaster area or rescuing people? A small measure of hope returned.

10:30. 11:30. No sign of help from the air or anywhere. The water ceased to rise but did not fall. The danger was far from over. We had to do something.

The porch held. For many minutes we vigorously waved the living-room curtains back and forth, out over the railing as far as we could reach. Through the eye-level foliage of the street, we saw the man. He was more than a few hundred yards away. If only we could get his attention! Just when it seemed utterly hopeless, someone began flashing a mirror. We had been seen!

After nine hours of anguish, our relief was short-lived. One by one a number of tremors shook the house. Plaster fell, followed by a crackling as of thunder. Through the living-room door to the attic came light. When the trembling stopped, we went to the attic door and looked up into sky. The roof had split open.

The next two hours seemed as long as the preceding nine. Intermittently, the tremors continued. Would help ever come?

At last it did. At 1:30 P.M. a Navy helicopter hovered over our house, coming in as close as the trees would allow. A voice shouted, "We're going to throw you a line. Grab it and step into the seat belt. Get a tight hold, and we'll pull you up. Don't worry; it's safe."

With a splash, the thing that was to pull us to safety hit the water just outside the porch railing. I fished it out, helped my mother into it, tugged on the line after she was straddling the railing, and up she went.

Minutes later the sling was dropped again. Stepping into the canvas belt that served as a seat, I, too, straddled the railing. I gripped the small wheel-like disk and tugged on the line. Straight up over the house and treetops I swung. Soon they had reeled me up to the open door of the craft. A hand reached out and grasped mine. It was over.

∞

FRANK LESLIE'S
ILLUSTRATED
THE CONNECTICUT VALLEY FLOOD.
NEWSPAPER

Entered according to the Act of Congress, in the year 1874, by FRANK LESLIE, in the office of the Librarian of Congress, at Washington.

No. 974—VOL. XXXVIII.]   NEW YORK, MAY 30, 1874.   [PRICE, 10 CENTS, $4 00 YEARLY. 13 WEEKS, $1 00

The Milk Wagon Hero

BY JAMES J. HAWTHORNE

The historic ride of Paul Revere rousing the Massachusetts countryside was made in 1775. In that same state at Williamsburg, just less than a hundred years later, there occurred another dramatic ride of warning, pregnant with a danger more immediately lethal and relentless than that which had motivated Revere. Both rides have been celebrated in poetry. It was New England's own Henry Wadsworth Longfellow who helped immortalize Revere. But it was John Boyle O'Reilly, Hoosier poet, who extolled the heroic excursion of the Williamsburg rider—Collins Graves.

Revere rode horseback. A horse also sped Graves on his message of alarm, but he was not on horseback. His horse was attached to a milk wagon, and Graves interrupted routine early morning deliveries to grasp in his reins the fateful role thrust upon him. He rode just a step before the surging waters of the Mill River, alerting all ahead to the imminent danger invading ruthlessly from the north. The sudden floodwaters, which he was barely able to outdistance, had soon inundated a wide area in the route from Williamsburg south to Florence, in western Massachusetts.

Though unsung in poetic annals, other heroes helped Graves sound lifesaving alarms for unsuspecting residents. George Cheney, Robert Loud, Myron Day, Jerome Hillman, and a little boy, James Ryan, were all listed with the brave who gave special selfless service to their imperiled neighbors. But, despite their efforts, 138 lives were lost in the flood, which subsided less than two hours after the first alarm. Fifty-seven of the dead were from Williamsburg, 30 from Skinnerville and Haydenville, and 51 from Leeds.

The death-dealing, terror-laden waves soared more than 20 feet high and in one place touched a tree branch 40 feet above the ground. The onslaught of the angry waters caused a dense, enveloping foglike mist. Sickening, stagnant odors permeated the area, starkly underscoring the nightmarish quality of the abrupt uprooting. According to Phyllis Baker Deming's *History of Williamsburg,* one survivor described the accompanying sound as the tearing of shingles from many buildings, while another heard in it the heavy foreboding thunder of a summer storm. Years later, an eyewitness, a little boy at the time, described his reaction to the event: "A great mass of brush, trees, and trash was rolling rapidly toward me. I have tried many times to describe how this appeared. Perhaps the best simile is that of hay rolling over and over as the hay rake moves along the fields, only this roll seems 20 feet high, and the spears of grass in the hay rake enlarged to limbs and trunks of trees, mixed with boards and timbers."

An engraving from Harper's Weekly *of June 6, 1874 dramatizes watchman George Cheney's frantic ride to warn the townspeople below the Williamsburg Reservoir that the earthen dam had crumbled. Cheney's portrait appears top left; at top right is Collins Graves, "The Milk Wagon Hero."*

Williamsburg, Massachusetts, where the first settlers had built their homes on the hills, was rapidly developing as an industrial community. A silk mill, brass works, sawmill, button shop, and flour mill, among other industries, had come to Williamsburg. These manufacturing enterprises required more power, which resulted in a demand for a reserve water supply. The massive dam structure settled upon for this purpose was erected on another hill, some three miles north and at a level 300 feet above that of the town. It was built in 1865, designed to hold one billion gallons of water. Although the builders made confident claims that the walls were as safe as a solid shaft of granite, the townspeople remained skeptical. In an effort to alleviate their fears, the reservoir was rip-rapped (given a sustaining wall of stones) shortly before May 1874.

May 1874 was a rainy month. This followed upon a winter of heavy freezing and sudden thaws. On Saturday morning, May 16, it was raining again. George Cheney, with three years' experience on the job, was the watchman on duty that day at the dam. He was known to share the common apprehension concerning the reservoir. However, on his rounds at six o'clock that morning, Cheney found nothing amiss nor any cause for alarm.

It was sometime after seven, when the ascetic-looking, mustached watchman was back at his home, eating breakfast with his father, that the first sign of disaster appeared. The older man, facing the window, suddenly exclaimed, "For God's sake, George, look at the dam." About 40 feet of the earthen section at the base had given way, and streams of water were seeping through. Immediately guessing that the dam was about to go, he threw open the gates to relieve the pressure of the waters, then mounted his horse and headed wildly for town.

Meanwhile, Robert Loud, who resided near the reservoir, had caused some stir in the town. He had run all the way on foot. Ironically, this effort muted Mr. Loud, causing him to lose his voice, and the only way he was able to communicate the danger was by pointing frantically toward the reservoir. Loud's health was permanently impaired by the experience.

Cheney was at Belcher's when Collins Graves rode up with his milk wagon and overheard the news. "If the dam is breaking, the folks below must be told of it," he yelled, and was off at once for Haydenville. Cheney, having changed horses, was on the road right behind him. So close were the onrushing waters, which now hurtled angrily after him, that he had to turn off the road to avoid being engulfed.

By now it was quarter of eight, just as the bells from the Williamsburg Congregational Church, sounded by Jerome Hillman, tolled their ominous warning. While those yet alive in Williamsburg scurried to shelter, Graves, still aboard his wagon and still in good voice, gave to all in earshot his dire warning. "This the cry," says poet O'Reilly, "that he flings to the winds, / 'To the hills for your lives, the flood is behind.' / He cries and is gone, but they know the worst, / The treacherous Williamsburg dam has burst."

When Graves, at Haydenville, was forced to turn up a hill to avoid being swallowed by the pursuing waters, there was another to take up the relay. Myron Day rode in his wagon on to Leeds and Florence, the last outpost affected by this destructive flood that was contained entirely within Hampshire County.

Less than two hours after the dam broke, the waters had left in their path a sorely wounded human habitation, a place of utter misery composed of death, destruction, and desolation. Before noon on that gray Saturday, the worst fears of the wary dam watchman and his apprehensive fellow townsmen had been realized.

The eight miles from Williamsburg to Florence were marked by demolished homes and factories, crumpled bridges, and obliterated highways. In Leeds, only three buildings were left standing on the main street. Florence was the terminal point of the flood, and on its meadows were washed up the bodies of 42 victims.

The disaster brought to light the slipshod construction and unsafe design that led to the dam's collapse. All over Massachusetts, critics expressed the smoldering resentment that had been harbored so widely because of fear engendered by the reservoir's location. The home of O.G. Spelman, overseer and agent of the reservoir company, had to be guarded to save him from possible harm at the hands of vengeful townspeople.   ∞

Two scenes of the destruction caused by the Mill River flood. **Bottom left:** *The ruins of Cook's Dam, in the village of Leeds.* **Bottom right:** *On the sight of the silk mill in Skinnerville. William Skinner's house stands in the background; amazingly, it was only slightly damaged in the flood, while the mill itself was utterly swept away.*

An artist's rendering of the broken dam at Williamsburg, Massachusetts, from Harper's Weekly. *Following the initial shock of the tragedy, lengthy hearings revealed that the careless design and slipshod construction of the dam had caused the disaster.*

The Mill River Disaster

The death and destruction caused by the dam break and flood of 1874 affected five villages in two western Massachusetts towns: Williamsburg, Skinnerville, and Haydenville in the town of Williamsburg, and Leeds and Florence in the town of Northampton. Of the five villages, only Florence, where the floodwaters deposited the wreckage carried from upstream, suffered no fatalities.

In Williamsburg, only three miles south of the dam, 57 persons were listed as lost in the flood. A large flour mill was destroyed, and 25 houses were swept away as the water tore down the length of Main Street. So great was the force and volume of the water that the river actually abandoned its old bed and cut a new channel on the other side of the valley, leaving a surviving mill without waterpower. The estimated loss of property at the time was more than $150,000.

Four persons died in the village of Skinnerville. William Skinner's silk factory was destroyed, his house was damaged, and 21 other houses were carried away. Total losses were estimated at nearly $250,000.

Two miles farther downstream, at Haydenville, the greatest loss occurred at the Hayden, Gere & Co. brass works, which employed 250 men. Two large boilers were in use at the brass works, one carrying 70 pounds of steam on the day of the flood. The heated boiler exploded with a loud report, while the cold boiler was carried more than 600 feet into the yard of one of the mill's owners, Joel Hayden. Twenty-six people died at Haydenville, and the damage to the brass works, other mills, and private homes came close to $350,000.

The main street of Leeds was so thoroughly destroyed that survivors who returned in an attempt to locate their old house sites were unable to recognize the landscape or determine where their houses had stood only a short time before. Seventeen houses and several other structures were swept away, for a total loss of more than $100,000. Fifty-one people lost their lives.

In Florence, where the great flood washed up the debris from the upper four villages, property damage was relatively light, though all three of the town's bridges were swept away. At least 100 acres of the town's best farmland were rendered useless, covered with anywhere from four inches to three feet of sand and gravel that had washed downstream in the flood.

As with any sudden and destructive tragedy that affects so many people, there were remarkable and even miraculous anecdotes associated with the tragedy. A cow reportedly floated from Williamsburg to Florence, uninjured except for one broken horn. And a certain Charles Brady was carried on a pile of debris for nearly one mile, finally landing in a tree. He was later rescued, alive but quite insane.

They Took to the Hills

BY HOLCOMB B. NOBLE

Clint Ballou peeled off his wet clothes and got into bed, exhausted. But he didn't plan to sleep long. It had poured sheets of rain all day. In fact, it had rained steadily all fall, and now there was a grave danger that the reservoir dam high above town would collapse. He knew there would be little chance for sleeping until the threat had passed—if it passed.

In November of 1927, rains bore down on the New England mountain towns of Vermont and Massachusetts as they rarely had before or have since. Every stream and brook was full, and rivers began overflowing their banks. Residents of some of the valley towns had been able to move out when the flooding became bad. They waited for the sun to reappear, the water to recede, and the chance to move back to wet but substantially undamaged homes. Ballou and the residents of Becket, a town in the Berkshire Hills of Massachusetts, knew they would have no such privilege. If there was going to be a flood, there would be no moving out and moving back. In their case, there would be nothing to move back to.

They had a beautiful town in a valley amid three wooded hills that rose at some points almost straight up from the beds of three mountain streams. Even in normal times one of the streams swirled and foamed down some 250 feet of moss-grown ravine. It joined another that flowed cleanly, harmlessly, along a main street shaded with maples, and all three streams came together in the center of town. There were summer homes scattered among the hills and five lakes, but most of the residents lived in the valley. Up near the end of one of the gorges, winding into the hills, lay the highest body of water in the state, the Wheeler Reservoir, held back by an earthen dam. Normally, the reservoir fed the stream on the main street as it flowed gently down over a series of waterfalls and under a series of bridges. But if the dam burst, it would unleash a body of water from its height of 1,800 feet that would crush everything in its path—in this case, the main part of a town of 700 people.

On November 3 it began to rain as though someone, somewhere, had decided to put New England under a great swamp. About four o'clock in the afternoon Clint Ballou and two employees of one of his basket shops drove up in the pelting rain to check the reservoir. They went out onto the 30-foot-high, 200-foot-long stone wall that held the earth and stone dam in place. Everything looked all right. There, stretched out behind them, was a 50-acre body of water, not peaceful in the rain and wind, but harnessed and harmless. Despite the rainfall, only a little water was going over the spillway. The dam showed no signs of weakening, but just to be safe they opened the main sluice gate at the base of the dam to a two-thirds head. They then returned to town and a dry change of clothes.

At about ten o'clock the downpour ceased—"the rain factory stopped for lack of raw material," as one of the townspeople put it—and by 11:30 the stream had begun to subside. Ballou and his brother, Will, went back up to the dam and found the reservoir had risen four inches since late afternoon and the spillway was now taking in a river. But the rain had let up. That was the important thing, and, because of it, they thought the worst was over. They opened the gate a full head, returned to their homes, and by 1:30 A.M. Clint Ballou was finally getting the sleep that had been so long in coming.

At 3:30 he jumped out of bed and called his grain store man, Fred Crochiere. When they arrived at the reservoir, the water had gone down two inches. The night was still in darkness—beautiful after the rain. The water was peaceful, like a sleeping lion, and the air was light again as they walked along the top of the dam.

Then they saw what they had come up there so many times not to see—what generations before them had feared as well. There, along the top of the dam, like a long, lethal dagger, was a crevice about 2 feet wide and nearly 12 feet long, the first indication that something was wrong underneath. At that moment the dam was probably honeycombed and, if it let go, the men would be hurled into a pit below.

Ballou and Crochiere hurried down to the gate house to see whether the water was discharging through the gate and cylinder all right. Ballou peered through the gate house flood with his flashlight and heard something crack, like timber snapping.

"For God's sake," Crochiere said, "let's get out of here! I don't like those sounds!"

A second crack warned them that it was time to move. No sooner had they gotten out of the gate house than part of the wall burst and smashed the little building like an eggshell. The two men, less than 30 feet away, broke into a run, reached the first house directly in line with the dam, and banged on the doors and windows.

If the dead sleep like that, Ballou thought, Gabriel would have some trouble waking 'em up. He thought the water would be upon them at any moment. Finally, the man of the house came downstairs and let them in. Ballou and Crochiere blurted out what was happening and told him and his family to hurry to high ground. Ballou rushed for the telephone.

Mac McCormick, who operated the town switchboard from a room in his house in the valley, answered on the first ring. He was not sleeping much that night either.

"Mac, this is Clint. Something terrible has happened here at the dam. The water is coming down on us just as sure as there is a God in heaven. Call my wife first, my brother second, then everybody on the low ground. Do you get it?"

Mac said he did. He called the Ballous and roused his own wife and two daughters and sent them up to Middlefield Hill. Then, although his house was bound to be in line with the onrushing water, he sat back down at his switchboard and one by one rang the bells on every circuit in the village.

Meanwhile, Ballou and Crochiere raced their Paige touring car around the eight narrow curves and over the narrow bridges on the road down to town, blasting their horn and shouting the warning to everybody. "If I live to be a thousand years old, I shall see the lights flashing in the houses and see the people leaving their homes as we came down the street," Ballou said. Most of the people did leave their houses, but some did not.

Frank Prentice couldn't believe there was so much danger. Although he thought he probably ought to get out of his house near the main railroad line, he was in no great rush. A 90-year-old man and his wife, whose house was right on a bank of the swollen, angry stream, respected the danger all right but insisted that, if anything was going to happen, they would prefer that it happen with them together in their own house. A housekeeper, Mrs. Justine Carroll, had been caught in a flood once before in another town and thought she would be safer inside than out. Repeated attempts to persuade them to leave were to no avail.

Others rushed to the hills. Generally, they were able to take nothing with them except the clothes they were wearing. Some brought personal papers or a trinket or two. One man in the confusion brought his neckties and a bag with one onion in it. It was still dark, and they could not see what was happening below. Esther McCormick, from a friend's backyard, could not pick out her own house from among the others in the darkness. She could not see that her father still had not left the telephone switchboard or that Ballou was still below trying to get everyone to safety. Finally, Ballou joined his wife on higher ground, but McCormick would not leave.

They all waited. And waited.

"Now and again I would see a lantern bobbing rapidly along the main street. . . . An automobile would speed by, carrying others seeking refuge in the hills," McCormick said. "An hour passed and nearly two. The suspense was terrible."

Perhaps the alarm had been false. Perhaps the dam was going to hold after all. Only one chunk of it had collapsed, and perhaps the rest of it would stand. Perhaps the town was safe. Gradually people began to go back to their homes. And Ballou, with five others, headed back up to the mountain reservoir for another inspection.

They got to within about a quarter of a mile of the dam when they saw in a sickening instant that the alarm had indeed been true. The dam had fallen, and water was rolling straight at them. Some of the men jumped from the car and dashed up the bank, and others urged that they all do the same. But there was a wide place in the road with a good place to turn around, and Ballou decided to try it. He thought he could beat the flood if he did not stall the engine in turning around. Then with the big wave in sight and water already up to the running board, he wheeled the car around and raced for town. Down the mile and a half of narrow winding road he sped, blowing the horn all the way, like Paul Revere in a touring car, sounding the warning, with the water rushing down the valley behind him.

The Reverend Charles Ramsay and his family, who had gotten cold waiting on a hilltop after the first alarm and returned home, thinking the danger was over, had just started eating a breakfast of oatmeal and coffee when they heard Ballou's horn. They hurried up the hill behind their house, turned, and saw the water. For them, and for most of the townspeople of Becket, there came—at just about dawn—the worst sound they would ever hear or sight they would ever see.

A great roar boomed out, and what seemed like a cloud of black smoke appeared at the head of the valley and approached in a dark mass bordered with seething white foam some 40 to 50 feet high. It pushed through

Main Street in Becket, Massachusetts, after the flood of November 1927. When the rain-swollen Wheeler Reservoir burst its dam, the waters tore through the very heart of town.

the first bridge and crushed the house from which Ballou had first telephoned McCormick. It rolled across the gorge and began tearing out the road behind Ballou, then collapsed a two-story sawmill, shooting lumber and logs into the air. As the water poured down toward the village, it sliced the front porch cleanly off the Ramsay house, but left the rest of it intact. Next came the big brick silk mill. The giant wave splashed into the millpond in front and stormed inside, knocking out bricks, pushing out walls, and caving in the roof as though the mill were a child's sand castle crumbling with the brush of a hand. Then another bridge. Then the Lyman house. Then Will Ballou's house. Here and there a great root or chunk of rock or concrete would stick out for an instant, only to be sucked under again. With irresistible force, the water crushed building after building.

Clint Ballou and his men had beaten the flood to the center of town by several minutes and taken to high ground. McCormick, however, was still at his post at the telephone switchboard, still trying desperately to get word to everyone, still apparently in the path of destruction himself.

Before he fled, Bob Burnham, whose house was not far from the reservoir, telephoned McCormick to tell him the dam had broken. The water was coming down on the town for sure. The operator decided he would not leave his switchboard. He told himself he was not afraid. The water was not going to hit his house anyway, he said; it would bank off before it got there and head for the opposite side of the valley. He began checking the circuits again and found almost everyone had gotten the warning of Ballou's auto horn and hurried to the hills. Now he was nearly alone. But there was still Mrs. Carroll, who had already refused all urging to leave, and there were others to call.

Suddenly he heard the mighty roar. He looked up the street, and the water had just come into sight. It was striking the silk mill, knocking bricks in all directions. There was an explosion, black smoke, and then nothing but the steady roar and crashing of the water. Somehow, he thought, it didn't seem to be coming very fast. But before he knew it, water had torn away the front half of the house next door. His switchboard went dead, and water swirled in around his knees. McCormick threw his headphone aside and raced for the back porch, but the water outside was already some 15 to 20 feet high. He was trapped.

Frank Prentice was still in his house, a few doors down, when the torrent picked it up and began bobbing it about like a toy boat. The water forced him to the second floor. From a bedroom window he just managed to grab the branch of a tree that had held fast and pull himself to safety. Seconds later the house broke into pieces when it crashed into the railroad bridge at the lower end of town.

Opposite page: *Fierce flooding, as at this mill site, was widespread throughout New England in November 1927.*
Below: *When this photograph was taken, the raging waters of the Merrimack River had already risen to within a few inches of the windows of this mill in Lawrence, Massachusetts. A few hours later, the river began swirling through the lower stories.*

Floodwaters washed out these Central Vermont Railroad tracks, leaving them suspended in midair.

The Vermont Flood of 1927

The Vermont Flood of 1927 caused the greatest death toll of any natural disaster in the state's history. Of the 88 persons reported dead throughout New England, 84 died in Vermont. Damage estimates around the state listed a property loss of around $28 million.

The month of October 1927 had been a particularly wet one, and the ground was already saturated by the time rain started to fall in earnest on November 3. Rivers quickly flooded their banks, and residents of low-lying areas had virtually no warning until the floodwaters were upon them. Montpelier received 4.24 inches of rain in only nine hours on November 3, and Somerset recorded an incredible 9.65 inches of rain from the storm. It is estimated that well over half the state received rain in excess of six inches.

Within Vermont itself the worst flooding occurred in the Winooski and White River valleys. From Winooski to Barre and Montpelier, 48 persons died as a result of the flood, and $12 million in property was destroyed.

Other buildings—homes, barns, and stores—followed the same pattern. They were picked up whole or in sections by the powerful, demented force and floated almost lightly and gently away—to be suddenly broken apart against the railroad bridge or Middlefield Hill as the water veered to the right and headed down toward the Connecticut Valley.

Mrs. Carroll's house floated airily away, then rolled on its side, and finally broke into shreds and washed away. She was never seen again.

Ballou and his family stood on a hill between the Baptist and Congregational churches. They saw the water strike the little dam above his gristmill. Like a volcano, it shot logs, rocks, trees and timbers, bricks, silk, machinery, furniture, and sacks of grain into the air. Ballou stood in a trance, watching helplessly as the work of a lifetime was washed away before his eyes. The basket shop collapsed. Then his house rose off its foundation, and he watched as it floated slowly, easily away and smashed against the twisted iron remains of the railroad bridge.

"My God, our property!" he murmured.

In what was once the center of town, a tall tree withstood the force of the thousands of pounds of water hurtling against it, and because it did, the old couple who insisted on staying together in their own home were saved. So much debris began piling up against the tree that it split the wave in two, one half going on one side of their house and the hotel and the other half on the other side. Neither building was damaged, and the old man and his wife—against all reasonable odds—were not harmed.

McCormick was still on the porch of his house when the crest of the high wave approached. Seconds before it reached him, the current twisted, and the bulk of it missed his house entirely—just as he had predicted. Houses on both sides of him were washed away, but his was spared. He left the porch and went back inside. Although the telephone switchboard and most of the first floor were covered with water and mud, he tried by force of habit to make a connection. Most of the lines in town were down, and the entire exchange was out of order.

McCormick waded out into the main street, the first to survey the awesome damage. Slowly, others began coming back to see the village that was no longer there. Many wept. Many had lost all they possessed. The more fortunate had lost nothing personally, but the shock of losing the land they had walked on and the stores where they had shopped—in fact, the very existence of the community they had known—was almost too much to bear. Most just stared and said little.

Above: *Several dead bodies were found beneath this mass of wreckage in Waterbury, Vermont. Hundreds of homes and businesses in the Winooski River Valley were destroyed.* **Below:** *Snow and cold weather followed on the heels of the 1927 flood, adding to the bleakness of the landscape and the misery of the homeless.*

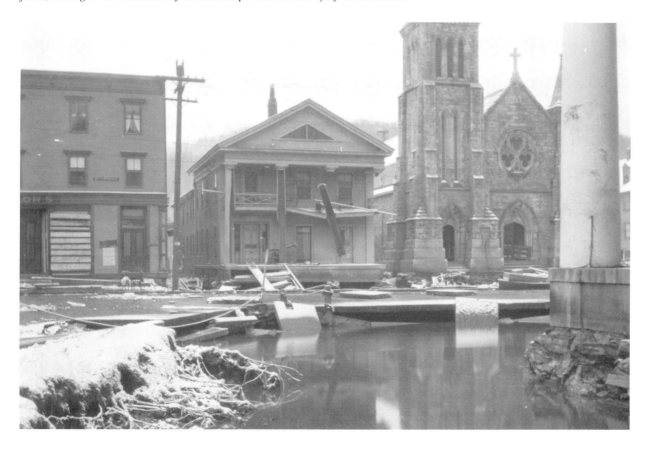

Above: *A team of horses provides a tow for a waterlogged truck on a flooded highway near Berlin, New Hampshire.* **Bottom:** *In New England, you never can tell when a rowboat may come in handy around the house.* **Opposite page, bottom:** *A broad flood near Northampton, Massachusetts.*

What was once their town was now a wide, deep gully of boulders, tree stumps, debris, and aimless, eddying, flowing water. A solitary hen walked up and down, looking as though she had been through a clothes wringer. A dog roamed around and around the spot where his master's house had once stood. People wandered aimlessly, too—wondering what they were going to do, what was going to happen to them now.

The town was a ruin. Forty-eight buildings were gone, along with 11 bridges, 2 miles of roadway, and 3 miles of railroad. Except for Mrs. Carroll, the people of the town were all right. The bulk of the raging flood had passed, and they were safe. No one had been hurt. The alertness and brave action of Ballou, McCormick, and others had saved scores of lives.

One employee of one of the Ballous' two basket shops, the one that was damaged but not destroyed, came to him the morning after the flood as he stood amidst the rubble. She was in tears and asked, "Mr. Ballou, what are we going to do?"

"I'll tell you what we're going to do," he replied. "We're going to open that basket shop Monday morning and go to work." ∞

The New England Flood of 1936

After the disastrous flood that devastated Vermont and parts of western New England in 1927, experts and local officials confidently predicted that another flood of such magnitude was unlikely to strike the region—at least for many years to come. Less than nine years later, the experts were proven wrong.

The winter of 1935-36 had been particularly severe throughout New England. By late fall, plunging temperatures had frozen many streams, and rivers were choked with ice. Heavy snows blanketed much of the region, especially the Vermont and New Hampshire hills.

On March 9, 1936, the spring thaw came—in one fell swoop that brought misery, not relief, to the region. Unseasonably warm temperatures had already started melting the snow cover, but on March 10 a hard, steady rain began to fall. By March 12 most upland streams had flooded their banks, and the spring runoff surged down the hillsides toward the icebound Connecticut River.

At Mt. Tom Junction in western Massachusetts, an ice jam 30 feet high and a quarter mile wide backed up the river for six miles, flooding farmland and threatening the city of Holyoke. On March 15, with a thunderous roar, the jam broke, hurling blocks of ice skyward and splintering trees, but the freed river passed by Holyoke, sparing it from destruction.

A second rainstorm followed closely on the heels of the first, and on March 18 the Connecticut River was rising again, this time to record levels. Water rushing through a dike at Hatfield, Massachusetts, swirled three feet deep around the town hall, trapping 150 people inside. At Brattleboro, Vermont, the water was rising at the rate of two feet every hour, and the cresting river had completely isolated the town of Bellows Falls. Sandbag crews worked furiously throughout the night as the flood waters surged down the river valley toward the cities of the south.

By 6 P.M. on the next day, March 19, the Connecticut River at Hartford had already reached its highest level ever, surpassing the old mark of 29.8 feet above normal recorded in May of 1854. Bushnell Park and East Hartford resembled one huge lake, and the waters threatened the city's downtown district. Two feet of water stood in the lobby of the Bond Hotel, and bellboys worked in hip boots; rowboats shuttled between flooded hotels and the railroad depot. And the river just kept rising—eventually climbing to over 37 feet above flood stage at its peak on Saturday, March 21.

Coast Guard whaleboats evacuated residents of flooded East Hartford. In Northampton, Massachusetts, the Coast Guard got help from a flotilla of Gloucester fishermen and boats from the Boston Navy Yard. Also in Northampton, a Smith College professor identified a corpse washed out of a shallow grave as that of an eighteenth-century Indian girl. At nearby Deerfield a young student from the Eaglebrook school rode a polo pony through the flood waters to rescue five people from a house on the riverbank. And in Wethersfield, Connecticut, a condemned murderer won a reprieve when the execution chamber became too flooded to proceed.

At the time, the Flood of '36 was the worst in memory, and even today it remains the most damaging and widespread in New England's history. Twenty-four people died as a result of the flood and 77,000 were left homeless. Damage to homes and businesses exceeded 60 million dollars. And, occurring at a time when the region had just started to rebound from the depths of the Great Depression, the Flood of '36 wreaked psychological as well as physical damage on the people of New England.

Right: *A roadsign on the outskirts of Northampton, Massachusetts, greets swimmers and aquatic fowl.* **Below:** *After the waters receded, this tavern was left high and dry.* **Bottom:** *An aerial view of the swollen Connecticut River at Bellows Falls, Vermont.*
Opposite page, top: *This residential neighborhood in Northampton resembled a placid lake during the flood of 1936.* **Opposite page, bottom:** *Seen from above, the besieged city of Hartford, Connecticut, with the Colt Arms factory in the foreground.*

Buildings standing near the ruptured molasses tank were coated to the second story with the viscous amber liquid.

We couldn't resist including one of the all-time favorite
stories from *Yankee,* the account of Boston's great
Molasses Flood. Whether the unseasonably
warm January temperatures contributed to the tragedy
is arguable, but the disaster exploded (literally) once
and for all the old expression "as slow as molasses
in January."

The Molasses Flood

BY ALTON HALL BLACKINGTON

As long as people work, live, and play in the vicinity of North End Park in Boston, no winter will pass without someone recalling the catastrophe that took place there on January 15, 1919. The scene of this tragic accident was that low-lying section of Commercial Street between Copps Hill and the playground of North End Park.

Looking down from Copps Hill on that mild winter afternoon, you saw first the tracks of the Boston elevated railroad and the old houses nearby. Across the street were the freight sheds of the Boston and Worcester and Eastern Massachusetts railways, the paving division of the Public Works Department, the headquarters of Fireboat 31, and the wharves with patrol boats and minesweepers moored alongside. In the background to the left was the Charlestown Navy Yard. And towering above the freight sheds was the big tank of the Purity Distilling Company—bulging with more than two million gallons of crude molasses waiting to be made into rum.

In the Public Works Department, a dozen or more horses munched their oats and hay, as flocks of pigeons fluttered around to catch the stray kernels of grain that fell from the feed bags. Stretched out on the running board of a heavily laden express truck, Peter, a pet tiger cat, slept in the unseasonably warm sunshine.

This was the fourth day that the mercury of the thermometer on the sunny side of the freight shed had been climbing. On January 12 it was only 2 degrees above zero. But on the thirteenth the temperature rose rapidly from 16 degrees to 40; now, at 12:30 P.M. on Wednesday the fifteenth, it was 43 degrees above zero, and so warm in the sun that office workers stood around in their shirtsleeves talking about the weather. Even the freight handlers had doffed their overcoats, and sailors from the training ship *Nantucket* carried their heavy pea jackets on their arms.

Mrs. Bridget Clougherty put her blankets out to air and smiled at little Maria Di Stasio gathering firewood under the freight cars. She waved to her neighbor, Mrs. O'Brien, who was dusting her geraniums on a dingy windowsill.

At the pumping station attached to the big molasses tank, Bill White turned the key in the lock and started uptown to meet his wife for lunch. He bumped into Eric Blair, driver for Wheeler's Express, and said, "Hello, Scotty. What are you doing around here at noontime? Thought you and the old nag always went to Charlestown for grub."

The young Scotsman grinned. "It's a funny thing, Bill," he said. "This is the first time in three years I've brought my lunch over here," and he climbed up on the bulkhead and leaned back against the warm side of the big molasses tank—for the first and last time.

Inside the Boston and Worcester freight terminal,

Percy Smerage, the foreman, was checking a pile of express to be shipped to Framingham and Worcester. Four freight cars were already loaded. The fifth stood half-empty on the spur track that ran past the molasses tank.

Smerage had just told his assistant to finish loading the last car when a low, deep rumble shook the freight yard. The earth heaved under their feet, and they heard a sound of ripping and tearing—steel bolts snapping like machine-gun fire—followed by a booming roar as the bottom of the giant molasses tank split wide open and a geyser of yellowish brown fluid spurted into the sky, followed by a tidal wave of molasses.

With a horrible, hissing, sucking sound, it splashed in a curving arc straight across the street, crushing everything and everybody in its path. In less time than it takes to tell it, molasses had filled the five-foot loading pit and was creeping over the threshold of the warehouse door. The four loaded freight cars were washed like chips down the track. The half-loaded car was caught on the foaming crest of the eight-foot wave and, with unbelievable force, hurled through the corrugated iron walls of the terminal.

The freight house shook and shivered as the molasses outside, now five feet deep, pushed against the building. Then the doors and windows caved in, and a rushing, roaring river of molasses rolled like molten lava into the freight shed, knocking over the booths where freight clerks were checking their lists.

Like madmen they fought the onrushing tide, trying to swim in the sticky stuff that sucked them down. Tons of freight—shoes, potatoes, barrels, and boxes—tumbled and splashed on the frothy, foaming mass, now so heavy that the floors gave way, letting tons of the stuff into the cellar. Down there the workers died like rats in a trap. Some tried to dash up the stairs, but they slipped—and disappeared.

As the 58-foot-high tank split wide open, more molasses poured out under a pressure of two tons per square foot. Men, women, children, and animals were caught, hurled into the air, or dashed against freight cars, only to fall back and sink from sight in the slowly moving mass.

High above the scene of disaster, an elevated train crowded with passengers whizzed by the crumbling tank just as the molasses broke loose, tearing off the whole front of the Clougherty house and snapping off the steel supports of the "El" structure. The trestle

Commercial Street in Boston as it looked before the great Molasses Flood. The Atlantic Avenue El tracks stand overhead at left; at right is the building that housed the paving division of the city's Public Works Department. The Purity Distilling Company's storage tank, holding 2,500,000 gallons of crude molasses, looms in the background.

snapped, and the tracks sagged almost to street level, but the motorman of an approaching train, seeing the danger, managed to throw his train in reverse and prevent further catastrophe.

The roaring wall of death moved on. It struck the fire station, knocked it over on its side, and pushed it toward the ocean until it fetched up on some pilings. One of the firemen was hurled through a partition. George Leahy, engineer of Fireboat 31, was crushed to death under a billiard table. In the Public Works Department, five men eating their noonday meal were smothered by the bubbling, boiling sludge that poured in upon them.

Up at fire headquarters, the first alarm came in at 12:40 P.M. As soon as Chief Peter McDonough learned the extent of the tragedy, he sounded a second and third alarm to get workers and rescue squads. Ladders were placed over the wreckage, and the firemen crawled out on them to pull the dead and dying from the molasses-drenched debris. Amidst a mass of bedding and broken furniture, they found the body of Mrs. Clougherty—killed when her house collapsed. Nearby lay the body of Peter the cat.

Captain Krake of Engine 7 was leading his men cautiously along the slippery wreckage under the elevated railroad when he saw a mass of yellow hair floating on a dark brown pool of molasses. He took off his coat and plunged his arms to the elbows in the sweet, sticky stream. It was Maria Di Stasio, the little girl who had been gathering firewood.

Over by the Public Works Building, more than a dozen horses lay floundering in the molasses. Under an overturned express wagon was the body of the driver.

Fifteen dead were found before the sun went down that night, and six other bodies were recovered later. As for the injured, they were taken by cars, wagons, and ambulances to the Haymarket Relief and other hospitals in the vicinity.

The next day the firemen tackled the mess with a lot of fire hoses, washing the molasses off the buildings and wreckage and down the gutters. When hit by the salt water, the molasses frothed up in yellow suds. It was weeks before the devastated area was cleaned up.

Of course, there was great controversy as to the cause of the tank's collapse. About 125 lawsuits were filed against the Purity Distilling Company. The hearings were the longest in the history of Massachusetts courts. Judge Hitchcock appointed Colonel Hugh W.

After the rupture, the tank and everything around it lay in a heap of twisted rubble. Even today, more than 70 years after it occurred, the Molasses Flood of 1919 remains one of the most macabre and tragic episodes in Boston's history.

Benjamin Franklin reported in his newspaper, the *New England Courant,* No. 83, one of the worst floods in Boston's history, and couldn't resist poking fun at some of the bizarre theories that attempted to explain it.

A Dutch Conspiracy? The Great Tide of 1723

On Lord's Day, the 24th past, we were surprized with the extraordinary Heighth of the Tide, which fill'd most of the Streets as well as Cellars near the Water, insomuch that many People living in Drawbridge Street, Union Street, and some other Places, were carry'd to their Houses in Canooes, after the Morning Service was over.

In some Houses the Water rose so high in their lower Rooms as that they were oblig'd to run away with their Meat half dress'd upon their Spits and in their Potts into some of their Neighbours, or into their upper Rooms, their Fire being all put out, and the Wood floating about the Rooms.

The Cordwood, Shingles, Staves, &c. were all wash'd off the Wharffs and carry'd into the Harbour, or left in the Streets after the Tide was down. The Water rose so high in the Ship Carpenters Yards, that they fear'd the Vessels would be carried off the Stocks, and made them fast with Ropes to the Tops of the Houses.

The Loss sustain'd by this Tide (in Town and Country) is reckon'd by some to be as great as that by the Fire in 1711. Charlestown likewise suffer'd very much; and we hear a great Number of Whaleboats have been carry'd from the shore towards Cape Codd, where the Tide was never known to come before. They write from Newport on Rhode-Island, that the Tide has entirely wash'd away several Wharffs, and done great Damage in several Warehouses and Dwelling Houses near the Water.

By an Article in the Boston News-Letter of Thursday last, we are told, that, *The many great Wharffs which since the last overflowing Tides have been run out into the Harbour, and fill'd so great a Part of the Bason, have methinks contributed something not inconsiderable to the Rise of Water upon us.* And upon the Authority of this News Letter, some begin to blame the Dutch for damming out the Sea, and sending the Tide over the Atlantick upon us: Some more reasonably conclude, that a large Fleet of Ships have been sunk in the Storm off our Coast, (the Wind blowing hard at North East,) which occasion'd the rising of the Tide. Others have upon this Account, framed a new Hypothesis to solve the Phaenomena of Noah's Flood, and very rationally suppose, that the Antediluvians brought the Deluge upon themselves by running too many Great Wharffs out into their Harbours. So that the Notions *(which were not without their Probabilities)* of *Burnet, Warren, Whiston,* &c. who were troubled with the Distemper called *Hypothesimania,* seem now less probable than ever.

Ogden to act as auditor and hear the evidence. It was six years before he made his special report.

There were so many lawyers involved that there wasn't enough space in the courtroom to hold them all, so they consolidated and chose two to represent the claimants. Never in New England did so many engineers, metallurgists, and scientists parade onto the witness stand. Albert L. Colby, an authority on the amount of structural strain a steel tank could sustain before breaking, was on the witness stand three weeks—often giving testimony as late as ten o'clock in the evening.

Altogether, more than 3,000 witnesses were examined and nearly 45,000 pages of testimony and arguments were recorded. The defendants spent more than

$50,000 on expert witness fees, claiming that the collapse was due not to a structural weakness but to a dynamite bomb.

When Ogden made his report, he found the defendants responsible for the disaster, because the molasses tank, which was 58 feet high and 90 feet across, was not strong enough to withstand the pressure of the 2,500,000 gallons it was designed to hold.

The owners of the tank eventually paid nearly a million dollars in damages, and at that point the great Molasses Flood might have passed into history. But some North End residents swear that, on certain summer nights, you can still smell the faintly sweet aroma of molasses in the air. ∞

While workers began cleaning up the cloying, disgusting mess, officials inspected the site of the disaster, searching for answers. The resulting litigation became the lengthiest in Massachusetts court history.

CHAPTER FIVE

The Good Old Summertime

When Mount St. Helens in Washington State erupted in 1980, it sent this grand plume of smoke and ash into the atmosphere. The much larger eruption of Mount Tambora changed world weather patterns and is thought to have caused the infamous Cold Summer of 1816.

1816:
The Year
without a Summer

BY ANDREW E. ROTHOVIUS

On April 10, 1815, the 13,000-foot volcanic cone of Mount Tambora in the East Indies—on the island of Sumbawa, east of Java and Bali—blew off its top in the most cataclysmic volcanic eruption of the past 500 years—certainly the one with the most widespread effects on humans around the globe.

One year later, this eruption—through its enormous cloud of ejected volcanic dust—led to the famous Summerless Year of 1816, of which the greater portion of New England continues to preserve traditions and anecdotes: about snow falling in June, overcoats worn on the Fourth of July, and cornfields blackened by August frost.

Far less generally known, however, is that the season was even more bleak over most of Europe, and that the resulting crop failures caused the last real famine in western European history. Although true famine did not occur in New England, the abnormal summer did cause great hardship and spurred a large emigration of people who feared that even worse times might lie ahead.

To understand fully the scope and context of the Summerless Year, it is necessary to assess its cause—the Tambora eruption. The fact that we possess some reasonably complete information about it is due entirely to the lucky accident of the East Indies then being under the temporary military occupation of British forces, as a consequence of the Napoleonic Wars then winding down. The British governor happened to be Sir Stamford Raffles, a man with enormous curiosity, who was interested in practically everything.

When, at his headquarters on Java, he heard the tremendous blast of Tambora blowing up more than 750 miles away and saw the sun hidden for almost two days by an inky pall of ash that sifted down to a depth of several inches, he realized that a disaster of uncommon magnitude had occurred, and he sent out a relief vessel to investigate. Making its way through an ash layer two feet thick that floated on top of the Sunda Sea, the ship arrived at Sumbawa to find the island smothered in three feet or more of muddy ash. The peak of Tambora, which had before been visible far out to sea, was gone, leveled off to a plateau 9,000 feet high.

Ten thousand of Sumbawa's 127,000 residents had perished in the cataclysm, and 82,000 more were to die there and on nearby islands over the next 10 to 12 months from disease and starvation. They were the first of what was to be a long and grim parade of victims of Tambora's eruption.

Later in 1815, Raffles published a full compilation of firsthand accounts of the eruption and its effects. It was not until 1847, however, that a Swiss geologist actually examined the still-smoldering stump of Tambora. He found a crater 5 miles across and 1,800 feet deep; from this had come the explosive force that pulverized an estimated 25 to 36 cubic *miles* of mountain into volcanic ash that blanketed an oval area a thousand miles in length.

This is by far the largest amount of ash from any recorded eruption, at least two and a half to three and a half times as much as from the famous Krakatoa eruption of 1883. A substantial part of Tambora's ash was carried into the stratosphere and for up to two years

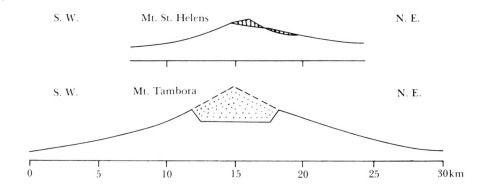

S. W.　　　Mt. St. Helens　　　　　　　　N. E.

S. W.　　　Mt. Tambora　　　　　　　　　N. E.

0　　　5　　　10　　　15　　　20　　　25　　　30 km

Above: *This illustration compares the scale of the recent Mount St. Helens eruption with the cataclysmic explosion of Tambora in 1815. In the eruption, Tambora threw about 25 cubic miles of debris into the atmosphere, losing the top 4,200 feet of its height.* **Opposite page, bottom:** *The smoking crater of Mount St. Helens.*

dimmed the sun, causing the freakishly cold summer of 1816.

No one at the time understood this connection. Forty years earlier, Benjamin Franklin had suggested that the unusual cold of 1784–85 might be linked to the great eruption of 1783 in Iceland, but his idea had not been followed up and by 1816 had been forgotten.

Tradition has exaggerated the true degree to which summer failed to materialize in 1816 in New England. There were actually many very hot days during the season. Nevertheless, overall it was the coldest summer on record, not only in New England but also over much of the rest of the Northern Hemisphere.

The lasting fame of 1816 in New England rests on four main events: a cold May; a uniquely unseasonable incursion of arctic air on June 6–11; and two episodes of killing frost, one in early July and another in late August. Snow did fall widely across northern and central New England in June, and possibly in the high Green·Mountains of Vermont during the August cold snap. But contrary to some claims, snow did not fall in every month of the summer, though widespread frost did occur.

May in New England was chilly and discouraging for planting, more so than most Aprils, but the last week of the month and the first days of June were seasonable, and farmers put in their tender seeds, such as corn, beans, and pumpkins. What these farmers didn't know was that, not far north of the Canadian border, winter had returned, having never really departed. Hudson Bay was still ice-locked, and adjacent parts of Quebec and Ontario lay under a snow cover. A large dome of frigid air formed over these frozen surfaces and began sliding southeastward.

Ahead of it warm air was pulled north into New England. On June 5 temperatures rose to 90°F. in many places, but things changed drastically when the cold front crossed the Green Mountains after midnight. Squalls of cold rain changed to snow flurries as far south as the Berkshires, and temperatures held in the forties all day. In northern Vermont, snow accumulated and did not melt. It was Inauguration Day in Concord, New Hampshire, for the new governor, William Plumer, and so cold in the unheated State House that the teeth of those present chattered. Few stayed to hear the conclusion of Plumer's inaugural speech, most preferring to flee home through streets swept by freezing gusts and snow flurries.

To the north a major snowstorm was occurring at Quebec City, halting all road traffic. The next day this storm extended south into northern and central Vermont, with the snow accumulating up to 20 inches in some of the mountain valleys, as at Cabot and Williamstown. Snow squalls and flurries continued as far south as Worcester and Salem in Massachusetts. This was followed by widespread killing frosts on the tenth and eleventh, which wiped out virtually all plantings, even down into Connecticut.

Temperatures rebounded into the eighties on the twelfth, and ten days later were in the scorching high nineties. Replantings sprouted rapidly, and it seemed as if a reasonably good harvest could be salvaged.

For many, if not most, farmers these hopes were dashed by the cold spell of early July. It was so chilly on the Fourth that men pitching horseshoes—then a common holiday amusement—had to wear topcoats to keep warm. Frost followed on four successive nights and wiped out the majority of the June replantings. Some, however, survived—especially on upland, south-facing slopes—and certain crops such as oats and barley were actually thriving. Apples also withstood the cold amazingly well, and many farmers had bumper crops of them. These factors ensured that none would actually starve in New England, despite the total loss of what remained of the corn crop in the late August freeze.

Normal summer weather had prevailed after the July frosts, and surviving plantings of corn were doing well. Then, on August 20, a sharp cold front that dropped temperatures 20 or more degrees in a couple of hours swept south across Vermont and New Hampshire. The ensuing frost destroyed all unharvested corn and severely damaged beans, potatoes, and squash.

New England's abundant coastal fisheries contributed to our ancestors' preservation from famine during the difficult winter that followed. Those who came closest to real starvation were the Indians of eastern Maine and upper New York State, who were saved by government and private donations of food and seed corn. Tens of thousands of Yankee farmers were resolved, however, not to face again so close a brush with destitution. They abandoned or sold (when buyers could be found) their homesteads and headed for the Midwest, which by all accounts had not been anywhere near as severely affected by the chilly summer as the eastern states.

Some towns were virtually depopulated—Granby, Vermont, lost all but three families out of more than a hundred—and overall Vermont lost more than 12,000 residents. Indiana gained more than 42,000 new inhabitants, largely from Maine.

Canada, where white settlement was then principally limited to the St. Lawrence Valley, suffered more than New England. Some ponds near Quebec did not become free of ice until August, and it became necessary on July 9 to proclaim a 60-day export embargo on grain, so as to hold on to the old stock to cover some of the almost total loss of the new harvest.

Even so, there is no record of actual famine in Canada. It was far different in Europe, where in Hungary alone an estimated 44,000 people perished from starvation. The crisis there commenced with the terrible "Brown Blizzard" of January 31, 1816—an enormously deep snow of tan or light brown color resulting from the presence of Tambora volcanic ash. This storm caused the loss of up to a million sheep, cattle, and horses in winter pasture. The loss was compounded by a cold, wet summer in which grain and potatoes rotted in the fields.

By mid-August it was apparent that a general failure of harvests was imminent from France to the Balkans. The Rhineland and Switzerland were particularly hard hit. It was the summer when Byron, Shelley, and their lady friends were trying to amuse themselves during the dismal Alpine weather by writing ghost stories and *Frankenstein* was born from the pen of Mary Shelley. But real-life horror outdid the fictional: 30,000 are said to have starved in Switzerland, and up to 200,000 died (65,000 of them in Ireland, where cold rain fell on 142 out of 153 summer days) in the ensuing epidemic of typhus, always a famine-generated disease. Up to 10,000 are said to have starved in northern Italy, where no grain ripened. The one saving factor was that the Russian Ukraine was favored with moderate rains and temperatures only a little below normal, and thus was able to export enough grain to prevent an even worse disaster in the rest of Europe. ∞

The following account of the Cold Summer of 1816 was
first published in the 1966 edition of *The Old Farmer's
Almanac*—150 years after that remarkable year.

"Eighteen Sixteen and Near Froze to Death"

Of the fourteen great events of 1816, its cold summer will be longest remembered. Even now that year is spoken of as "1816 and near froze to death." At least one Vermont farmer, according to the recollection of his nephew, James Winchester, *was* frozen to death in the great snowstorm in June of that year:

"I was at my uncle's when he left home to go to the sheep lot, and as he went out the door he said, jokingly, to his wife: 'If I am not back in an hour, call the neighbors and start them after me. June is a bad month to get buried in the snow, especially when it gets so near July.' Three days later, searchers found him . . . frozen stiff."

One old man, James Gooding, became so hopeless over the unseasonable weather that he killed all his cattle and hanged himself. The Reverend Thomas Robbins of East Windsor, Connecticut, kept a diary of that cold year. It tells of a man in Maine freezing to death, of a foot of June snow in the Berkshires, and of ice in Massachusetts that would bear the weight of a man. The entire corn crop, except in fields near ponds or the ocean, failed. Suicides were common: Drought, financial panic, and lack of food goaded many to desperation. Hailstones beat the blossoms of all fruit trees. All through July heavy frosts—and occasional ice storms—were commonly seen. Most people took off their winter clothing, only to have to put it on again. So many young (and old) birds were frozen that but a few birds were found in New England during the following three years.

Caleb Emery of Lyman, New Hampshire, visited a well in his town that was completely frozen over on the Fourth of July—eight feet below the surface of the earth—and it remained that way until the twenty-fifth. The 120-day drought, which began in August, created fearsome forest fire conditions, leading to fires only the November snows could quell. Sheep froze to death in their pastures. Mackerel had to be introduced as a main course instead of pork and beef, thus earning the abnormally cold summer another nickname—"The Mackerel Year."

The price of hay skyrocketed. Emerson Hale, a Rindge, New Hampshire, farmer who had held his over in large barns for 20 years, even sold that at a healthy profit. "Going down to Egypt" was how these cropless farmers put it when they found they had to buy hay for the first time in their lives.

One farmer near Tewksbury, Vermont, built fires around his cornfield to keep off the frost. Every night he and his men kept up those fires. His reward was in harvesting the only crop of corn in that region. On Indian Hill (now Christian Hill) in the village of Ashland, New Hampshire, there is a gravestone in honor of Reuben Whitten (1771–1847). The inscription reads: "Son of a Revolutionary Soldier, a pioneer of this town. Cold Season of 1816 raised 40 bushils [sic] of wheat on this land which kept his family and neighbours from starvation."

Elisha Clark of China, Maine, according to his granddaughter, Nellie Clark Strong of Somerville, Massachusetts, "often picked Baltimore orioles off the branches of orchard trees in that cold summer and brought them into the house to warm them up."

Elder Job Seamans of Grafton, New Hampshire, recorded in his diary of August 18, 1816: "The heaven that is over our heads is as the earth under us, as iron, and the rain of our land has become as powder and dust. We are anxiously inquiring what shall we eat, what shall we drink, and where with all shall we be clothed."

In sum, as one anonymous poet put it:

The trees were all leafless, the mountains
*   were brown,*
The face of the country was scathed with a
*   frown;*
And bleak were the hills, and the foliage
*   sere*
As had never been seen at that time of year.

Little more perhaps may need be said about this year of 1816, except that its January was one of the warmest on record and that it was not without its humor. According to Sidney Perley, Jacob Carr of Weare, New Hampshire, used to boast of potatoes he picked that year that ran 500 bushels to an acre, and nary a one was picked up until it was the size of a teakettle. However, the subject of this cold summer should not be passed over without at least a cursory examination of what were thought to have been the causes of this freakish weather.

"The sun's rays seemed to be destitute of heat throughout the summer; all nature was clad in a sable here." Thus reads a report in the *Albany* (New York) *Almanac* of 1852, which was based on its old-time records.

"During the entire season the sun arose each morning as though in a cloud of smoke, red and rayless, shedding little light or warmth and setting at night as behind a thick cloud of vapor, leaving hardly a trace of

its having passed over the face of the earth." So reads the back file of the *American Magazine of History*.

"What would happen," speculated the *North American Review* in that year, "if the sun should become tired of illuminating this gloomy planet?"

Nobody, apparently, had an immediate answer. The anonymous author of the *Physician's Almanack*, published in Boston in 1817, quoted one Mr. Ferguson—a prominent astronomer of that time—to the effect that planets in the same quarter of the heavens, from their mutual attractions, create disturbances. This book also pointed out that the ancients believed that the varying distance between moon and earth might influence the seasons. And it referred, as Dudley Leavitt (another astronomer and almanac writer of that day) felt, to the numerous spots on the sun which were observed in 1816. Some thought them to be supernatural—and ominous. These spots were usually observed by telescopes, and on some days with the naked eye. Leavitt attributed the Cold Summer of 1816 to these spots. It was his contention that their number and sizes were such that they could easily have caused this cold season.

It remains difficult at this writing to agree with Leavitt. Sunspot counts of much greater numbers have not, since then, provided the world with any such phenomenon as this one. Modern science recognizes a correlation of sorts—just what, nobody knows—between sunspot cycles and weather. So Leavitt's surmise someday may be proved correct.

The almost certain cause seems to have been the volcanic eruption of Mount Tambora, a 13,000-foot volcano on the island of Sumbawa, near Bali, in the East Indies. This happened in April of 1815 and was one of the greatest volcanic eruptions in history. The volcanic dust from this eruption was blown into the stratosphere in such quantities that it covered the earth like a great cosmic umbrella, dimming the sun's effectiveness that whole cold year. Such an eruption would explain the appearance of the 1816 sun as "in a cloud of smoke."

To which must be added the conjectures produced by a complete eclipse of the sun on May 26, 1816, and of the moon on June 9, as well as the "greater number of conjunctions of the planets than usual," which would favor, wrote Robert B. Thomas, editor of *The Old Farmer's Almanac,* "old maids and bachelors." Thomas, according to a completely apocryphal story that goes back to as early as 1846, had predicted for July 13, 1816 (while fighting a fever as well as a printer's deadline) "Rain, Hail and Snow"—all three of which, to his great amazement, did fall on that day.   ∞

The temperature of a massive lightning bolt can reach 30,000°F., or nearly five times that found on the surface of the sun.

Hit by Lightning

BY BOB WYSS

Every year lightning strikes and kills 150 persons in this country. New England has fewer storms than the rest of the country, but scientists say that we make up for that lack of frequency by the intensity: Our storms have greater force and violence. A lightning bolt, which can be 20 miles high yet only 4 inches in diameter, can carry 100 million volts of electricity, with accompanying heat 5 times greater than the surface temperature of the sun, and can zip along at 90,000 miles per second. Yet the bodies of lightning's victims show no markings.

People struck by lightning are either killed instantly or else recover completely, their stories intact. *Yankee* talked with a few of the latter, and here are their stories:

John Hannon, Jr.
Pawtucket, Rhode Island

The animals moved restlessly in their cages inside the main building at the Slater Park Zoo in Pawtucket, Rhode Island. Outside the wind was howling and the rain was pouring down on an August afternoon in 1978.

Park policeman John Hannon, Jr., was huddled in the main office of the zoo building with Ed St. Pierre, another park policeman, and two caretakers. Hannon was getting out of his chair to leave when a bright light filled the small room. He did not know what was happening, but his muscles contracted, and he jumped into the air. "I literally came right off the floor," he recalled later.

It passed quickly, and one man swore later that he had seen the lightning bolt exit through a storm drain in the concrete floor. Hannon did not know; he had not seen a bolt. Besides, he was dizzy and had pains in his chest. Within a few minutes he calmed down and soon was back at work.

But the animals seemed to know what had happened. The lion roared, and the elephant unleashed a trumpet cry. The baboon cried and ran back and forth in her cage. She did not quiet down for hours.

Lucille and Sal Pereschino
Johnstown, Rhode Island

Lucille Pereschino was worried when her parents drove up to the Johnstown, Rhode Island, house that she and her husband, Sal, had recently bought. It was June 1972, and a violent thunderstorm was passing overhead. Just then a lightning bolt hit the fence across the street, tossing four white pickets carelessly into the air.

They talked about that in the living room as Lucille prepared coffee in the kitchen. A loud pop interrupted them. Lucille turned and watched a lightning bolt streak from the open kitchen window through the room and hit the clock over the stove. The dials spun crazily. It was over in seconds, and the bolt disappeared. Except for the clock, nothing had been disturbed.

Three months later, the Pereschinos were awakened around midnight when the drone of the air conditioner stopped. Sal opened the bedroom door and switched on the hallway lamp. It burst with a bright, burning light. The cat in the cellar screamed. The light faded, but they could still see light from the kitchen.

They crept a few steps down the hall. Eerie orange fireballs were dancing on the linoleum floor. Smaller than a fingertip, the balls bounced two to three inches off the floor. The couple stood in a stupor, watching until the balls disappeared.

More than the stove and the electrical wiring were ruined after this second lightning strike.

"We were petrified," recalled Lucille. "Every time we heard a storm coming we would get out. We finally sold the house."

The Pereschinos have stayed in touch with the new owners. The house has not yet been hit by lightning again. ∞

IN NEW ENGLAND YOU SHOULD NEVER SAY HOW YOU WANT TO DIE

☞ James Otis, a hero of the Revolutionary War, often told family and friends he hoped his death would be the result of a bolt of lightning. On May 23, 1783, Otis was leaning against a doorway at his home in Andover, Massachusetts. Lightning hit the chimney, coursed through the frame of the house, and killed Otis.

Arthur McCain
Fairfield, Connecticut

Arthur McCain was watching brilliant yellow and white lightning bolts strike the choppy blue surface of Yawgoog Pond. It was twilight on a day in August 1980, and he was under a tent canopy with 13 Boy Scouts—one of them his son, Scott—and another scout leader in Hope Valley, Rhode Island.

He had turned to take his canteen when the bolt struck, a force strong enough to spin him to his knees. "We've been hit!" he yelled.

McCain could not feel anything in his left leg, but he forced himself to look at it. The shoe had been blown off and so had the sock, except for one section near his big toe. The skin was gray but still there.

Looking around, he saw boys in their khaki uniforms sprawled on the tent platform, moaning and crying. Most of them revived within a few minutes. McCain and two other scouts were the most seriously injured, and investigators discovered why later.

They found that the bolt had struck a 20-foot pine and then leaped onto the tent support. It had traveled down and then under the platform, eventually grounding into a granite boulder on the other side.

"My left leg was on a nail," McCain related. "The electric current, which could only have been a small spark from the bolt, came up the nail. It apparently came up the instep, went across my foot, and came out next to my big toe."

A huge blister formed, and McCain could not walk for two months. After it popped, he could see the canyon that had been carved in the sole of his foot.

James Otis, a New Englander who made an electrifying exit.

John Packard and John Tilton
Salem, New Hampshire

The four golfers stood under pine trees on the third tee, the highest point at the Pine Valley Golf Links in Pelham, New Hampshire. The rain was coming down so hard that it obscured the green ribbon of fairway before them.

They knew they should have quit, but the three older golfers, Warren George, John Packard, and John Tilton, pushed on because of young Tim Cronin. Tim needed only seven more holes to qualify for an upcoming tournament. It was July 1982.

When the bolt struck, Packard recalled that it "hit like a bomb." Feeling the pressure, he opened his mouth to relieve the compression just the way the U.S. Marines had taught him years ago in boot camp.

The lightning ran down a pine, peeling back the bark, and then it jumped to George, who had been leaning against the tree. It pushed him into the mud.

It leaped next to Packard, sent him sprawling, and split open his shoe. He was out for only a second, but when he came to, his left leg was numb. At first he could not look at it, but when he did, he saw it was still there. He breathed more easily.

Cronin and Tilton also were knocked down. Tilton could feel an electric shock hit and travel up his legs until it reached his waist. Then it stopped and went back down and out of his leg. The lightning ran along the ground and then went 20 feet up another pine.

Packard looked toward George. His face was wedged next to a rock, his skin was purple, and he did not look as if he were breathing.

Tilton called out and asked what was wrong. Cronin began yelling about his foot, but the two other men could not see any damage. They agreed that Tilton should go to the clubhouse for help.

Packard rolled George onto his back. He placed his two hands near George's rib cage and pressed in even strokes, beginning the rhythm of cardiopulmonary resuscitation (CPR).

"I thought he was a goner, but you never know about electricity, so you keep working just in case," he explained.

George never came out of the coma, and he died one week later. Packard had a second-degree burn on his left foot and could not walk right for a month. But he was back in a golf cart and on the course within two days. The other two men also soon returned to the golf course.

A Word to the Wise

If a lightning storm catches you outside, don't assume you are safe by standing near a high object. Experts report that lightning could just as well strike a 6-foot man as the 80-foot church steeple he is standing next to.

Stay indoors. The safest place to be during a storm is inside a car, a metal-frame building, or a structure protected by lightning rods.

Even if you're inside, take care. Stay away from open windows and doors. Don't sit near a fireplace. In particular, don't use plug-in electrical equipment or the telephone during a storm. Don't run the water and stay out of the shower.

If you do get caught outside, avoid the highest objects in an area. Stay away from an isolated tree, but high clumps of trees in an open forest are fairly safe. Avoid hilltops and open space. It's also dangerous to be near metallic conductors such as wire fences, ski lifts, and railway lines.

Anytime you feel an electrical charge, particularly if your hair stands on end or your skin tingles, you may be about to be hit by lightning. If you're in an open area, do *not* lie down. If you are flat on the ground, even a near miss could send enough power radiating through the ground to injure you. Squat with your head between your knees or as low as possible. In this position you are low, and yet you have only minimal contact with the wet ground.

Benjamin Franklin, scientist, editor, patriot, bon vivant . . . and inventor of the lightning rod.

Cotton Mather, 1663-1728.

A Word on Lightning

New-England hath been a countrey signalized with mischiefs done by thunders, as much as perhaps most in the world. If things that are smitten by lightning were to be esteemed sacred, this were a sacred countrey. Rarely a summer passes, without some strokes from the thunders, on the persons, or houses, or cattel of our people.

To enumerate the instances of damages done by thunders in this land—houses fired, cattel slain, trees pull'd a-pieces, rocks pulverized, bricks vitify'd, and ships mortify'd—would be to fill a volume.

—*Cotton Mather*
Magnalia Christi Americana

We Think
They Should Still Be Called "Franklin Rods"

Benjamin Franklin is chiefly remembered today for his patriotism, his service to his country, and his wit as an editor, author, and humorist. He also is remembered fondly as the man who flew a kite in the middle of a thunderstorm and "discovered" electricity. Unlike other stories about our country's founding fathers (like the fanciful one about George Washington and the cherry tree), this story is entirely true. Well, almost.

The theory that lightning was really a form of electricity did not originate with Ben Franklin. As early as 1708, an English scientist named William Wall had suggested a connection between the two forces, as had Sir Isaac Newton. But it was Franklin who first conceived of a way to prove experimentally that lightning was an electrical phenomenon.

In a 1750 letter to the Royal Society in London, Franklin presented his idea for a metal rod that could be used to attract and safely ground a bolt of lightning. As a result of this letter, a French team led by Thomas-François D'Alibard set up a 40-foot lightning rod at Marly, near Paris, in an attempt to collect and contain electricity from a lightning bolt in a Leyden jar. On May 10, 1752, they succeeded, thus proving conclusively that lightning is electricity.

Meanwhile, Franklin, unaware of the results of the French experiment, was conducting his own famous kite and key experiment, standing inside a barn door and holding a satin ribbon in his hand as an insulator (albeit a poor one) to protect himself from the lightning. Franklin performed his experiment in June of 1752 and published his results in an essay titled "Securing Houses Against Lightening" in his *Poor Richard's Almanack* for 1753. The article advocates the wisdom of protecting houses and other structures from lightning by means of grounded iron rods topped with coiled brass wire. Soon thereafter, the first lightning rods in America (dubbed "Franklin rods" in his honor) appeared on the lower spires of Christ Church in Philadelphia.

At first, Franklin's lightning rods were not universally welcomed. In 1755, Reverend Thomas Prince of Boston's South Church warned against such rods as a foolhardy attempt by man to circumvent the divine wrath of God. According to Prince's theory, earthquakes were a result of electricity in the earth, and so, in trying to avoid God's judgment from the skies, man only transferred his destruction to the ground. Professor John Winthrop of Harvard College, however, took Prince to task for suggesting that there was anyone so foolish "as ever to have entertained a single thought, that it is possible, by the help of a few yards of wire, to 'get out of the mighty hand of God.' "

In 1760 the real utility of Franklin rods was proven when the house of a Mr. West in Philadelphia took a direct hit from a bolt of lightning. The top three inches of brass wire atop the lightning rods burned, but the house remained unscathed.

Interestingly enough, Franklin never tried to patent his invention. The accolades that he received both at home and overseas, though, rewarded him richly. King Louis XIV of France sent Franklin a complimentary letter, and the Royal Society in London awarded him the Sir Godfrey Copley gold medal for his research. As great and varied as his talents and accomplishments were, it's interesting to think that Benjamin Franklin's most valuable and lasting contribution to the world might be the simple piece of metal that we so often take for granted.

Some Facts about Lightning

☞ Scientists estimate that the earth is struck by lightning somewhere on the average of 100 times a second.

☞ In dry climes clouds tend to be higher above the earth, and cloud-to-cloud lightning is much more frequent than in temperate zones. It is estimated that, in these arid regions, less than 20 percent of lightning bolts strike the ground. Bolts that do strike the ground from these high clouds can be quite impressive, some having been measured as 20 miles in length.

☞ A typical lightning bolt lasts less than one-half of a second and can release on the order of 250 kilowatt-hours of energy (or enough energy to light a 100-watt light bulb for three months).

☞ About three-quarters of the energy from a lightning stroke dissipates into the air as heat. The temperature of the lightning channel can rise to 15,000°F. In the case of giant discharges, it can reach 30,000°F., or nearly five times the surface temperature of the sun.

☞ While a massive charge of electrons shoots down to earth in a lightning stroke, the visible light of the bolt actually moves *up* the channel as a return stroke.

☞ A lightning strike actually consists of a number of leader and return strokes, but all these strokes are visible only as a single flash.

☞ The world record for being struck by lightning belongs to the late Roy Sullivan, a Virginia park ranger. Between 1942 and 1977, Sullivan was struck no fewer than *seven* times by lightning. He died not by lightning but by suicide in 1983.

☞ Fires caused by lightning strikes account for more than 10 percent of all the fire insurance claims filed each year.

☞ The first demonstration of artificial lightning (ten million volts) occurred in Pittsfield, Massachusetts, on June 10, 1932. The experiment was conducted by General Electric.

Hot Saturday

BY TIM CLARK

Saturday, August 2, 1975, was the hottest day on record in New England. My wife, May, and I didn't know that when we started our long-planned bicycle trip from Lee, New Hampshire, to Blue Hill, Maine. All we knew was that it looked like a scorcher, and we wanted to get away early. We started before dawn, rolling through the deserted streets of Dover and down a long hill into the valley of the Piscataqua River, which serves as the boundary between the two states. We hoped to make it to our first night's stop, a friend's house outside Portland, before the hottest part of the day.

It was cool enough then, with a coppery sun coming up in the mist on our right, keeping an easy ten-mile-per-hour pace. We stopped for a rest by the Civil War Monument in South Berwick and had a good breakfast at a little place in Alfred. By the time we came out and saddled up, though, the sun was well above the horizon and the heat was intense.

I don't remember much about the ride between Alfred and the outskirts of Portland. It just got hotter and hotter. Our first indication that it was more than the ordinary heat of an August day came in Gorham, when we passed a bank thermometer that read 105°F. That was still before noon. We stopped somewhere near there for a drink, and I downed a quart of lemonade without pausing for breath.

The last hour of the ride was a shimmering white haze. I seem to recall that the narrow wheels of our racing bikes left ruts in the softening asphalt of the road. We reached our friend's house around 2:00 P.M. and stumbled into a cold shower, almost delirious with exhaustion and thirst. We stayed in the shower a long time, drinking the water as it sprayed into our faces.

We decided that we wouldn't risk riding the next day in such temperatures, but we needn't have worried. The next morning dawned rainy and cold. We went from sunstroke to hypothermia in 24 hours. This was New England, after all.

IT'S NOT THE HEAT, IT'S THE HUMIDITY

☞ In a controlled study of 40,000 crimes committed in a metropolitan area, medical climatologists noted that on:

Warm and muggy days/murder and aggravated assault . . . . +45%
Overcast humid days/violence . . . . +30%
Dry, clear days/overall crime rate . . . . −75%

Conclusion: Humidity may be an accessory to violent crime.

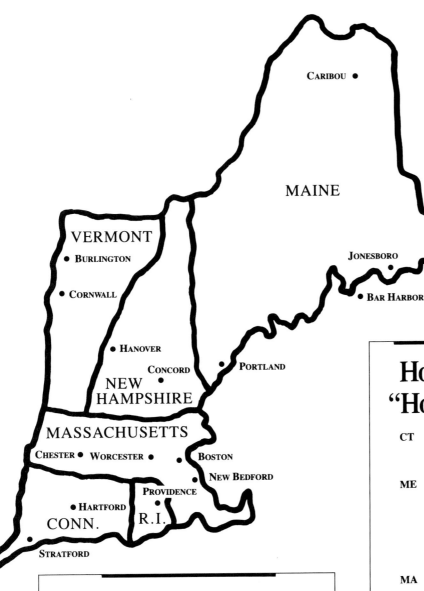

MAINE

VERMONT
● BURLINGTON

● CORNWALL

● HANOVER
CONCORD
●
NEW
HAMPSHIRE

JONESBORO

● BAR HARBOR

● PORTLAND

MASSACHUSETTS

CHESTER ● WORCESTER ● ● BOSTON

● NEW BEDFORD

PROVIDENCE

● HARTFORD

CONN. R.I.

● STRATFORD

CARIBOU ●

How Hot Was "Hot Saturday"?

CT	●	HARTFORD, 101°F.
	●	STRATFORD, 96°F.
ME	●	BAR HARBOR, 101°F.
	●	CARIBOU, 95°F.
	●	JONESBORO, 104°F.
	●	PORTLAND, 103°F.
MA	●	BOSTON, 102°F.
	●	CHESTER, 107°F.
	●	NEW BEDFORD, 107°F.
	●	WORCESTER, 96°F.
NH	●	CONCORD, 101°F.
	●	HANOVER, 103°F.
RI	●	PROVIDENCE, 104°F.
VT	●	BURLINGTON, 99°F.
	●	CORNWALL, 100°F.

In New England We Never Say *Hot*, We Say *Warm*

☞ Here are the all-time record highs for each New England state.

State	Temperature (degrees Fahrenheit)	
Connecticut	105	(Waterbury, July 22, 1926)
Maine	105	(North Bridgton, July 10, 1911)
Massachusetts	107	(Chester and New Bedford, August 2, 1975)
New Hampshire	106	(Nashua, July 4, 1911)
Rhode Island	104	(Providence, August 2, 1975)
Vermont	105	(Vernon, July 4, 1911)

The Dark Day of May 1780

BY HERBERT A. WISBEY, JR.

For a generation of New Englanders, Friday, May 19, 1780, was a date never to be forgotten. On that day the sun was blotted out by a strange darkness, varying in intensity and length from place to place, but extending from New Jersey and New York across Connecticut, Rhode Island, Massachusetts, and southeastern New Hampshire into Maine. This phenomenon, which frightened some, excited the curiosity of others, and caught the attention of all, became known as "The Dark Day."

For several days before The Dark Day, the sun was obscured by smoky clouds, and the moon took on an unusual reddish color. At Ipswich, Massachusetts, the unusual darkness began to attract attention by eleven o'clock in the morning, following a light rain. By eleven-thirty, it was too dark to read or do household tasks such as weaving, and candles were lighted for the noon meal. Wild birds and barnyard fowl went to roost, frogs peeped their night chorus, and woodcocks whistled as they do only in the darkness. "In short, there was the appearance of Midnight at Noonday." Adding to the terror of the superstitious was a strong smoky smell that brought to mind visions of hellfire and brimstone. The deepest darkness lasted from three to five hours, depending on the location.

In Providence, Rhode Island, the darkness began at about ten in the morning and increased in intensity until "common business was wholly suspended, and that which was necessary, obliged to be performed, though at Noon-Day, by candle-light." People gathered in groups in the streets to discuss the strange event. A distraught man approached President James Manning of Rhode Island College (later Brown University) and asked, "How do you account for this darkness, sir? What does it mean?" Dr. Manning's reply, uttered "with great solemnity of manner," did not quiet the man's apprehensions. "I consider it, sir, as a prelude to that great and important day when the final consummation of all things is to take place," he declared.

Another college president, Ezra Stiles of Yale, was also in Rhode Island on that day, visiting his old parish in Newport. Always the curious scholar, Stiles made careful observations of the event and wrote an account of it for the next day's newspaper. He recalled other strange appearances of darkness on the coast of Africa and in Europe, but believed that such a phenomenon had not happened in New England since the first English settlement. "And it is not recollected from history that a Darkness of equal Intenseness & Duration has ever happened in any parts of the World, except in Egypt, and at the miraculous Eclipse at the Crucifixion of our Blessed Savior." He warned, "However this Darkness is undoubtedly a phaenomenon, which may be accounted for by the Laws of Nature, without having recourse to any Thing miraculous or ominous." Professor Daggett of Yale, who wrote a description for a New Haven newspaper, also warned against public hysteria. "The Appearance was indeed uncommon, & the Cause unknown," he admitted. "Yet there is no reason to consider it as supernatural or ominous. It is therefore hoped that no persons, whether of vapoury Constitution of

Body, or an enthusiastic Turn of mind, will be in the least terrified by it, or inspired to prophesy any future Events, till they come to pass."

It could hardly be expected that such advice would be heeded. Jemima Wilkinson, the Publick Universal Friend who had been predicting the beginning of the millennium about the first of April 1780, declared that The Dark Day was the fulfillment of her prophecy. She may even have hoped to restore life to Susannah Potter of South Kingstown, Rhode Island, who died on May 19, by praying for a miracle at the coffin of the young girl. The day seemed made to order for prophets and preachers who had been warning about the temporal nature of this transitory, wicked world.

Elder Peleg Burroughs, pastor of the Baptist church in Tiverton, Rhode Island, used the awesome event as an excuse to compose a 17-verse hymn warning sinners to repent.

The Connecticut legislature was in session at Hartford on May 19, 1780, and, when the darkness fell, the House of Representatives was unable to transact business and adjourned. A commonly expressed opinion was that the day of judgment was at hand. When a proposal to adjourn was brought upon the council, however, a Colonel Davenport spoke up. "I am against an adjournment," he declared. "The day of judgment is either approaching, or it is not. If it is not, there is no cause for an adjournment; if it is, I choose to be found doing my duty. I wish therefore that candles may be brought." A Yale student reported that the General Assembly of New York, meeting in Poughkeepsie, noticed the darkness but did not adjourn.

All across New England observations of the phenomenon were recorded. In Ipswich "several Gentlemen of Liberal Education at the House of the Rev. Mr. Cutler" described the deepening darkness and accompanying circumstances from about eleven in the morning until after four in the afternoon. They spent an enjoyable few hours speculating about possible causes, although people in a nearby tavern were much agitated. A traveler who compared accounts of the event along his route through Norwich, Providence, Boston, and Portsmouth thought that the darkness must have been greatest at Newburyport, where it "differed very little from the Darkness of a common Starlight Night." "A sickly, melancholy gloom overcast the face of Nature," wrote a Worcester, Massachusetts, observer.

Some spectators thought the day should be called "Yellow Friday." In some places the clouds that ushered in the darkness were shades of red, brown, or yellow. During the darkness, objects that usually appeared green seemed to be of deepest green verging on

blue, and, as the darkness receded, an eerie light cast a yellow tinge over the landscape.

The night that followed The Dark Day was no comfort to the fearful. At Worcester it was noted, "Nor was the Darkness of the *Night* less uncommon or terrifying than that of the day: notwithstanding there was almost a full Moon, *no Object was discernable* [sic], but by the help of some Artificial Light, which when seen from some of the neighboring houses and other places, at a distance, appeared through a kind of Egyptian Darkness which seemed almost impervious to the Rays." The unusually black darkness was also noticed in Providence, where it was observed that a candle in the window seemed to give no light outside, the glow not penetrating more than six inches beyond the window. Nothing could be seen of a large building 20 feet across an alley. At Groton, Massachusetts, the darkness at eight o'clock was so great that traveling was impractical. "Although the moon rose nearly full about Nine o'clock . . . yet it did not give Light enough to enable a person to distinguish between the Heavens & the Earth."

The next day, in several places, a distinguishable film was discovered on barrels and tubs of exposed water. At Barnstable, Massachusetts, where the darkness at midday was so great that the people had to stop planting corn because they could not see the kernels they dropped, a fine sulfurlike substance was noticed on the edges of water in open kettles and tubs. The rainwater at Ipswich had a sooty smell and was covered with a light scum that seemed to be composed of black ashes or burnt leaves. The only reports of adverse effects of The Dark Day, however, came from Portsmouth and Dover, New Hampshire, where a number of birds died after flying against houses.

The first theories offered to explain The Dark Day included speculation that it was an aftereffect of a comet or had some relation to the aurora borealis. The duration of the darkness quickly ruled out an ordinary solar eclipse. Even the earliest guesses about the possible causes, however, considered smoke from forest fires as one of the probable factors. An Ipswich observer speculated, "The vast Body of Smoke from the *Woods which had been burning for many days,* mixing with the common Exhalation from the Earth & Water, and condensed by the Action of Winds from opposite points, may perhaps be sufficient Causes to produce the surprising Darkness."

With his characteristic, indefatigable curiosity, Ezra Stiles collected newspaper accounts, interviewed Yale students and faculty for their observations, and corresponded about The Dark Day with friends far and wide. On June 28, 1780, he gave a lecture in the chapel at Yale on "the memorable Darkness of May 19th 1780," in which he read all the published accounts as well as others he had collected. Stiles compared The Dark Day with a similar phenomenon near Detroit in 1762. "I gave it my opinion," he remarked, "that the Cause of both was the Conflagration of the Woods of an extensive Territory. That, in the fall of 1762, by the Indians for hunting Deer; this by the English Settlers in clearing Lands."

Forest fires extending across a vast area from New Hampshire and Vermont into New York State burned furiously for a week or more before The Dark Day. No rain had fallen in northern New England since the fall, and "a profusion of Settlers pushing back into the Wilderness were everywhere clearing land and burning Brush." The fires got out of control and burned over a great expanse, creating great suffocating clouds of smoke. Evidently, an unusual atmospheric condition trapped the smoke in a cloud cover over New England until it reached sufficient density to blot out the sun on The Dark Day of May 19, 1780. This explanation, offered by Stiles, was elaborated upon by Professor Samuel Williams of Harvard in an article published in the first volume of the *Memoirs of the American Academy of Arts and Sciences* in 1785. The learned professor's paper presented a logical explanation of the various aspects of the strange event, and was designed to put an end to the speculation about it. But to many New Englanders who lived through it, The Dark Day was an inexplicable mystery never recalled without a strange feeling of awe.   ∞

Other Remarkable Days

☞ **The Dark Day of 1716 (November 1, 1716; October 21, Old Style):** Caused (as were all of the dark days listed) by western forest fires, this event was observed by Noah Webster and reported to the Royal Society in London by Cotton Mather.

☞ **The Two Dark Days of 1819 (November 2 and November 9, 1819):** The darkness was most noticeable on both these days over Vermont and southern Canada. On the day of November 2, candles were needed for illumination in the Champlain Valley.

On November 9, Frederick Hall, professor of mathematics and natural philosophy at Middlebury College, reported that students at the college had to study during the day by candlelight. The sun, when visible at all, shone a deep blood red.

☞ **The Yellow Day (September 6, 1881):** Destructive forest fires around Lake Huron in Michigan caused this widespread atmospheric phenomenon. Artificial lighting was needed by mid-morning in western areas of New England. Grass and foliage took on a brassy hue, and daylight was a luminous yellow haze that cast no shadows. The Burlington (Vermont) *Free Press* described the sun as looking like a "crimson wafer."

☞ **The Blue Sun and Moon (September 26, 1950):** Also known as The Great Smoke Pall, this unusual event occurred due to forest fires in the Canadian northwest. Its full effects were felt over the eastern United States from September 24–30, but this date marks the beginning of the phenomenon in New England.

Unlike other dark days on the list, visibility at ground level was good, but the sun and moon took on what observers described as a blue, purple, or violet hue. Scientists believe that particles of smoke in the atmosphere selectively scattered light rays, depleting the greens and yellows in the spectrum and making the blues and violets visible.

Fog Along the Maine Coast

BY EDIE CLARK

During the summer along the coast of Maine, the air and the sea never seem to come to terms. Provoked by the Labrador currents, the temperature of the water remains frigid throughout the summer while the air warms up, at times becoming tropical. As a result, coastal Maine spends much of its summer waiting out the fog. The highest number of hours of fog anywhere on the Atlantic coast are tallied there. For instance, during June, July, and August of a recent year, Portland recorded a mere 280 hours shrouded in mist—not bad when you consider that in Eastport, which is just shy of the Canadian border, 750 hours of the summer were locked in the clouds.

Fog *is* a cloud, a mass of tiny raindrops suspended by their lightness. If it's in the air, we call that a cloud, but if it's down around us, it's fog. Meteorologists sometimes refer to fog as "horizontal precipitation": If the drops of moisture were any heavier, they would become rain.

Fog is defined by its density: If you can't see farther than a kilometer, that's fog; otherwise it's merely gray skies. In most places fog comes at the change of seasons, before the earth and the air can come back into balance with each other. Yet fog has no season of its own. It can come at any time of the year without surprise.

Along with lighthouses, Maine has foghorns, sometimes stacked two or three on top of each other to increase volume. These hidden beacons are on buoys, towers, lighthouses, or the ends of jetties. The moan of the horn can call as far as four miles into the blur, throbbing a timeless lullaby to fogbound tourists and guiding the men at sea, who know the sound as they know their own voices.

There are those who say fog is the most dangerous kind of weather, ranking it above such killers as hurricanes and tornadoes, not only because it is often unpredictable, but also because it seems benign in its stillness, a harmless veil that lacks the fury and violence we equate with life-threatening conditions. So we don't take care. On highways, cars collide one after the other in chain-reaction collisions. Air traffic, in spite of modern control devices, still waits in obeisance to fog, unable to take off or land until visibility clears to a quarter mile. And perhaps nowhere does fog make the landscape more unfamiliar than it does at sea, where landmarks are blotted out more than on a moonless night.

It is human nature to despair of anything so independent, so uncontrollable. Though an ageless inspiration for artists and poets, fog nonetheless does all the things that we human beings mistrust in others of our kind. It veils; it distorts; it hovers; it conceals; it dis-

Fog-shrouded scenes, like this one at Stonington on Deer Isle, are commonplace in the summertime along the coast of Maine.

guises and covers up. It's no wonder that moviemakers lean heavily on its effect in order to imply mystery and invoke stealth. Meteorologists say that they can pinpoint conditions that will produce fog, but they find it hard to be accurate about when it will begin—or end. And once it's there, it's there.

Richard Rooney, the manager [in 1984] of the Portland International Jetport, knows this quite well. He expressed it as a matter of practicality: "Snow, you can plow it back down to the pavement, salt it, or sand it. But fog, you just have to accept it. You can't plow fog. You can't wish it away. All you can do is just sit there and watch it until it goes away."   ∞

When We Don't Get Enough Weather the Usual Way, We Make It

Indoor Fog: If the Boston Bruins make it to a late round in the Stanley Cup play-offs, they can count on playing a cloudy game or two. A warm spring day will combine with the ice on the rink at Boston Garden to make fog. During the 1983 play-offs with the New York Islanders, exhaust fans were placed around the Garden perimeter, and players were encouraged to skate in circles whenever a stop in play occurred.

Bruins goalie Andy Moog peers through the murk during a late-season game in Boston Garden.

The Sunny Months . . .

☞ Based on a compiled average, percentage of sunshine for daylight hours:

Month	Northeast	Southwest	Pacific Northwest
January	46	69	25
February	50	72	36
March	48	73	45
April	50	70	51
May	52	66	56
June	55	65	54
July	57	82	69
August	58	83	64
September	56	79	60
October	55	73	42
November	47	74	30
December	46	71	21

Least sunshine on record for a month in New England: 21% (April 1901)
Most sunshine: 77% (June 1971)

Occurring early on a pleasant summer afternoon, the famous Vineyard Waterspout delighted vacationers and photographers alike in 1896.

The Vineyard Waterspout

BY DAVID M. LUDLUM

Waterspouts occur infrequently, and they usually form well out at sea in a tropical climate where few or none at all can witness the awesome spectacle. Imagine, then, the appearance of not one but three distinct spouts in a temperate latitude, in full view of a vacation resort at the height of the season, and close to the midday mealtime, when a maximum number of people were up and about! Certainly no such phenomenon ever chose a more propitious time and place to exhibit its wonders to an appreciative audience.

The event took place early on Wednesday afternoon, August 19, 1896, off the southeast coast of Massachusetts, between Cape Cod and the popular vacation isle of Martha's Vineyard. The pillar of water and vapor joining cloud and sea rose only five miles from the northeast point of Martha's Vineyard near Cottage City, a resort community. Now known as Oak Bluffs, it overlooks the body of water where Nantucket Sound and Vineyard Sound join off the promontory called East Chop.

The first spout, appearing from a threatening shower cloud at 12:45 in the afternoon, served as a preview to alert vacationers and local residents. The rumor quickly spread of untoward doings offshore, and many hurried to vantage points. When a larger and grander spout appeared at exactly one o'clock, a sizable group of people were on hand. For some there had been time to secure cameras and film so that valuable photographic records of the marine funnel could be made. At least ten reproducible photographs were made despite the unfavorable lighting conditions. A number of discerning eyewitnesses supplied their impressions to the local and national press. Finally, a thorough technical study of the physical dimensions and nature of the three waterspouts was prepared by a leading meteorologist of the Weather Bureau in Washington, D.C., and published in July 1906, ten years after the event.

The following descriptions are excerpted from eyewitness accounts:

"A large mass of heavy black cloud hung above the ocean between Nantucket and Cape Cod. Suddenly it was seen to project a circular column of its own dense vapor perpendicularly downward, rapidly but not precipitantly, until sea and cloud were connected by a cylinder one or two hundred feet in diameter, straight as a pine tree, and at least a mile high. It was a waterspout indeed, of most unusual proportion and indescribable beauty."

*****

"The sea was perfectly calm, the air almost motionless, the sun shining brightly, light summer clouds hanging here and there over the deep blue sky; and in strange contrast with all the rest, was the lofty mass of black vapor with its absolutely perpendicular support. To add to the weird effect, occasional livid streaks of forked lightning shot athwart the black monster cloud above. The column was only slightly funnel-shaped just where it joined the cloud, and was of equal diameter the remainder of its length. At its base the sea was lashed into a mass of white foam and spray that mounted upward as high as the masts of a large schooner."

*****

"From Cottage City it seemed about six miles distant, but careful observation through a glass from the writer's view-point showed that it was nearly in line with the light-ship off Hyannis harbor, and still farther distant, its foot resting upon the sea beyond the horizon line. It must have been 20 or 25 miles away, but such was its magnitude that it seemed not more than one quarter of that distant.

"It moved slowly eastward, and continued with little change in form for 17 minutes. Then it gradually attenuated till it looked like a dark ribbon hanging out of the cloud, and at length disappeared. The lashing of water into foam and spray where its base had rested continued unabated, which was evidence that the water-spout was still there, though now invisible, and that it might be expected to reappear. Surely enough, after an interval of about ten minutes, the cylindrical form of black vapor began to push its way downward again from the cloud and continued until it stood again upon the white mass of foam and spray mounting up from the sea surface. This time its top was more funnel shaped and curved to the eastward. It continued eight minutes and disappeared.

"The old sea captains of Martha's Vineyard said that this waterspout exceeded in size and grandeur anything of the kind they had seen during all their seafaring experience."   ∞

I Survived
a Waterspout

BY QUENTIN DEGRASSE,

AS TOLD TO CHESTER SCOTT HOWLAND

uentin DeGrasse rolled up his pants' legs and uncovered the thick parts of his feet and lower ankles. An ugly network of scars covered them.

"These have never left me," Quentin said. "As I grow older I do not like to look at them or think of the fearful days and nights in the mid-Atlantic when I was helpless to prevent pilot fish from viciously biting my body. Whenever I am reminded in the daytime of the details of that experience a half century ago, I relive it all in bad dreams at night."

The story of Quentin DeGrasse is the story of the New Bedford whaler *Alice Knowles,* caught in the nuclear force of a giant waterspout in the Atlantic Ocean, 35 degrees north of the equator. The bark *Alice Knowles* was built in 1878, a good ship of 302 tons. She sailed April 19, 1915, out of New Bedford bound on a whaling voyage.

Twenty-one days after leaving her home port, the vessel lay off St. Vincent, one of the Cape Verde Islands. Captain Horace Haggerty was taken ashore, and, as was common in the last years of whale hunting out of New Bedford, he recruited supplies and men to make up a full crew. Quentin DeGrasse, a lad 17 years old, carried with him his mother's consent to put out on a New Bedford whaler, and he signed shipping papers in the cabin of the *Alice Knowles* as a foremast hand.

Five months after leaving New Bedford the vessel was hunting whales on the western whaling grounds in the Atlantic Ocean, 28 to 36 degrees north of the equa-

tor. The ship had 1,600 barrels of sperm oil aboard— a total cargo so great that some of the casks had to be stowed on deck, considered a risk in case of bad weather.

Quentin proved himself to be a strong, capable, and willing hand. He was a skillful boatman, quick to observe and learn. He reports that the needed pig iron ballast deep in the hold of the *Alice Knowles* was removed to make room for oil that would be taken from whales captured during the six-week journey back to the home port.

I listened to the story of the wreck of the *Alice Knowles* as told to me by Quentin, the only surviving member of the crew.

"Our ship had been at sea five months, when on September 1, with Cape Hatteras 40 miles due west, the barometer dropped rapidly. The southwestern horizon became black with a solid cloud mass, and heavy winds began to strike the *Alice Knowles* and pick up the sea.

"Captain Haggerty spoke with the chief mate, who ordered, 'Take in all light sails and rig in studding-sail booms.'

"The squall passed off to the southeast, but in spite of a brief calm Captain Haggerty sang out: 'Clew down topsails—haul out reef tackles and haul up courses.'

"During the next 12 hours the storm seemed to remain stationary and did not change in its intensity.

"September the third the wind suddenly increased in strength. The man at the wheel was whirled to the

The ill-fated whaler Alice Knowles, *photographed at dockside in 1908. She sailed out of New Bedford in 1915, never to return. Only Quentin DeGrasse, a young Cape Verde shiphand, survived to tell her story.*

deck. Two men were sent to stand by but could not hold the wheel steady. The wheel was lashed to hold the vessel into the wind.

"About noon a huge funnel-shaped cloud even blacker than the sky itself was sighted four or five miles from the ship. The men on the second watch paced the deck apprehensively in the threat of a hurricane. There was an uneasiness aboard. Orders were given to double-reef the fore topsail and furl the mainsail.

"At midnight the sea moderated. Captain Haggerty called the ship's company aft.

" 'Men,' said the captain, 'I cannot predict the moderation of the weather means a favorable change in the wind. The officers are to remain on deck with me through the night; any of you who want to can remain with us or go below to the forecastle.' The men talked among themselves, and most of the crew went down into the forecastle.

"At two o'clock a terrific roar came out of the blackness. No man could hear another's shouts. The waterspout enveloped the ship, dragging her onto her beam-ends. She remained there a brief moment, and the captain attempted to smash in the cabin skylight to release his son in the steerage and any others of the crew. Before he had struck a half dozen blows, the vessel had turned keel up—the crew was trapped below or thrown from the deck into the boiling ocean.

"Six crew members had chosen to remain on deck with the officers. I was one of these. We had climbed into a whaleboat hanging in the davits just before the waterspout struck. This boat and the crew members in it floated free, but a great wave picked both men and boat 50 feet into the air, and when the wave rolled on before the storm, the boat and men dropped like a plummet, crashing onto the upturned keel of the *Alice Knowles*. The boat flew into pieces, and the men disappeared into the ocean.

"I was a powerful swimmer, trained from babyhood off the ocean shores of St. Vincent Island, and was not injured in the crash. I struggled to the surface of the ocean. I could not see one inch in front of me. The waterspout and gale had passed, but a thundering noise still deafened me. When the light of the morning came, I found myself near half of a whaleboat that six months before had been crushed by a whale's tail and had been kept on the after upper deck (house) of the mother ship for repairs.

"I had hung onto it 10 or 15 minutes when I heard a cry and my name. 'Quentin, help! Help!' I looked around and saw Jules Lopes, one of the *Alice Knowles'* harpooners.

"Jules was exhausted and floating with the great ocean swells. I swam over to him and helped him get onto my half-boat raft. There had been no wind since sunrise.

"The weight of Jules and me in the open-ended half boat submerged it so that, although it supported us, only our heads were above the surface of the sea. We feared sharks might smell us, although neither of us had been more than bruised in the smashing of the whaleboat on the keel of the wrecked and sunken ship, and none of our blood was in the water.

"The glare of the sun in a bright, clear sky was painful. Jules kept his eyes closed. He was much weaker than I. I would close mine for a few minutes at a time and then search the sea, hoping to discover floating wreckage from the *Alice Knowles* or a ship on the horizon.

"Mid-afternoon of our first day in the water I sighted a cask filled with whale oil that had floated from the deck of the *Alice Knowles* when it capsized. I thought it would be more buoyant than the broken boat and swam over to it and pushed it with my head and body toward the boat. However, when Jules and I attempted to climb onto it, we could not get a grip, and it rolled in the water. It was a large cask, more than four feet in diameter. If we could have gotten onto it, we might have been able to keep our bodies out of the water. We returned to the broken half boat.

"As we drifted away from the cask, large pieces of pork floated toward us. These pieces of salt meat had been soaking in the galley aboard the *Alice Knowles* the day of the wreck.

"I again left my position in the half boat and swam out to the floating pork. Although it was soft, I was able to hold a piece between my teeth and swim back to the half boat. As I reached out to hand the pork to Jules, he shouted, 'Quentin—a shark is following you.' I turned to see his fin above the surface of the ocean. I shouted and beat the water with my arms and legs, clapping my hands in the commotion. The shark fin disappeared, and I expected to feel his teeth ripping at my abdomen as I lay flat in the water. I was not attacked. Jules and I took bites of the sea-soaked pork.

"Fighting the shark in my weakened condition robbed me of my strength, and I did not recover. After the first 24 hours Jules and I locked our arms around each other's body and our legs under the only thwart remaining in the broken boat. This would keep us from falling into the water if the sea became rough. We had no strength for further swimming.

"We remained in this position 48 hours under a burning sun by day and through the damp, shivering cold nights, without food or water. Our eyes were becoming sticky, and it was difficult to keep them open. The horizon was growing indistinct and blurred. It seemed that we might be blind before we died, with no chance to sight and hail a passing ship. We mumbled prayers we had been taught as boys in church on the island of St. Vincent.

"On the fourth day, September 7, we sighted a vessel coming toward us. We could not make any sounds above a gruff whisper forced from our feverish throats. As the ship approached us the master shouted, but we could not answer him. We saw the crewmen lower a boat and row toward us. They thought us dead, as we could not move or make any sound.

"We had been in the water so long we could not release our arm grips around each other or our legs from the boat thwart. The men in the rescue boat towed us to their vessel, and we were hauled aboard by tackle ropes and painfully pried apart.

"Captain Charles Gilbert, master of the six-masted schooner *Fred W. Thurber*, slowly nursed us and took us to Pernambuco on the Brazilian coast."   ∞

Editor's Note: *Jules Lopes died from the effects of his terrible ordeal, and Quentin DeGrasse alone survived to tell of the fate of the* Alice Knowles.

MEMORABLE QUOTES

☞ I'd like to live in a house that was so well insulated that all it would take to heat it would be the daily burning of the *New York Times*.

—*William Shurcliff*

☞ Everybody talks about the weather, but nobody does anything about it.

—*Charles Dudley Warner*

☞ If you are newly married people, go to bed. You need neither electric heat, nor light.

—*Power Board of Sweden*

☞ It hain't no use to grumble and complain,
It's jest as easy to rejoice;
When God sorts out the weather and sends rain,
Why rain's my choice.

—*James Whitcomb Riley*

COAL! DUCK!

☞ Bennington, Vermont, witnessed an unusual hailstorm on June 27, 1950. The hail that fell contained bits of slag and coal, most likely caused by the combination of a strong uprising wind current and the high stacks of a coke company in Troy, New York.

COLD DUCK!

☞ On December 15, 1933, an ice-encrusted mallard duck fell from the sky in Worcester, Massachusetts—literally a waddling hailstone. It fell at the feet of Roscoe Blunt, who took the duck indoors. When Roscoe and his dad were sure the bird had regained the capacity to flap, they let it go.

September Salt Storm

BY MARY LOUISE KITSEN

On a late September afternoon in 1815, the sun suddenly disappeared, and a heavy layer of black clouds settled in. The people of Southington, Connecticut, expected a late electrical storm.

At first it looked as though they were to be proved correct. A wind of gale force came up, and a driving rain began to fall.

It was a son of farmer James Smith, tarrying outside with two friends who had walked home from school with him, who first alerted the farmer that something was indeed "funny." According to the farmer's notes in his journal, the lad ran in shouting, "It's raining salt, it's raining salt!"

"I thought the boy daft," wrote the farmer in his journal.

Farmer Smith went outside and tested the rain in his face. It did indeed taste salty. In fact, other people throughout the community and into the outlying areas of nearby towns were discovering that, as improbable as it seemed, it was indeed raining salt in Southington!

The strange storm continued through the night. In the morning, what a strange sight greeted the people of the unfortunate village! The salt crystals covered entire buildings; even the windows were covered over.

The crops were destroyed as though struck by a huge frost. It was the end of the 1815 harvest season.

Later, the probable explanation became known. A salt spray had blown inland from Long Island. It seems the ocean had been extremely calm that day, but the tide had reached a great height—a height never before seen. Then a sudden strong offshore wind had lifted the salt spray and carried it over the Southington area, where it simply "let go."

CHAPTER SIX

The
Prognosticators

Above: *Bob Minsenberger checks his rain gauge up on Hollister Hill.* **Previous pages:** *A U.S. Weather Bureau observer prepares to launch a weather balloon from the deck of a Coast Guard cutter.*

The Weatherman
of Hollister Hill

BY MEL ALLEN

I n the early afternoon of April 13, 1984, Bob Minsenberger readied his first weather forecast for his
Washington County neighbors in north-central
Vermont by taking a long, sweeping look out the
window. He lives high above a valley on a ridge of
Hollister Hill. His house is handmade from rough-
sawn lumber with a room tucked on top that he
calls "my tower." The view to the west is of river-
valley farms and forests, 25 miles distant. The clouds
he saw sweeping over the peaks of Camel's Hump,
Glen Ellen, and Sugarbush told of impending rain. His
meteorological training was zero. He felt, however,
that hundreds of hours looking out the tower windows
had given him "a sense for the weather."

Sometimes he passed entire days in the tower,
binoculars pressed to his eyes, watching rain pelt distant ridges while he basked in sunshine. With his neighbors he shared an irritation with the National Weather
Service reports from Burlington, 40 miles away on the
other side of the mountains. The reports were repeated
by local radio stations and newspapers even though
Burlington, with mountains to the east and Lake Champlain to the west, often had weather dramatically different from what Bob Minsenberger saw outside his windows. He thought he could do better. And, like other
homesteaders, he was always searching for an angle, a
need to fill, a craft to peddle. Friends sold eggs, hard-
crusted bread, dolls. Minsenberger, who made a modest living cleaning houses, thought just maybe he could
sell the weather. With people able to learn the weather
nationwide at the touch of a dial, he would narrow his
world to a chunk of Vermont that lay east of the Green

Mountains, west of the Connecticut River, north of
Route 107, and south of Route 15.

He advertised his phone-in service, Weatherwatch, in the local weekly, with a number (454-7707)
he hoped people would remember. His goal was to
attract enough callers to interest advertisers in sponsor-
ing the forecasts. At the time he had neither electricity
nor phone. He left the house and walked a quarter of a
mile down a mud-thickened drive. At the end of the
drive was a telephone pole. Beside the pole Minsenberger built a wooden box, two feet tall and two feet
deep, and stood it beneath a tree. Inside the box he
placed a telephone answering machine hooked to the
telephone line.

Minsenberger is a shade under six feet and well
fed. He crammed his head into the box while the rest of
him straddled the mud. He is generous with words, and
his forecast calling for increasing clouds with showers
by evening ran two minutes.

The next day the answering machine clicked 75
times, a number that grew daily. He updated reports 6,
8, 12 times a day depending on conditions. Callers who
heard wind, rain, and thunder in the background thought
Weatherwatch had nifty sound effects. They were unaware that their weather forecaster, who always concluded "from a tower on Hollister Hill," lay prone getting soaked as he spoke.

On June 9, 1984, Minsenberger awoke at 4:00 A.M.
The ground was waterlogged after five days of steady
rain. The rain gauge read four inches, with no letup in
sight. Hours before other warnings, "I said I better tell
people in the valleys to get ready for flooding." He

slogged down the drive and wedged his head into the box. "Later that morning we had the worst flood in decades. That day convinced me I had something important to do."

He began adding weather notes and observations to his forecasts, as if he were drinking coffee in a diner speaking with a friend. What began as an angle turned into something like love.

Loyal callers and weather enthusiasts took to driving along Hollister Hill Road looking for the tower. One neighbor, a dairy farmer named Bob Light, recalls, "I was outside, and an elderly couple wanted to know where the weatherman was with his tower. I said I knew nothing about it. I called the number and thought, By God, that voice sounds awfully familiar. Then my wife dialed it, and she said, 'That's Bob Minsenberger.' He'd been afraid to use his real name. Called himself Bob James. I said, 'You've got to come clean.' "

One day Minsenberger programmed his machine to receive messages. After giving his forecast, he asked for listener responses.

"You have the most accurate weather report we have ever caught. We are from Lake Woodbury, and we thank you very much."

"I call during haying season three times a day, sometimes more. If I cut hay and it rains, the minerals and vitamins and protein leach out. Sometimes I've called planning to cut and changed my plans. It helps us farmers a lot."

"My husband is a contractor. When he starts out in the morning, he has to know if he can rip out a wall and not have rain pouring in. We count on you."

"The radio station's weather line is always busy. It's really frustrating to always get a busy signal when your husband is a logger and depends on the weather to plan his day. So now I use you. But why do you always sound like you have a cold?"

Late in autumn, before the first snows, Bob Minsenberger had phone service extended to his house. And when he gave the forecasts, he began using his own name.

He doesn't know for certain how many people listen to his forecasts. He guesses "maybe a thousand off and on." He works part-time in a hardware store in the village of Plainfield, and sometimes a customer will look closely at him and say, "Your voice sounds *awfully* familiar. Do I know you from somewhere?" During storms his answering machine clicks 500 times a day, one after the other, with barely a pause. He'll sit in the tower just listening to the clicks. For a year and a half he drove 70 miles a day along back roads delivering the *Times-Argus* in his pickup. He learned the "muddiest

roads and the roads that will be closed first from drifting," and he thinks he is probably the only weatherman who, when he gives a forecast—especially during storms—pictures the people along his old paper route listening.

He wakes each morning to static from the clock radio beside his pillow, since the local station, WNCS from Montpelier, does not go on the air until 5:00 A.M. His wife and daughter are accustomed to his "morning chores" and slumber on. Upon waking he feels a little anxious, having slept through six hours of north-central Vermont's weather. In winter the first clue in a house heated solely with wood is immediate and personal: Is he cold?

The bathroom window faces south, and at first light he looks to the sky, comparing what he sees to what he thought he would see when he went to bed. Flashlight in hand, he checks the thermometer in the bedroom and, if necessary, fires up the parlor stove. In spring and fall he steps outside to check for frost. "We don't frost that easily," he says. "A neighbor not a thousand feet away gets double our frost. If I have frost, I know others have."

He keeps two other thermometers outside, one deep in the woods that he consults in summer. He has recorded 15 degrees difference between his house and the woods, and during heat waves he likes to remind people how easily they can find relief. One thermometer probe sinks eight inches into the ground, useful for telling people the temperature of the soil for planting. He plans on putting a probe into a sugar maple, too, as tree temperature is crucial to sap flow. In sap season he counts drops per minute in a test bucket and calls neighbors to compare. When he thinks the best sugaring weather is coming—teens to 20 degrees at night, 40 to 45 during the day, with sun and calm or light winds from the north or west—he tells listeners to call their helpers.

If it has rained during the night, he checks his rain gauge. If there is mixed precipitation, he goes to the driveway, where he sets a washcloth on a tray. Big flakes tell him wet and warm; small flakes dry and cold. Trees, clouds, and chimney smoke all speak of wind, but he looks at his wind sock, 30 feet high on a small open knoll, with a father's pride. "I made two dozen treks into the woods searching for the right tree for the pole," he says. "I found it in the middle of a big cedar clump and stripped the bark by hand."

By 5:00 A.M. he is in the tower for the day's first forecast. He knows now what is happening on Hollister Hill, but he needs to know what fronts are advancing and from where. For that information he looks not to the sky but to a shelf where he keeps a television and a weather radio. "It would be great if I could do this just by instinct," he says. "Sometimes I wonder—if we were cut off for days, what kind of forecaster would I be? But I need those satellite pictures. The livelihoods of a lot of people who call me depend on the weather. They expect me to be right."

From the weather channel on television he gains a national perspective; the radio tells him what Burlington, with its team of three meteorologists, computers, and radar, sees. "But if the Weather Service says, 'At present winds are from the south but will be shifting, becoming northwesterly by noon,' which means cold Canadian air, I can look out the window and see it *already* has shifted, winds *are* out of the northwest, and cold *is* here. I can give weather in the present tense."

In a corner of the tower is a rack of cassette tapes, dated and titled. These memorable forecasts and caller responses serve as a sort of audio album. One is titled "October 4, 1987, Storm," which dumped from six to ten inches of snow over much of central Vermont, a record breaker for that early in the year.

"The day before began to look interesting," he says. "Unseasonably cold air moving up the coast. Could be rain, maybe sleet, maybe snow. I woke at 2:00 A.M. I knew then a storm was coming, but its nature was still uncertain. I woke again at 5:00, and it was raining. But I heard the temperature for Montreal and knew the cold air was coming. The uncertainty of the storm meant it could be snowing in the Mad River valley while raining here. So I set the answering machine to receive messages. I asked people, 'Where are you? What time is it? What's happening?' "

11:45 A.M.: "Rain on East Hill."

12:00 noon: "Lots of icy sleet in Calais."

12:07 P.M.: "Middlesex, snowing hard and it's sticking."

1:00 P.M.: "I'm in Northfield. It's a blizzard!"

3:15 P.M.: "Barre. Power's out and tree limbs down."

4:30 P.M.: "This is Hookerville. Five inches of snow."

5:00 P.M.: "Six inches on Spruce Mountain Road. Trees are down. Cars off the road everywhere."

"I gave 20 different reports that day," Bob says. "Imagine. I was listening to the storm live! It was like I had windows open all over the county."

Sometimes there is so much he wants to say about the weather of the day and what is to come that he runs past the machine's three-minute tape. He wants people to know that they can expect a spectacular sunset, just as he wants them to know that in 1966 north-central Vermont had three straight snow days in May. He saves some of the weather lore that fills his days for a 6:30 A.M. "Live from the Tower" weather spot on WNCS. He receives no money, only publicity. It is his chance to have an audience of 5,000 ponder topics such as how many gallons of water fell on Washington County during a recent two-inch rainstorm (24 billion).

He gives the forecasts in the tower from a six-foot-long, three-foot-wide nook that is crammed with weather books, a cloud chart, a moon chart, maps, an imported German barometer (a gift from his in-laws), binoculars, and an answering machine, his eighth since Weatherwatch began. "I want to ground myself in Washington County climate," he says. "I want to build up climate records for north-central Vermont. I want to be the one person people call when they need to know records and patterns."

His dream seems a trifle ambitious. After four years he has attracted only two steady advertisers, the local hardware store and a nearby eatery called Lickity-Split, which combined pay him the sum of $26 a week. (He also gets $30 a week from the *Times-Argus* for a weather column.) Recently he applied for a job-start loan, defining himself as a weatherman. He hopes to borrow $1,000, maybe more, to set up a sophisticated weather station with instruments hooked to a computer, a wind-speed indicator with memory, and a self-dumping rain gauge. He hopes to hook a computer into a national service that offers weather maps in an instant. "I want to be able to tell people, 'Call me by 7:00 P.M. Leave your destination and I'll tell you what the weather will be.' "

While he waits for that day, Bob watches from his tower post. He has learned the truth about weather forecasting—that it is not just about wind and rain and heat and cold but about people. And in a corner of Vermont Bob practices being a good neighbor the way it must have been long ago. He keeps his windows on Hollister Hill open to all who care to listen in.   ∞

Our Favorite Homegrown Prophets

Above: *Ray Samson learned the art of reading pig spleens from his father-in-law, the late Leon Wolejko* **(left).** *Leon claimed 99 percent accuracy for his winter weather predictions.* **Opposite page:** *Bill Pomeroy won't reveal much about his secret method for predicting snowstorms. All he'll say is that it hinges on the phases of the moon and is remarkably accurate.*

Half a century ago, having a feel for the weather was crucial to the survival and success of a fisherman, logger, or farmer. Today, of course, the weather radio has all but replaced intuition. The weather sages are dying out, and with their passing goes weather lore of generations, lore that is part science, part craft, and part mystery. Here and there, mostly in inland villages and along the sea where the old ways die hardest, the weather prophets can still be found, their abilities known mostly to their neighbors.

Reading Pig Spleens

Late in the fall of 1987, when Ray Samson butchered his pigs, he set aside on a table in back of his house in Sunderland, Massachusetts, a piece of bitter fat found near the intestine that his father-in-law always called "pork melt." In fact, it is the spleen. It resembles a tongue approximately 12 to 18 inches long, 1/2 to 3/4 inch thick, and 2 1/2 to 3 inches wide. Such dimensions are important to Ray Samson, just as they were to Leon Wolejko, his father-in-law, and to Leon's father. In "reading" the variations in the pork melt's width, Ray Samson foretells the severity of the coming winter.

The spleen is divided into eight equal sections, representing October through May. Thick segments predict cold, tapered portions a milder time. "Last winter," Samson said, "I said we'd have a pretty mild winter, which it was. No long cold spells. Sometimes the spleen just about folds over, and then watch out! That's a long cold snap. We didn't have any. It tapered off nice and slow, and I knew our spring would be long and steady, which it was."

Leon, who died in 1987, claimed to be 99 percent accurate. "I don't know how to explain it," he once said. "It's just one of those things in nature." Leon's widow, Margaret, who still keeps the farm with Ray Samson's help, says the whole family helps read the weather now. "I'm not a believer in many things," she adds, "but after more than 40 years, I'm a believer in this."

His Secret's in the Moon

In 1935 there were 28 snowstorms in the village of Millers Falls, Massachusetts. Fred Pomeroy had predicted there would be 28. In 1972 there were 30 snowstorms in Millers Falls. Fred's son, Lewis "Bill" Pomeroy, had foretold that number. In 1987 Bill predicted there would be 25 snowstorms. There were only 22. "But a couple missed us and turned out to sea," he quickly explains.

Like his father before him, Bill carefully records each storm in a small black ring binder, the second volume of the book his father used, marking down how many inches and whether it was slush, corn snow, or just a dusting. To count as a storm it has to measure at least a quarter of an inch, and if there are two storms back-to-back, he figures the sun has to come out between them in order to call them two separate storms.

"As soon as we get the first cat-tracker, I can work up my prediction," says Bill. "It takes me less than an hour after I see that first snowfall. I can't tell you the formula. It's a family secret. But I can tell you this much: It has to do with the phases of the moon."

Bill's predictions are relevant only to the area around Millers Falls. "If I moved to Maine, I guess I could still make a prediction," he says, "but you really have to know the territory, the way the storms come through the hills. Maine is different country. This is the territory I know." ∞

Maine innkeeper Steve Wight holds one of his uncanny balsam weather sticks.

Weather Sticks Tell All

Since 1972 guests at Steve Wight's Sunday River Inn in Bethel, Maine, have not needed to listen to a weather report to know whether fair weather or foul was in the offing. All they needed was a glance at what the inn calls its "Maine Woodsman Weather Stick," which is fastened perpendicular to an outside wall. The pencil-thin stick is 10 to 16 inches long and cut from a balsam fir. If a dry spell is coming, the stick points up; if rain is imminent, it curls down. Sometimes, as a storm brews, the stick will, in Wight's words, "really put on a show," arching until it is nearly vertical.

Wight learned about the weather sticks from a guest, an old Maine guide. At the end of a trip the guide would ceremoniously cut down a weather stick and tell his sport that the stick would foretell the weather if he promised to return.

So many guests expressed fascination with the sticks that Wight soon began mass production. As soon as cross-country skiing season ends, he and his crew cut as many as 15,000 sticks from local balsams. "Luckily the balsam is considered a weed by pine growers here," Wight says. "They're happy to have us come in."

Each tree produces several sticks, which, Wight says, "last forever. That is, if a house painter doesn't take them away. House painters are the enemies of weather sticks."

His sticks are in every state and many foreign countries, and his files are filled with testimonials. "You have to learn the personality of your stick," says Wight. "Each one will act a little differently. I have a letter from a man who said he was sailing and his stick started going wild. He had a 20-minute warning of a sudden squall."

A weather stick and simple directions can be ordered for $3.50 each or three for $10 (add $2 for shipping) from Maine Line Products, Main St., Box 356-Y, Bethel, ME 04217.

The Sea and Sea Gulls

Clarence Bennett lives on Vinalhaven Island in Maine. He is 75, the son of a lighthouse keeper, and has spent his life on the island fishing first for lobster, then sardines. Now retired, he still fishes a string of gear in summer and has no need to rely on anything besides his senses to know the coming weather. He says after so many years living by the water he has learned that different seas have different sounds, and by listening to the crashing waves from his bedroom he often knows the coming weather.

He said he watches four things: the air, the sea, optical effects over the water, and gulls. He proceeded to outline one old fisherman's weather sense, of which we can offer only a part.

"Horsetails and a mackerel sky: strong southeast winds, gale force within 24 hours.

"Thick, small, heavy clouds that we call 'sheep': when they're in the north, heavy northwest winds coming soon. Get in off the water.

"Engine smoke drops to the water's surface and hovers: moderate southerly breeze coming in the next afternoon.

"'White days,' those dead-flat calms all day long with a light overcast: 24-hour notice for strong southeasterly storms. We call these days 'weather breeders.'

"Sea vapor at sunrise leaps up into fluffy, deep red smokes: two to three days of severe cold ahead.

"Short, steep, choppy waves: a southwest blow, 15–25 knots coming.

"Distant islands appear suddenly through a haze and seem to leap out of the ocean: light, variable warm breezes over the next 48 hours.

"Evening lights reflect in a long line along the ocean's surface toward the viewer: warm drizzle or fog by morning.

"A far-off lighthouse at predawn looks yellow and doesn't shimmer: gentle, variable winds in the offing; same lighthouse is white and wiggles: good strong northwest wind.

"'Sun dogs,' the second or third sun that appears on either side of the sun: gale coming within three days.

"Gulls playing high air currents: strong northwest winds the next day; gulls washing themselves: rain within 24 hours."

Vinalhaven Island native Clarence Bennett doesn't need any special charts or gimmicks to predict what kind of weather's coming. After living on or near the ocean all his life, he just relies on his senses.

"Our weather continues to be dominated by a slow-moving low pressure system sweeping down out of Canada . . ."

THE *REAL* SIGNS OF A STORM

Courtesy of the Springfield (*Massachusetts*) Union, *March 15, 1888*

☞ Foxes barking at night indicate a storm.

☞ Soot burning on the back of a chimney indicates a storm.

☞ Peafowl utter low cries before a storm and select a low perch.

☞ Coals becoming alternately bright and dim indicate an approaching storm.

Other Surefire Methods for Predicting the Weather

☞ The Disgusting but Effective Way

For 50 years Gordon (Bear Fat) Wimsatt of Weed, New Mexico, has been predicting the weather pretty accurately by studying bear fat in glass bottles. He says he learned the method from a local Apache Indian friend, the late George Hightower. If the fat lies heavy on the bottom of the jar, there will be no change in the weather for the next two or three days. When the fat begins to build up in the center or along the sides, expect a storm. Specks of grease drifting above the fat mean wind—a few specks, a light breeze; many specks, a big wind. It doesn't matter what part of the country the bear comes from.

—Courtesy of Charles Hillinger of the Los Angeles Times

☞ Digging Holes Sometimes Works

Elmer Reiter, an atmospheric scientist at Colorado State University, says that deep soil temperature can be used to predict rainfall patterns months ahead. You just dig a hole 40 inches deep and take the ground's temperature. Warm winter soil means a wet spring. Cool summer soil means a dry fall. Warm fall soil means a wet winter. Cool fall soil means a dry winter. This method works nine out of ten times—he says.

—Courtesy of Science Digest

☞ The Old Equinox Method

Lovers of the equinox all over the world swear by this one. It provides, for instance, a method for predicting the weather for the six months following the vernal and autumnal equinoxes:

If the wind is from the south at the *exact* time of the equinox, generally warm weather will prevail. If it is from the north, expect cool weather. If it's from the west, expect a lot of clear weather. If it's from the east, there will be lots of storms. If there's no wind at all, expect little change.

Lost on
Mount Washington

BY CHRISTOPHER R. STEWART

Pretend it's just a dream. A bad dream. Pretend you're 66 years old and wandering alone on a mountainside. The December sun hangs half an hour above the horizon, and each tick of the clock drops the temperature closer to zero. Your muscles ache with exhaustion.

You try to push forward, but the thin crust on the drifts gives way to thigh-deep snow. When you look up searching for the path, hundred-mile-an-hour gales blast icy crystals into your eyes. The tips of your fingers grow numb, and you doubt rescuers will ever arrive. Perhaps they've given up the search. Perhaps they think you're dead.

By this stage in the dream, fear shakes you awake. Phil Labbe wasn't so fortunate. This "dream" was his, and it was as harsh and real as Mount Washington in winter.

New Hampshire's Mount Washington dominates all other peaks in the White Mountains. Its treeless 6,288-foot summit is the year-round home of the Mount Washington Observatory and the permanent transmitting station for WMTW-TV and Radio. By 1981 Phil Labbe had spent more than 30 years as WMTW's chief of maintenance—a unique occupation in a unique location.

His work demanded the skills of an electrician, plumber, mechanic, steeplejack, repairman, and driver, and Labbe was equal to the task. If ten inches of rime ice coated the radio tower, Labbe would scale the 80-foot ladder and chip away. If the summit's diesel engine conked out at midnight in the middle of February, Labbe would leave his Gorham, New Hampshire, home, drive his Thiokol Sprite snow tractor up the eight-mile Mount Washington Auto Road, and coax the engine back to life.

"He was the man who kept the station on the air," observatory director Guy Gosselin explained. "He could do anything. It didn't matter what was broken; he could fix it."

Labbe's maintenance chores and commutes up and down the mountain were usually routine matters during the summer. Then, snarled traffic or a faulty water pump might be the toughest problems he faced. His wintertime work was never as easy. The mountain didn't allow it.

Peter Randall writes in *Mount Washington* that conditions atop this peak deliver "the most severe combination of wind, cold, and icing to be found at any permanently inhabited place on earth." He doesn't exaggerate. Here a major storm track unleashes its power, here December temperatures *average* 5.6 degrees, and here were recorded the world's highest winds—231 miles an hour. Here, too, more than a hundred people have lost their lives.

Phil Labbe knew this well. From the driver's seat of his Thiokol, carrying crews and supplies to the summit, he had seen and felt nearly every winter extreme visited upon the mountain. Avalanches, hurricanes, ice storms, and blinding whiteouts—when wind and snow

relieve fellow employees already on the summit. Moderate winds and light snows indicated nothing unusual on top.

The first four-mile leg of the journey went without a hitch. This stretch of the Auto Road crisscrosses the mountain's lower eastern flank, where dense forests provide shelter from the wind. While packed ice and snow blanketed the road, the Thiokol's steel treads held the vehicle firmly on track. Beyond the Halfway House at the Auto Road's midpoint, however, the weather grew nasty.

Above the forest buffer, gusting winds rocked the Thiokol as it chugged along the mountain's upper ridges. The higher they drove, the more often drifting snows—backed by gale-force winds—cut visibility of the road to quick glimpses. Labbe eased back on the accelerator and gently eased the machine forward, moving only when the wind paused. By 11:30 A.M. he'd seen enough.

A mile from the summit, Labbe decided to scrub the trip. Constant wind speed had reached 100 miles an hour, and further advance was impossible. If they ventured higher, Labbe knew they'd be exposed to the full force of the storm.

Their retreat was no picnic. "I turned around at the Seven Mile Post and made it across the Seven Mile Stretch," Labbe said, "but as we came around the Hairpin Turn, I lost the road." He halted on this icy plateau not knowing—literally—which way to turn. One choice remained.

Leaving the Thiokol idling, Labbe stepped outside and walked a few yards ahead, looking for any sign of the road. He'd done this dozens of times before under similar conditions and had always found the way. But not this time.

"Usually I never walk farther than a point where I can look back and see the machine," Labbe explained. "But when I walked forward, I stepped on a patch of ice and slid. I couldn't say how far I slid, but it was far enough, and I got twisted around, so I didn't know which direction to go when I stood up."

Except for bruises, the fall left Labbe unhurt. But he was lost. The wind drowned out the sound of the Thiokol's engine, and blowing snow was all he could see. Labbe did the most sensible thing.

"I walked in one direction, then another, to find the machine. I did that for 15 or 20 minutes until I realized this wouldn't work. Then I decided to head downhill because I figured I'd eventually cross the road."

Despite his predicament, Labbe had several advantages. He wore a snowsuit, cap, and gloves, which

churn together as if mixed by a giant Cuisinart—were as familiar to him as the Auto Road itself.

In his career, he had survived everything the mountain threw his way. And then one day several winters ago a routine trip almost became his last.

Wednesday, December 16, 1981, didn't begin like other twice-monthly shift changes. "Everything went wrong that morning," Labbe remembered. "Something should have told me to stay away from the mountain.

"First, I had to pick up groceries at the store, but the delivery truck was half an hour late. Then, when I got down to the Glen House and loaded all the supplies onto the Thiokol, I locked the snow machine keys in my Ranchero." Another half hour passed before the keys were retrieved, but that wasn't the final snafu. When Labbe went to gas up the Thiokol, he discovered that the pump was frozen; 30 more minutes were lost in thawing out the lines. As it happened, these delays were nearly fatal.

Close to two hours behind schedule, Labbe steered the Thiokol onto the Auto Road and began his ascent. With him were four WMTW-TV crewmen coming to

Opposite page, top left: *Long plumes of rime ice feather a water tank atop New Hampshire's Mount Washington.*
Above: *Phil Labbe, a veteran and a survivor of the mountain, pilots a Snowcat on a routine descent from the summit.*

gave him reasonable protection from exposure. He also had memorized the mountain in his mind's eye so that, even in a whiteout, he could look for a landmark pointing the way to safety. Most important, he kept calm and focused his attention on escape. "Scared? I didn't have time to get scared."

Labbe plotted his downhill course and began slogging through the snow. By keeping his left shoulder to the wind, he calculated he'd soon walk to the road. In fact, his calculations were correct, and he probably did reach the road near the Hairpin Turn, but the wind's ferocious blasts hid it from view. Between one and three o'clock that afternoon, observatory records show that winds were shrieking at a mean velocity of 103 miles an hour.

To make matters worse, Labbe's vision was impaired. He had forgotten his glasses in the Thiokol, and his unprotected eyes were being repeatedly doused with ice crystals. To see anything, he had to peel congealed ice from his eyes again and again, yanking out all his eyelashes in the process.

Instead of angling to the road as he had planned,

Labbe's route led parallel to the road, traversing the alternately rocky then snowy flats bordered by the Nelson Crag Trail. Here, northeast of the summit cone, he bent his six-foot two-inch frame into the wind just to maintain his balance. The first hour of this effort produced only more confusion.

Kicking a trail through drifts, Labbe discovered his first clue. A telegraph pole was sticking upright out of the eerie arctic landscape. His spirits soared. He believed it was one of a string of poles running up the northern slope of the mountain—a sign directing him to help. It was a false hope. This pole was on the south side of the road—apart from any others—where the mountainside dropped into a forested wilderness.

"From the pole I went out in two or three directions, but I couldn't find a thing," he said. "So I kept on moving with the wind to my shoulder."

Movement was slow and fatiguing. By one o'clock, when rescue teams had begun to assemble, Labbe realized his chances were shrinking. His survival was in his own hands. If he could simply maintain his pace, he reasoned, he'd escape. Like a blind man

Above: *Mount Washington, the highest peak in the Appalachian mountain range, seen from across the fields of Intervale, New Hampshire.* **Below:** *Even in the summertime, a sudden storm can whiten Mount Washington, and strong winds can swiftly turn its summit into one of the most forbidding places on earth.*

trapped in an obstacle course, his path took him close to more danger than he imagined. But he had to keep going.

When able, he leaned and hunched his way forward, shielding his exposed face from the violent wind chill of more than 60 degrees below zero. More often, he crawled. Every yard held tricks.

"I couldn't see anything clearly," he said. "I walked across rocks that I thought were ice and across snow that turned out to be the tops of dwarf fir trees, where I'd cave in up to my armpits. I'd dig out, move a little farther, then cave in again. I've never been so tired in my whole life."

In between his struggles to keep going, Labbe rested briefly. Several times he crouched with his back to the wind and his head tucked low, gasping for air. These short rests gave him time to gather his thoughts.

"There are a lot of things that go through your mind. I thought about my wife and my children and that I might never see them again . . . that I'd never get out . . . that this was the end." But he pressed on.

Two more hours sped by, and the battle started to take its toll. After driving his body against a wall of wind and extracting himself from countless holes in the snow, exhaustion grabbed hold. It required him to stop, and Labbe complied. At the foot of a boxcar-size snowdrift, he got down on his hands and knees and burrowed into the snow. In this warm cave he plunked down and savored the peaceful calm. For ten minutes a sense of relief and drowsiness prevailed. He was almost seduced.

"I thought I was going to stay there," Labbe said, "but I started to get cold and shiver." Luckily, thoughts of his family replaced the dull euphoria of rest. He also remembered what he knew from experience. "Once freezing starts, you get numb and fall asleep, and I knew that would happen if I didn't move."

Wrenching himself to his feet, Labbe went back into the whiteout. "I told myself, 'This old mountain wants me badly, but it isn't going to get me without a fight.' " His resolve paid off, and this time he finally discovered what he had been searching for. Not more than 200 yards from his cave, Labbe encountered another massive drift blocking his path. To keep on course he decided to plod on through. It was a wise choice.

"When I went into the drift, I couldn't see a thing, but coming out I ran into one of the wooden poles marking the side of the road," he said. There was no mistake. "I knew where I was."

That pole marked the edge of the Cragway Drift, a stretch of the road between the Six and Five Mile posts where as much as 30 feet of snow collects during the winter. Labbe was elated. "When I saw it, I went over and hugged it as if it were a woman," he said. "I couldn't have hugged it any tighter."

At last he knew where he was, and the knowledge energized him. He walked down the road for another three-quarters of a mile until he heard the welcome sound of a Thiokol's engine. "When I approached the machine, some fellow was shoveling snow to clear the road. All of a sudden he looked up and started yelling, 'There he is! There he is!' They picked me up and threw me into the machine." The ordeal had ended.

This Thiokol—manned by Al Oxton and Ken Rancourt of the Mount Washington Observatory and Motorola employee Frank Hobley—had followed behind Labbe's machine later that morning. Like Labbe, they had decided to retreat from the storm, though an avalanche and heavy snows slowed their descent. Chance found them near the Five Mile Post when Labbe appeared.

News of his rescue traveled fast. For the 30 volunteers who had been searching for Labbe, it was a profound relief. For the men in Labbe's Thiokol who had remained patiently at the spot where he disappeared, the radio report of his safety was a welcome signal to end their vigil and return to the Glen House.

For Labbe's wife, Germaine, it was something more. She had been sitting "like a stone" waiting by the telephone in Gorham for five hours. When the call came at 4:10 P.M., she remembered the fears she had been fighting. "People had given up hope," she said, "but I tried to think of his experience and know-how."

Aside from a mild case of exposure and fatigue, Labbe was none the worse for his time on the mountain. After a short stay in the hospital, he returned to work to finish his final year before retirement. Today Labbe considers himself a fortunate man.

"I miss the mountain since I was there for so long, but I don't miss it in winter," he said. "I feel I was lucky. If a stranger had been in my place—a person unfamiliar with the mountain—he might not have made it. I was lucky." Lucky and more. ∞

Mount Washington in winter. Wind velocities frequently exceed hurricane force on the summit, but on April 12, 1934, they hit the all-time record—231 miles per hour.

On April 12, 1934, the greatest wind ever measured on the face of the earth—231 miles per hour—was recorded by three weather observers atop Mount Washington, New Hampshire. The previous high of 152 miles per hour had been recorded only a year earlier. Although winds associated with tornadoes are believed to blow several hundred miles per hour, no wind higher than the 1934 howler has ever been recorded. Salvatore Pagliuca was the chief observer on the weather team in the hut on the mountaintop. Cook, forecaster, and repairman Wendell Stephenson and radio operator Alex "Mac" McKenzie were the other team members. This is Wendell Stephenson's account of the record-setting occasion.

We Recorded the Greatest Wind Ever Measured on Earth

BY WENDELL STEPHENSON

COURTESY OF FREDERICK JOHN

Nothing on the radio or the weather maps on April 11, 1934, gave any clue as to the extraordinary events that were about to happen. The temperature was warm for the mountain—low twenties—and a heavy, almost clear ice rime was rapidly covering everything. When we came back in the house after our routine inspection of gauges and recorders, the melting ice from our storm clothes left puddles everywhere.

Mac and I took a break from normal procedures in the late afternoon. This was tea and doughnut time, as we all were fairly free from duties before supper. Sal commented that if the wind kept increasing, we'd keep a 24-hour watch. He'd take the early shift, Mac would go from 1:00 to 4:00 A.M., and I, low man on the totem pole, would get the shift from 4:00 to 7:00 A.M. Well,

it kept getting wilder and wilder, with gusts around 100 miles per hour, so the all-night plan, a rather common occurrence in those days, went into action.

We were all young, in good shape, and happy with our munificent salary. (The first year it had been $5 a month, and now it was $5 a week!) We had no trouble sleeping in our unheated bedroom, so Mac had to thump me awake. In that half-awake state I stood by the stove to dress and attune myself to what was going on outside. I had the tingly feeling that it was blowing about as hard as I'd ever heard it. The house shuddered in a steady throb. You see, up there the wind blows steadily, not in gusts, so it has a tone for any given velocity. I had learned to guess quite accurately how fast the wind was going by, and I decided to check my guess of more than 100 miles per hour.

Above: *An early photograph of the Mount Washington Observatory, covered as usual with a thick mantle of ice.*
Below: *A more recent shot of the summit buildings. Weather observers and others have lived here year-round since 1932.*

Our anemometer sent electric impulses to a recorder in Mac's radio shack. At the passing of a mile of wind, a pen kicked up and made a short, straight line perpendicular to the line on the clock-driven recording sheet. A fast count of the straight lines over a five-minute span could easily be figured to miles per hour. I counted several of the more recent five-minute blocks but couldn't get much over 90 to 100 miles per hour. I knew that was inaccurate, which meant only one thing—so much ice had built up on the mast carrying the anemometer rotor that it was shielding the rotor from the full force of the wind. This happened whenever rime was forming rapidly, and one of us would go up the ladder to the roof, bash and beat the ice away, and scurry down to take a few fast stopwatch readings and make a note on the chart to explain the sudden increase in velocity.

I can wax dramatic from this distance, but then and there it was my job—so into the storm gear and out the door I went. I began to be suspicious of the situation when I could hardly get the door open against the vacuum of the wind screaming by. I was further convinced when I got knocked down as soon as I stepped out. I had leaned, as usual, into the northwest wind, but the blast was from the southeast and dead against the ladder. It took two tries to get started, with me carrying a club to break the ice and trying to keep my parka from blowing up over my head and arms. I wasn't afraid or apprehensive, just annoyed that I had to go so slowly. I hooked a leg around the ladder, hung on madly, and beat away the huge ice shield that had formed. I finally threw the club down, crawled back down the ladder, and ducked around the corner of the house and in the still-stubborn door.

Before I even took off my parka, I grabbed the stopwatch and began counting. The first time I tried I couldn't believe the answer. The second time it still seemed too fast. On the third try I whispered, "Ye gods, 186 miles an hour!"

And so it was. Had I known, I might never have gone out. But there was more. When Sal and Mac came down, I was almost out of control, and, if anything, the wind was even wilder. We sent the 186 figure on our morning weather report, and did we get reactions! The most important and fortunate break came when Dr. C. Brooks of the Blue Hill Observatory in Massachusetts called to check and Mac plugged the anemometer recorder into the radio to let Dr. Brooks time the gusts for awhile. Our new high was the famous 231 miles per hour at 1:21 P.M., which Dr. Brooks also timed to lend support to our claim. Sal held the stopwatch as the gusts' velocity climbed first to 229 and finally to 231.

In 1870 the U.S. Army Signal Corps (the precursor of the U.S. Weather Bureau) sent a team of observers to spend the winter on the summit, to gather weather data.

FROM AN EXPERT, THREE SUREFIRE WAYS TO AVOID CABIN FEVER

☞ According to Ken Rancourt, staff meteorologist at the Mount Washington Observatory (home of the world's worst weather), here's what to do when the weather keeps you indoors:

• Watch the Pitot-static anemometer.
• Monitor the Hayes draft recorder.
• Keep an eye on the anemoscope.

The wind blew ferociously into the afternoon of the twelfth, but by the thirteenth we were back to normal—which for Mount Washington is about 80 miles an hour. The house hadn't blown over, collapsed, or otherwise suffered, thanks to the 20 or more inches of heavy ice rime.

People are always asking me if I was frightened up there that day. Well, I was just a young man not too long out of the University of Chicago. McKenzie hadn't been too long out of Dartmouth either. We were all in our twenties and full of life. Do you know what we did when that wind hit a record high? We cheered! We had recorded the greatest wind ever measured on earth. ∞

Some Other Notable Mount Washington Records

At 6,288 feet above sea level, and smack-dab in the path of storm tracks, Mount Washington, New Hampshire, experiences some of the most fickle and extreme weather in the world. Just about every weather record associated with Mount Washington carries an asterisk next to it, precisely because the extremes of cold, snow, and wind are so much worse than those recorded almost anywhere else in the lower 48 states.

In 1870, the U.S. Army Signal Corps sent an expedition to the summit of Mount Washington to spend the winter tabulating weather information. After the Signal Service became the U.S. Weather Bureau, buildings were erected on the summit, though between 1892 and 1932 no year-round scientific installation was maintained. Here are a few of the records set at the summit since a private group decided to staff and maintain the Mount Washington Observatory in 1932:

Greatest wind speed (world) . . . . 231 mph
(April 12, 1934)

Greatest 5-minute sustained wind speed
(U.S.) . . . . 188 mph (April 12, 1934)

Lowest mean annual temperature
(lower 48 states) . . . . 27.0°F. (1943)

[**Note:** The second-lowest annual mean for *New England* was recorded at First Connecticut Lake in northern New Hampshire—37.3°F.]

Lowest mean summer temperature
(lower 48 states) . . . . 47.2°F.

Most annual precipitation (New England) . . . . . 130.14″
(1969, measured as inches of rain)

Greatest monthly snowfall (New England) . . . . . 172.8″
(February 1969)

Greatest seasonal snowfall (New England) . . . . . 407.6″
(winter of 1969–70)

Weatherwise and Otherwise: The American Almanac

BY ALAN LAKJER

No New England weather history would be complete without at least a brief account of the role almanacs have played in the all-important science of weather forecasting. Although the almanac didn't originate in the United States, it was in this country that it attained its highest form and most devoted and widespread following. Even today, right here in New England, America's oldest continuous publication, Robert B. Thomas's *Old Farmer's Almanac,* continues to entertain and inform, still making long-range weather predictions as it has for the past 200 years.

The almanac has existed in one form or another for a long time, with most scholars tracing its origins back 5,000 years to ancient Egypt. The origin of the word *almanac* is less certain, with various authorities having suggested Germanic, Greek, and Hebrew roots. The most likely of these is the Arabic *al-* ("the") and *manakh* ("reckoning" or "calendar"). (In modern Arabic, *al-manac* actually means "weather.") An almanac is very different from a calendar, however. Whereas a calendar only records time, an almanac actually predicts future events—tides, eclipses, planetary motions, and so on—based on calendar time.

Developed independently in both the Roman Empire and northern Europe, the early "clog" almanacs consisted of wooden blocks on which ancient almanac makers inscribed astronomical information for ready reference. The user could refer to the marks on one side of the block, then turn to another face to line up a second set of inscriptions, which would explain or correspond to the adjacent marks. In later times, scribes produced manuscript almanacs, but only with the introduction of printing in fifteenth-century Europe did the almanac really begin its career as a widely read and indispensable resource.

In America, as elsewhere, the almanac was one of the first fruits of the printing press. The Stephen Daye Press of Cambridge, Massachusetts, was founded in 1638, and one year later it issued an almanac drafted by Captain William Pierce. During the rest of the seventeenth century, almanacs continued to be published in Cambridge and were referred to as "philomaths" (*philomath* means literally, "lover of learning"). These philomaths were typically long on astronomical information and short on prognostication. In fact, although Harvard astronomer Thomas Brattle included a few meteorological notes in his 1694 almanac, he also expressed his disdain for weather forecasts: "Astrologicall Predictions . . . serve only to Delude and Amuse the Vulgar . . . [they are] not fitting to be joyned with Astronomical Certainties."

A great blow for "the Vulgar" was struck in 1674, when the Massachusetts General Court granted engraver John Foster the right to set up a printing shop of his own in Boston. Foster's almanac for 1676 offered some practical meteorological advice for farmers. Presented in a popular style, this advice distinguished his product from the Cambridge philomaths. In fact, Foster's almanac became the prototype for the great number of farmer's almanacs that soon came into being.

In 1687 John Tulley, a mariner from Saybrook,

1871. JUNE, Sixth Month.

Astronomical Calculations.

☉'s Declination.

Days.	d.	m.	Days.	d.	m.	Days.	d.	m.	Days.	d.	m.	Days.	d.	m.
1	22N.	4	7	22	46	13	23	13	19	23	26	25	23	24
2	22	12	8	22	52	14	23	17	20	23	27	26	23	23
3	22	20	9	22	57	15	23	19	21	23	27	27	23	20
4	22	27	10	23	2	16	23	22	22	23	27	28	23	18
5	22	34	11	23	6	17	23	24	23	23	27	29	23	15
6	22	40	12	23	10	18	23	25	24	23	26	30	23N.	11

○ Full Moon, 3d day, 1h. 43m., morning.

☾ Last Quarter, 9th day, 7h. 53m., evening.

● New Moon, 17th day, 9h. 45m., evening.

☽ First Quarter, 25th day, 6h. 0m., evening.

Day of the Year.	Day of Month.	Day of the Week.	☉ Rises. h. m.	☉ Sets. h. m.	Length of Days. h. m.	Day's Incre. h. m.	Sun Fast.	Moon's Age.	Full Sea, Boston. Morn h.	Full Sea, Boston. Even h.	☽'s Place.	☽ Sets. h. m.	☽ Souths. h. m.
152	1	Th.	4 26	7 29	15 3	5 59	3	13	$9\frac{3}{4}$	$10\frac{1}{4}$	sec.	3 23	10 54
153	2	Fr.	4 26	7 30	15 4	6 0	2	14	$10\frac{3}{4}$	$11\frac{1}{4}$	thi.	3 59	11 54
154	3	Sa.	4 25	7 31	15 6	6 2	2	○	$11\frac{1}{2}$	12	thi.	rises.	morn.
155	4	*SU*	4 25	7 31	15 6	6 2	2	16	—	$0\frac{1}{2}$	kn.	9 25	0 58
156	5	M.	4 25	7 32	15 7	6 3	2	17	1	$1\frac{1}{2}$	kn.	10 26	2 2
157	6	Tu.	4 24	7 33	15 9	6 5	2	18	$1\frac{3}{4}$	$2\frac{1}{4}$	legs	11 15	3 5
158	7	W.	4 24	7 34	15 10	6 6	2	19	$2\frac{3}{4}$	$3\frac{1}{4}$	legs	11 54	4 4
159	8	Th.	4 24	7 34	15 10	6 6	1	20	$3\frac{3}{4}$	4	legs	morn.	4 58
160	9	Fr.	4 23	7 34	15 11	6 7	1	21	$4\frac{1}{2}$	5	feet	0 27	5 48
161	10	Sa.	4 23	7 35	15 12	6 8	1	22	$5\frac{1}{2}$	6	feet	0 52	6 34
162	11	*SU*	4 23	7 36	15 13	6 9	1	23	$6\frac{1}{4}$	$6\frac{3}{4}$	h'd	1 18	7 18
163	12	M.	4 23	7 36	15 13	6 9	1	24	$7\frac{1}{4}$	$7\frac{3}{4}$	h'd	1 41	8 0
164	13	Tu.	4 23	7 37	15 14	6 10	0	25	8	$8\frac{1}{2}$	n'k	2 5	8 42
165	14	W.	4 23	7 37	15 14	6 10	0	26	$8\frac{3}{4}$	$9\frac{1}{4}$	n'k	2 28	9 24
166	15	Th.	4 23	7 38	15 15	6 11	S.	27	$9\frac{3}{4}$	10	arm	2 55	10 8
167	16	Fr.	4 23	7 38	15 15	6 11	0	28	$10\frac{1}{4}$	$10\frac{3}{4}$	arm	3 25	10 54
168	17	Sa.	4 23	7 38	15 15	6 11	1	●	11	$11\frac{1}{2}$	arm	4 0	11 41
169	18	*SU*	4 23	7 39	15 16	6 12	1	1	$11\frac{3}{4}$	12	br.	sets.	0 30
170	19	M.	4 23	7 39	15 16	6 12	1	2	—	$0\frac{1}{2}$	br.	9 10	1 20
171	20	Tu.	4 23	7 39	15 16	6 12	1	3	$0\frac{3}{4}$	1	br.	9 53	2 10
172	21	W.	4 23	7 39	15 16	Dec.	1	4	$1\frac{1}{2}$	$1\frac{3}{4}$	h'rt	10 31	3 0
173	22	Th.	4 24	7 40	15 16	0 0	2	5	$2\frac{1}{4}$	$2\frac{1}{2}$	h'rt	11 4	3 48
174	23	Fr.	4 24	7 40	15 16	0 0	2	6	3	$3\frac{1}{4}$	bel.	11 34	4 35
175	24	Sa.	4 24	7 40	15 16	0 0	2	7	$3\frac{3}{4}$	4	bel.	morn.	5 22
176	25	*SU*	4 25	7 40	15 15	0 1	2	8	$4\frac{1}{2}$	5	bel.	0 1	6 8
177	26	M.	4 25	7 40	15 15	0 1	2	9	$5\frac{1}{4}$	$5\frac{3}{4}$	rei.	0 27	6 56
178	27	Tu.	4 25	7 40	15 15	0 1	3	10	$6\frac{1}{4}$	$6\frac{3}{4}$	rei.	0 52	7 45
179	28	W.	4 26	7 40	15 14	0 2	3	11	$7\frac{1}{4}$	$7\frac{3}{4}$	sec.	1 20	8 38
180	29	Th.	4 26	7 40	15 14	0 2	3	12	$8\frac{1}{4}$	$8\frac{3}{4}$	sec.	1 53	9 35
181	30	Fr.	4 27	7 40	15 13	0 3	3	13	$9\frac{1}{2}$	10	thi.	2 32	10 36

JUNE hath 30 days. 1871

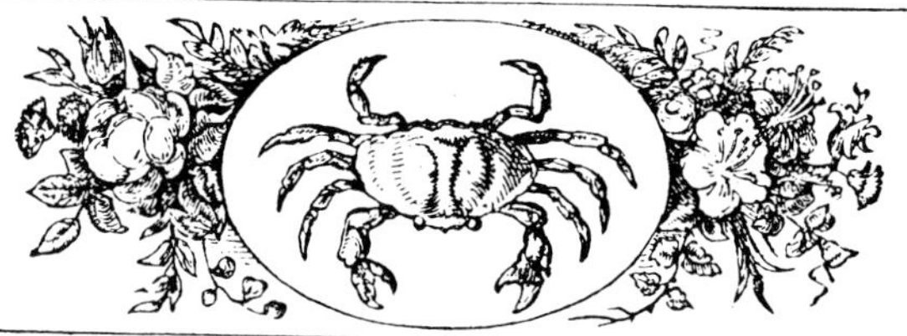

June is the pearl of our New England year.
Her coming startles. Long she lies in wait,
Makes many a feint, peeps forth, draws coyly back,
Then from some southern ambush in the sky,
With one great gush of blossom storms the world.

J. R. LOWELL.

D. M.	D. W.	Aspects, Holidays, Events, Weather, &c.
1	Th.	**Nicomede.** *High wind,*
2	Fr.	*with signs of rain.*
3	Sa.	Very hi. ti. ☽ in Perigee.
4	A.	Trinity Sun. ☽ runs low.
5	Mo.	[☌ ♅ ♀. ☌ ♄ ☽.
6	Tu.	*Much finer.*
7	W.	New Hampshire Legislature meets.
8	Th.	**Corpus Christi.** *Some rain*
9	Fr.	Charles Dickens died, aged 58, 1870.
10	Sa.	☿ gr. elongation W. *this*
11	A.	1st Sun. af. Tr. **St. Barna.**
12	Mo.	☿ gr. hel. lat. S. *time.*
13	Tu.	Very low tides. *Quite*
14	W.	Battle of Marengo, 1800. *warm.*
15	Th.	☌ ☿ ☽. *Cooler.*
16	Fr.	☽ in Apogee. *Very*
17	Sa.	☉ eclipsed, invis. at Wash.
18	A.	2d Sun. af. Tr. ☽ runs hi.
19	Mo.	High tides. [☌ ♃ ☽.
20	Tu.	☌ ♅ ☽. [Longest day.
21	W.	☉ ent. ♋. Summer begins.
22	Th.	{20th. Very severe thunder storm, with hail, in New England, 1870.
23	Fr.	*warm.*
24	Sa.	**St. John Baptist.**
25	A.	3d Sun. af. Trin. ☌ ♂ ☽.
26	Mo.	□ ♂ ☉. *Dull and*
27	Tu.	Low tides. *heavy weather.*
28	W.	☍ ♄ ☉. *Showers*
29	Th.	**St. Peter.** *in*
30	Fr.	☌ ♃ ☉. *many places.*

Farmer's Calendar.

PLANTING must now be hurried up and quickly finished. It is getting rather late to put in corn, yet many are still behind with that. The first hoeing presses also. In fact there is work enough at this season. As to Swedes, it is generally thought that the middle or 20th of the month is in season, but I have made up my mind that it is a good plan to get in the seed as early as the 10th, if you can. Turnips want a light, warm soil. Mangolds, on the other hand, prefer a stronger and heavier soil. They ought to go in earlier, too. It is a good plan to get through with planting so as to leave time for hoeing before the haying begins to press, and I like to begin the latter towards the end of this month, so as to get fairly into it before the Fourth of July. It is always best to keep a little ahead of work, and not be driven by it. If you begin late everything seems to drag, and it makes the summer go rather hard. If you keep up square with the work you feel greater pride and satisfaction in it, and everything goes smoother. I hope you sowed some fodder corn and millet, or some other crop for soiling. The pastures will be getting short by and by, and the cows need a little extra feed to keep up the milk.

Connecticut, issued an almanac with the first real weather forecasts in America, and other publishers soon followed suit. Tulley also added essays and humorous material to his almanacs, and, though still relatively short in length, the new farmer's almanacs began to bridge the gap between pure science and popular literature.

With Tulley's almanac came the convention of printing brief forecasts in a vertical column on the calendar pages of the book, next to the dates corresponding to the weather predictions. Space was at a premium, and a lengthy forecast, stretched out over a week or so of dates, could cover many contingencies and enhance the "accuracy" of the forecasts. Even Ben Franklin in his *Poor Richard's Almanack* for 1737 used this fudge factor, claiming that, if his forecasts were inaccurate, it

1990	JUNE, THE SIXTH MONTH

Anything north of the Arctic Circle receives 24 hours of daylight from the solstice on. Antares is in the southeast; its name ("not Mars") indicates that, like Mars, it is red and should not be confused with it. Spica, the brightest star of Virgo the Virgin, and Arcturus are high overhead, the Milky Way low in the east, and in it can be found the Summer Triangle consisting of the bright stars Deneb, Vega, and Altair. Saturn rises in the evening and stands very close to the Moon in the morning hours of the 11th. The summer solstice is on the 21st at 10:33 A.M. EST; on this day the Moon is at perigee (closest to the Earth). Uranus is at opposition on the 29th and Mars is at perihelion (closest to the Sun) on the 30th. Left of orange Arcturus in the south is the cup-shaped Corona Borealis, the Northern Crown.

ASTRONOMICAL CALCULATIONS

○	Full Moon	8th day	6th hour	1st min.
☾	Last Quarter	15th day	23rd hour	48th min.
●	New Moon	22nd day	13th hour	55th min.
☽	First Quarter	29th day	17th hour	7th min.

ADD 1 hour for Daylight Saving Time.

FOR POINTS OUTSIDE BOSTON SEE KEY LETTER CORRECTIONS — PAGES 80-84

Day of Year	Day of Month	Day of Week	☉ Rises h. m.	Key	☉ Sets h. m.	Key	Length of Days h. m.	Sun Fast m.	Full Sea Boston A.M.	Full Sea Boston P.M.	☽ Rises h. m.	Key	☽ Sets h. m.	Key	Declination of sun ° ′	☽ Place	☽ Age
152	1	Fr.	4 10	A	7 14	E	15 04	18	5½	6¼	12 P.M. 57	D	12 A.M. 29	C	22N.05	LEO	8
153	2	Sa.	4 10	A	7 15	E	15 05	18	6½	7	2 00	D	12 49	C	22 12	VIR	9
154	3	**G**	4 09	A	7 16	E	15 07	18	7½	7¾	3 02	E	1 09	B	22 20	VIR	10
155	4	M.	4 09	A	7 17	E	15 08	18	8½	8½	4 05	E	1 32	B	22 27	VIR	11
156	5	Tu.	4 08	A	7 17	E	15 09	18	9¼	9¼	5 07	E	1 57	B	22 34	VIR	12
157	6	W.	4 08	A	7 18	E	15 10	17	10	10	6 09	E	2 27	A	22 40	LIB	13
158	7	Th.	4 08	A	7 18	E	15 10	17	10¾	10¾	7 08	E	3 03	A	22 46	SCO	14
159	8	Fr.	4 08	A	7 19	E	15 11	17	11¼	11¼	8 01	E	3 48	A	22 52	OPH	15
160	9	Sa.	4 08	A	7 20	E	15 12	17	—	12	8 48	E	4 39	A	22 57	SAG	16
161	10	**G**	4 07	A	7 20	E	15 13	17	12	12½	9 27	E	5 38	A	23 01	SAG	17
162	11	M.	4 07	A	7 21	E	15 14	16	12½	1¼	10 00	E	6 42	B	23 05	SAG	18
163	12	Tu.	4 07	A	7 21	E	15 14	16	1¼	2	10 28	E	7 48	B	23 09	CAP	19
164	13	W.	4 07	A	7 22	E	15 15	16	2	2¾	10 53	D	8 54	C	23 13	CAP	20
165	14	Th.	4 07	A	7 22	E	15 15	16	2¾	3½	11 16	D	10 00	D	23 16	AQU	21
166	15	Fr.	4 07	A	7 23	E	15 16	16	3½	4¼	11 P.M. 38	C	11 A.M. 12	D	23 19	AQU	22
167	16	Sa.	4 07	A	7 23	E	15 16	15	4½	5	— —	–	12 P.M. 23	D	23 21	PSC	23
168	17	**G**	4 07	A	7 23	E	15 16	15	5½	6	12 A.M. 02	B	1 36	E	23 23	PSC	24
169	18	M.	4 07	A	7 24	E	15 17	15	6½	6¾	12 28	B	2 53	E	23 24	PSC	25
170	19	Tu.	4 07	A	7 24	E	15 17	15	7½	7¾	1 00	B	4 12	E	23 25	ARI	26
171	20	W.	4 07	A	7 24	E	15 17	15	8½	8¾	1 39	A	5 31	E	23 26	ARI	27
172	21	Th.	4 07	A	7 24	E	15 17	14	9½	9¾	2 29	A	6 44	E	23 26	TAU	28
173	22	Fr.	4 08	A	7 25	E	15 17	14	10½	10½	3 31	A	7 46	E	23 26	TAU	0
174	23	Sa.	4 08	A	7 25	E	15 17	14	11¼	11½	4 43	B	8 36	E	23 25	GEM	1
175	24	**G**	4 08	A	7 25	E	15 17	14	—	12¼	6 00	B	9 14	E	23 24	GEM	2
176	25	M.	4 08	A	7 25	E	15 17	13	12¼	1	7 17	B	9 44	D	23 23	CAN	3
177	26	Tu.	4 09	A	7 25	E	15 16	13	1¼	2	8 30	C	10 09	D	23 21	LEO	4
178	27	W.	4 09	A	7 25	E	15 16	13	2¼	2¾	9 39	D	10 32	D	23 18	LEO	5
179	28	Th.	4 10	A	7 25	E	15 15	13	3	3¾	10 45	D	10 52	C	23 15	LEO	6
180	29	Fr.	4 10	A	7 25	E	15 15	13	4	4½	11 A.M. 49	D	11 13	B	23 12	VIR	7
181	30	Sa.	4 10	A	7 25	E	15 15	12	5	5½	12 P.M. 52	E	11 P.M. 35	B	23N.09	VIR	8

OLD FARMER'S ALMANAC 1990

JUNE hath 30 days.	1990

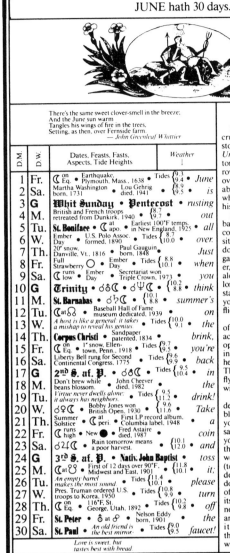

There's the same sweet clover-smell in the breeze;
And the June sun warm
Tangles his wings of fire in the trees,
Setting, as then, over Fernside farm.
— *John Greenleaf Whittier*

D.M.	D.W.	Dates, Feasts, Fasts, Aspects, Tide Heights	*Weather* ↓
1	Fr.	☾ on Eq. • Earthquake, Plymouth, Mass., 1638 • Tides {9.3 9.4 •	*June*
2	Sa.	Martha Washington born, 1731 • Lou Gehrig died, 1941 • {8.9 9.5 •	*is*
3	**G**	**Whit Sunday • Pentecost** •	*rusting*
4	M.	British and French troops retreated from Dunkirk, 1940 • {8.7 9.7 •	*out*
5	Tu.	**St. Boniface** • ☾ at apo. • Earliest 100°F temps. in New England, 1925 •	*all*
6	W.	Ember Day • U.S. Polo Assoc. formed, 1890 • Tides {8.7 10.0 •	*over.*
7	Th.	20″ snow, Danville, Vt., 1816 • Paul Gauguin born, 1848 •	*Just*
8	Fr.	Full Strawberry ○ • Ember Day • Tides {8.8 10.1 •	*when*
9	Sa.	☾ runs low • Ember Day • Secretariat won Triple Crown, 1973 •	*you*
10	**G**	**Trinity** • ☌♅☾ • ☌♆☾ • {10.2 8.8 •	*think*
11	M.	**St. Barnabas** • ☌♄☾ • {10.1 8.8 •	*summer's*
12	Tu.	☾ at ☊ • Baseball Hall of Fame museum dedicated, 1939 •	*on*
13	W.	*A host is like a general: it takes a mishap to reveal his genius.* • Tides {10.0 9.1 •	*the*
14	Th.	**Corpus Christi** • Sandpaper patented, 1834 •	*brink,*
15	Fr.	☾ on Eq. • 1″ snow, Ellentown, Penn., 1918 • Tides {9.7 9.5 •	*you're*
16	Sa.	Liberty Bell rung for Second Continental Congress, 1775 • Tides {9.6 9.9 •	*back*
17	**G**	**2nd S. af. P.** • ☌♅☾ • Tides {9.5 10.4 •	*in*
18	M.	Don't brew while beans blossom. • John Cheever died, 1982 •	*the*
19	Tu.	*Virtue never dwells alone: it always has neighbors.* • Tides {9.5 11.2 •	*drink!*
20	W.	☌♀☾ • Bobby Jones won British Open, 1930 • {9.6 11.6 •	*Take*
21	Th.	Summer Solstice • ☾ at peri. • First LP record album, Columbia label, 1948 •	*a*
22	Fr.	☾ runs high • New ● • Fred Astaire died, 1987 •	*coin*
23	Sa.	☌♃☾ • Rain tomorrow means a poor harvest. • {10.1 12.0 •	*and*
24	**G**	**3rd S. af. P.** • **Nativ. John Baptist** •	*toss*
25	M.	☾ at ☋ • First of 12 days over 90°F, Midwest and East, 1901 • {11.8 10.1 •	*it;*
26	Tu.	*An empty barrel makes the most sound.* • Tides {11.4 10.1 •	*please*
27	W.	Pres. Truman ordered U.S. troops to Korea, 1950 • Tides {10.8 9.9 •	*turn*
28	Th.	☾ on Eq. • 116°F, St. George, Utah, 1892 • Tides {10.2 9.8 •	*off*
29	Fr.	**St. Peter** • ♅ at ☍ • Nelson Eddy born, 1901 •	*the*
30	Sa.	**St. Paul** • *An old friend is the best mirror.* • Tides {9.0 9.5	*faucet!*

Love is sweet, but tastes best with bread.

Farmer's Calendar

In early summer the blackfly is the cruel overseer of gardeners and other stooped workers. Imagine a scene of *Uncle Tom's Cabin* inspiration: a cotton field; slaves bent over the endless rows; striding among them the fiend overseer, cracking his long whip just above the harvesters' heads so anyone who stands for a moment's relief from his work feels the sting.

In blackfly season that little humpbacked bug no bigger than a gnat becomes a slavedriver of a sadism exquisite and relentless. As long as you remain down close to the ground — weeding the garden, thinning, fixing the lawn mower, changing a tire — he will leave you alone. The moment you can finally no longer bear your bent-over position and stand, the flies descend on you. You find your head and shoulders in a cloud of flies. Quickly you kneel again.

No doubt the blackfly's persecution of gardeners who slack off their work is accounted for by some arcane force, operating automatically on the lives of insects, that makes them fly at a certain height above the ground at certain times. The effect on us is the same as though the fly's merciless hounding was bought with a planter's gold.

In the woods the mosquito and the deerfly work a subtle variation on the blackfly's cruel attentions. Suppose you are cutting wood, using a chain saw. You will find that the bugs spare you so long as the saw is running — that is, so long as you are actively at work on your task. Turn off the saw (to rest, say), and the mosquitoes and deerflies immediately close in. No doubt they are kept away by the racket of the saw's engine, by the smoke of its exhaust, and not by a deliberate neglect that lasts just as long as you are at your job. The effect is the same as it is with the blackflies outside the woods. Loggers know: the bugs work for the boss.

1990 OLD FARMER'S ALMANAC 63

Opposite page: *A typical calendar page spread, featuring astronomical data and weather predictions, from the 1871 edition of* The Old Farmer's Almanac. **Above:** *A calendar page spread from the 1990* Old Farmer's Almanac. *After two hundred years (and many different editors), very little has changed.*

was the printer's fault for rearranging the predictions to make room for holidays.

What methods or formulas did these early almanac makers use to devise their long-range weather forecasts? The answer varies from publisher to publisher, but in general almanac forecasts relied on the perceived influences of celestial motion and activity on the earth and its weather. In 1680 John Foster published an essay on the effect of the (then known) seven planets on weather. Later forecasters based their predictions on complex local weather observations, on cyclical theories of weather development, or on the famous lunar chart attributed to English astronomer Sir John Herschel (1792–1871). Herschel's lunar chart purported to predict weather for any location on earth, provided the times of the moon's phases were known.

HERSCHEL'S LUNAR CHART

In summer, if the new moon, first-quarter moon, full moon, or last-quarter moon occurs at the times listed in the left-hand column, the weather conditions in the right-hand column will prevail:

12 midnight to 2 A.M.	Fair
2 A.M. to 4 A.M.	Cold and showers
4 A.M. to 6 A.M.	Rain
6 A.M. to 8 A.M.	Wind and rain
8 A.M. to 10 A.M.	Changeable
10 A.M. to 12 noon	Intermittent showers
12 noon to 2 P.M.	Heavy rain
2 P.M. to 4 P.M.	Changeable
4 P.M. to 6 P.M.	Fair
6 P.M. to 8 P.M.	Fair (if wind northwest)
8 P.M. to 10 P.M.	Rain (if wind south or southwest)
10 P.M. to 12 midnight	Fair

In winter, if the new moon, first-quarter moon, full moon, or last-quarter moon occurs at the times below, you may expect:

12 midnight to 2 A.M.	Frost (if wind is not from southwest)
2 A.M. to 4 A.M.	Snow and wind
4 A.M. to 6 A.M.	Rain
6 A.M. to 8 A.M.	Stormy
8 A.M. to 10 A.M.	Cold (if wind west)
10 A.M. to 12 noon	Cold and high winds
12 noon to 2 P.M.	Snow and rain
2 P.M. to 4 P.M.	Fair and mild
4 P.M. to 6 P.M.	Fair
6 P.M. to 8 P.M.	Fair and frosty (if wind north)
8 P.M. to 10 P.M.	Rain and snow (if wind south)
10 P.M. to 12 midnight	Fair and frosty

The lunar chart attributed to English astronomer Sir John Herschel was said by some to be able to predict weather for any location on earth, provided only that the forecaster knew the times of moon phases.

Whatever formula, or combination of formulas, an almanac forecaster uses, he or she is bound to miss the mark with some considerable frequency. So frustrating is the art of making long-range weather predictions that more than a few almanac editors have been known to throw in the towel. Thomas G. Fessenden, the editor of *The New England Farmer's Almanac,* boldly asserted in 1832: "The time is rapidly approaching when the prognostications of Calendar-Conjurors will rank with the exploded fooleries and atrocities of witchcraft, palmistry, astrology, etc., etc."

He was wrong, of course. Even before 1832, weather forecasts had become so integral a part of American almanacs that the public demanded the predictions and felt cheated without them, regardless (it would seem) of their accuracy. A few years after his pronouncement, Fessenden was forced to reintroduce his forecasts in order to stay in business.

Even the venerable *Old Farmer's Almanac* at one time tried to stifle its weather forecasts. For a brief period during the 1930s, the publishers substituted U.S. Weather Bureau "weather averages" for the usual forecasts. "Put one foot on a cake of ice," wrote one disgusted reader in 1938, "and your other foot in a pail of boiling water, and the 'average' says you feel just right!" Since 1939, when the current publishers purchased *The Old Farmer's Almanac,* the weather predictions have been reinstated and expanded to encompass 16 weather regions in the continental United States.

When Robert Bailey Thomas founded *The Farmer's Almanack* in 1792 (the "Old" was added to the title in 1832 to distinguish the annual from its many imitators), his publication resembled many other almanacs of the day, particularly those of his Worcester neighbor, Isaiah Thomas (the two men were unrelated). In his preface to the first edition of 1793, Robert B. addressed the issue of weather predictions: "As to my judgment of the weather, I need say but little; for you will in one year's time, without any assistance of mine, very easily discover how near I have come to the truth."

Whatever his patrons may have thought of Robert B.'s forecasts for 1793, they obviously were sufficiently impressed to keep buying his almanac. By 1803, Thomas reported, sales of his publication had reached a level "unprecedented by any other Almanack published in the New England States." Today, approximately nine million people read *The Old Farmer's Almanac* each year. Current editor Judson Hale, Sr., isn't at all sure why the publication is so popular: "To try to explain why this little yellow-covered annual continues not only to endure but to remain a best-seller would be as difficult as it would have been to persuade Calvin Coolidge to sing tenor to 'Drink to Me Only with Thine Eyes.'"

The Old Farmer's Almanac weather forecasts are both the heart and soul of the book and a matter of the utmost interest to many readers, whether they actually trust the predictions or not. Every year in the early fall, before the *Almanac* goes on sale, mothers call in looking for favorable days on which to schedule their daughters' weddings. A few years ago the Milford, New Hampshire, town road agent telephoned to ask how severe the coming winter would be so he could figure out how much road salt to buy.

Just how accurate *are* the long-range forecasts in *The Old Farmer's Almanac* and other American almanacs? Analyzing the success of forecasts from old-time almanacs is next to impossible, given the fact that the National Weather Service (formerly the U.S. Weather Bureau) has maintained official records only for the last century or so. Tradition gives *The Old Farmer's Almanac* an 80 percent accuracy rating, and, as editor Hale often says, "We wouldn't *dream* of messing with tradition!" Skeptics often take the *Almanac* to task for missing major events such as the great midwestern drought of 1988, but these same skeptics are usually unwilling to admit that the forecast for June 9, 1953 ("Heavy Squall and That's Not All!") presaged the tornado that struck Worcester County in Massachusetts. Clearly, loose interpretation cuts both ways. Tradition aside, some readers have compared *The Old Farmer's Almanac*'s long-range predictions with National Weather Service forecasts over a period of time and either have found their overall accuracy to be about the same or have given a slight edge to the *Almanac*.

On one hand, the way in which long-range weather forecasts are prepared for *The Old Farmer's Almanac* hasn't changed much in almost 200 years. The current publisher still jealously guards the secret formula devised by Robert B. Thomas in 1792. On the other hand, the *Almanac* now uses the most modern scientific data available in formulating its forecasts. Dr. Richard Head, formerly chief solar physicist for NASA, provides calculations based on predicted solar activity, which in turn suggest what the weather on earth will be like, on a day-to-day basis, over the next 18 months. The procedure for making these predictions is extremely complicated and takes into account many factors, including sunspot cycles, seasonal variations of the earth's position relative to the sun, and the nature of atmospheric and ocean currents. The basic weather philosophy of *The Old Farmer's Almanac*, which appears in each year's edition, perhaps sums it up best:

> *We believe nothing in the universe occurs haphazardly; there is a cause-and-effect pattern to all phenomena, including weather. It follows, therefore, that we believe weather is predictable. It is obvious, however, that neither we nor anyone else has as yet gained sufficient insight into the mysteries of the universe to predict weather with anything resembling total accuracy.*

Robert Bailey Thomas, founder and first editor of The Old Farmer's Almanac.

The beauty and fascination of weather forecasting lies in the fact that it is not (and probably never will be) an exact and infallible science. Indeed, the art of prognostication—both weatherwise and otherwise—has exalted the almanac above its former status as a useful but rather dry astronomical tool and has helped create an American institution that is still read and revered today for its wit, wisdom, and tradition. ∞

One perennial concern among Americans is whether Christmas will be "green" (or, more accurately, "brown") or "white" (the better to indulge in nostalgia amid a Currier & Ives backdrop). In the December 1966 issue of *Yankee,* intrepid reporter Con Dent went in search of the man with the answers: Dr. C.G. Abbot, author of "A Long Range Forecast of United States Precipitation" (Vol. 139, No. 9, of the Smithsonian miscellaneous collections). Dent didn't find what he was looking for, but the trip did turn out to be educational.

Will This Christmas Be Green or White?

Upon the publication of the Smithsonian document, this writer betook himself to Washington, D.C., and looked up Dr. Abbot. The looking up took the better part of a day—for the Smithsonian itself is about as large as my hometown—and Dr. Abbot's office is private as well as carefully hidden. He was not there anyway, so the hunt became one of finding his house number in a suburb of carefully hidden numbers.

There he was, however. After I told him where I lived, he explained he was also a native of a New Hampshire town. Immediately we were friends. I explained I was interested in his long-range forecasts, and he suggested I join him at the landing of the front stairs on his second floor. There he produced two huge rolls of what I am certain was toilet tissue. He rolled one of these down the stairs. We followed, *not* rolling. He continued to ravel it up and down his 60-foot-long living room and, when the end of it came up, he had covered perhaps half the floor of that room. He then unrolled the second scroll. This finished the living room and spread over all of the dining room, the pantry, and part of the kitchen floors.

"There it all is," he then announced, "and you can see it for yourself."

I should love to have had a photograph of Dr. Abbot and myself during the next hour and a half. There we were, on hands and knees, following the tracings on these rolls as he explained to me (who little understood) the highs, the lows, the valleys, the peaks, the variations, the modifications, and all else, including absolute verification.

Exhausted, arthritic, lame, bedazzled, and confused, I left loving him, but with a belief unshaken to this day that, if anybody could tell in advance whether or not Christmas 1966 would be white or green, Dr. Abbot (and his Vol. 139, No. 9) could do so.

Out to Sea in Search of Weather

BY JAY F. BUTERA

fficially it was called the Atlantic Weather Project. It began in 1940, and for the next 37 years a fleet of specially outfitted Coast Guard cutters carried teams of meteorological observers into the North Atlantic. The ships would drift, steam, pitch, and pound in mid-ocean while Weather Bureau technicians launched weather balloons and gathered data, which they radioed to shore every three hours. Coast Guard crews of more than a hundred seamen operated the cutters and stood ready to assist passing ships and planes by providing weather bulletins, navigation aids, and—when necessary—rescue operations.

Some of the most dramatic rescues of maritime history were conducted by Coast Guard cutters on weather patrol. The project was mankind's way of wrestling with the great Atlantic Ocean—to save the lives it tried to claim and to sound the secrets of its weather.

A typical weather patrol lasted 30 days. The ship would spend 4 to 5 days steaming to its assigned ocean station, 21 days on station, and another 4 or 5 days running back home.

Ocean station was the name given to the area of sea assigned to a weather ship. Each station was a 100-square-mile patch of ocean situated, as a Coast Guard seaman once said, "between no place and nowhere." American ocean stations were located as far north as Greenland, with the southernmost station set in the hurricane track off Cape Hatteras, North Carolina.

The various ocean stations received names according to the phonetic alphabet: Alpha, Bravo, Charlie, Echo, and so on.

It was a weather ship's duty to remain on its ocean station—no matter what. Nature might kick up with a force that sent other ships scudding toward safer waters or limping into port, but a weather ship kept to its mark through thick and thin.

"You just sat out there," recalled Ken Gove of Warwick, Rhode Island, veteran of more than 130 patrols as a Weather Bureau observer. "And whatever came through, you knew you were going to ride it out. I saw winds out there of around a hundred knots. I saw seas that were probably 55 or 60 feet high. When that ship was bounding around like an empty beer barrel, all you could do was hold on. After bouncing off the bulkheads for 21 days, you'd come home from a trip, take off your shirt, and count up the bruises."

As it was, the worse the weather got, the more important a weather ship's mission became. Its chances of being called to a rescue increased with the wind speed and sea state. At the same time, the weather information the ship was gathering became increasingly important. "When the weather's good, nobody cares too much about it," said George Poole, who directed the project's logistics for the Weather Bureau. "But when it gets bad, everyone wants to know what's going on."

Consequently, there were only three conditions under which a weather ship could leave its ocean station. First, of course, would be when she was physically relieved by another cutter. The second condition would be if she were called off to search and rescue. Last of all would be if the ship were damaged, disabled, or in a situation that put the vessel in immediate danger.

Immediate danger, however, is a relative term; one man's danger is another man's routine. For weather ships on ocean station, the definition of the term was stretched to its upper limits. To illustrate this, here is an excerpt from a message transmitted from the weather ship *Humbolt.* The message gives some idea of conditions that did *not* constitute enough danger for the ship to abandon her mission:

Took exceptionally large sea aboard at about amidships . . . sea swept up and over superstructure . . . spray shield with two heavy stiffeners buckled . . . watertight doors to laundry and to athwartship passage together with door frames very badly buckled . . . ladder to superstructure deck bent . . . two boats broken out of chain gripes and holed . . . not possible to determine all damage due to darkness, heavy seas, and coating of ice . . . proceeding 13 knots with a 45-knot wind and average 30-foot-high sea. . . .

On station in the North Atlantic, freezing spray could quickly turn a cutter into a floating iceberg. Crewmen had to beat off the accumulated ice with baseball bats.

On the northern stations, ice was a constant threat. Freezing spray would coat the ship's deck, rails, and superstructure with heavy saltwater ice. It could build up as fast as two inches per hour, and if enough were allowed to accumulate, it could make the ship top-heavy and more likely to capsize. To avoid this accumulation, the cutters carried baseball bats. "Nothing breaks it better," said Poole. Crews would get out on deck and beat the ice off.

With gale-force winds screaming across icy steel decks while the ship pitched, plunged, and crashed through the sea, launching a weather balloon was no simple task. Inflated, the balloons had a diameter of about six feet. They caught the wind like sails and, once on deck, they had minds of their own. The radio instruments the balloons carried aloft were fragile, and many things could go wrong. Somebody might slip and drop the instrument. The balloon could brush against something and burst. Or the thing could get airborne, only to be hung up in the ship's rigging or caught in a gust and dashed against the deck. Sometimes the whole thing would blow right into the sea.

"So it wasn't just a matter of going outside and letting the balloon go," Poole explained. "It was a mat-

Unless disabled or called away for a rescue, a cutter had to sit tight and ride out whatever nature had to offer. Here, the cutter Pontchartrain *wallows in the trough of a following sea on Ocean Station "Baker."*

215

ter of filling it up in the shelter, getting the ship on a special course to get the proper movement in heavy weather with the wind coming off the quarter in a certain direction. Then you'd be crouching down inside the shelter. You held the balloon close to the deck in one hand and the radio transmitter and train in the other. You had to get the rhythm of the vessel, waiting for the stern to come up. And then, when everything was right, you'd bounce out of there just as the wind hit the deck and swept up so it could catch the balloon and carry it away. If you got out there at the wrong time, the wind would take it right down into the water."

After the launch, the weathermen had approximately 90 minutes to work up their calculations and get their report to the ship's radio operator. The calculations were done by hand in the cramped quarters of the weather shack. "There were about 10,000 chances for error," recalled Herb Chadwick, Weather Bureau veteran of more than 130 patrols. "We had to check our work constantly." When the ship was pitching and rolling in a violent sea, things became even more difficult. "You'd put something down on the table, and the next thing you knew it was across the room." Sometimes it was all the men could do just to hang on.

One incentive that lured the weather observers to sea was money. By sailing on the weather ships they earned approximately twice what they could make on shore. As a group, they were the highest paid in the entire Weather Bureau. But there were other motives that kept them returning to the weather ships year after year, spending as much as seven or eight months of each year at sea.

Many of the weathermen agreed that a large part of the lure was the chance to be their own bosses. "We were working for the government," said Henry Chapman of Westport, Connecticut, who weathered more than 150 patrols, "but we had a lot of freedom. We made our own decisions, and we had to use our own judgment. And when somebody gives you a chance to do that, it's satisfying. And we did something that was needed. It needed to be accurate, and it needed to be done on time. You got a feeling that your work was worth something."

Meteorological information from the weather ships was distributed to American forecasters and also to those abroad. In fact, a major reason for starting the Atlantic Weather Project was to aid Great Britain's military planners in forecasting the weather moving their way. Until that time, merchant ships crossing the Atlantic made surface weather observations along their route and radioed the information back to land. Forecasters used the reports in advising transatlantic avia-

For the men of the U.S. Weather Bureau who worked aboard the cutters, the duty was hard and physically demanding, but the pay was good and the importance of their work made the job worthwhile.

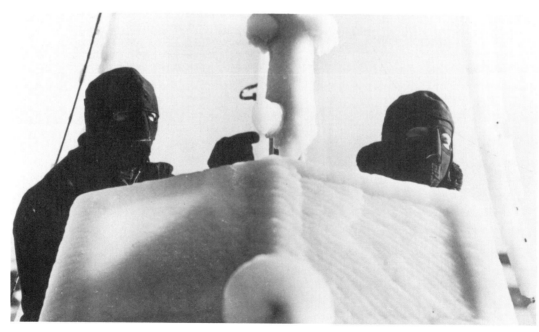

tion and in forecasting the weather moving toward Europe.

But with German U-boats plaguing the seas, merchant ships stopped making the weather reports in order to maintain radio silence and avoid revealing their positions. This proved an effective defense for shipping, but the forecasting data were sorely missed.

President Franklin Roosevelt ordered the inception of the Atlantic Weather Project. Two ocean station sites were selected along the northern air route to Britain, and by 1940 Coast Guard cutters were making the first weather patrols. At the peak of the war effort, there were 22 ocean stations in the Atlantic, 13 of them manned by the United States and the rest maintained by Britain.

Surprisingly, the weather ships were never harassed by the German submarines. It is said that the Nazi navy valued the weather reports from the ships too highly. The U-boats would intercept and decode the transmissions, and some speculate that the Germans became heavily dependent on the information.

After the war, a reduced network of ocean stations was maintained by the United States, Canada, and European countries. But whether the world was at war or at peace, life on the ocean station was a constant battle.

It was grinding—both physically and mentally—knocking about in mid-ocean for 21 days at a stretch. When a ship at sea is going nowhere, morale can sink into the deep troughs. Time passes slowly. The eleventh day on station was called "hump day" because it marked the halfway point of the patrol. Hump day was often celebrated with a party of sorts, and something special was cooked up in the galley. Morale tended to pick up on the "downhill" side of hump day. "But, of course," said Herb Chadwick, "it was still a long time before you saw that relief ship."

The monotony of a patrol could be shattered at any moment if the ship picked up a distress call on its radio. In 1947 Americans held their breath as the Coast Guard cutter *Bibb* battled giant seas and a screaming gale to rescue 69 people from the airplane *Bermuda Sky Queen*. The passenger plane, en route from Britain to the United States, had been forced down 800 miles northwest of Newfoundland.

It was 6:47 A.M. on October 14 when the *Bibb* received this message: "Aircraft call KFG going to make emergency landing at sea at Station Charlie at approximately 0800." Retired Coast Guard captain Paul B. Cronk, commander of the *Bibb* at that time, remembers feeling numb when he heard that the *Sky Queen* had 69 persons on board. "Planes at that time were carrying 10 to 12 passengers at a time," Cronk said.

Launching a weather balloon that carried delicate and expensive scientific instruments was no picnic in the North Atlantic, even under relatively calm conditions like these.

"But then this one plopped down in the North Atlantic carrying over 60 passengers plus pilot and crew. It was unheard of."

"When the thing came down, it was the worst possible weather for a rescue operation," Cronk recalled. A gale that had been blowing for 56 hours had built up steep, fast-running, crossing seas. "The wind was driving such that it set the plane drifting at better than five knots. We had to chase her for over a hundred miles before we could complete the rescue."

The sea was in such a wild state that the *Bibb* could not get near the plane. Some survivors were rescued by a rubber raft attached to the cutter by a line and allowed to drift down upon the plane. But, on the fourth crossing, the raft broke loose. A motor surfboat was sent to rescue the 16 people in the raft, but the surfboat

The 180-foot Coast Guard tender Citrus, *on a search-and-rescue mission.*

swamped and began sinking. Captain Cronk decided to move in with his ship, to try and rescue those in the boats. The *Bibb* was rolling heavily in the seas, listing as much as 45 degrees, but crewmen lowered boarding nets and scrambled over the cutter's side, forming what Captain Cronk called a "vertical bucket brigade" that plucked all 16 passengers and the boat crew from the sea.

The entire fight lasted 25 hours. In the end, every one of the 69 persons on the *Sky Queen* was taken safely aboard the *Bibb*. Four days later, the cutter received a hero's welcome as it steamed into Boston Harbor with a new broom lashed to her mast—the maritime symbol for "clean sweep."

In recent decades, as aircraft became more reliable, navigation became more exact, and the jet age took aviation above the clouds to altitudes beyond the reach of surface weather, ocean stations played smaller roles in transatlantic commerce. At the same time, satellites circling the earth began giving meteorologists global weather pictures. With each ocean station costing the United States millions of dollars per year to operate, the weather ships had become white elephants in the eyes of many people.

By 1974 all the northern stations had been dis-

banded, and only ocean station "Hotel," located between Cape Hatteras and Bermuda, remained in operation. Hotel was the station used to track storms and hurricanes moving up the coast toward New England and the Georges Bank fishing grounds, according to Rod Winslow, meteorologist in charge of the southern New England forecast office of the National Weather Service.

In 1977 the automated deep-ocean buoy EB-07 was deployed near the weather ship on ocean station Hotel. The buoy was far less expensive than manning the ocean station, but it could transmit only surface observations. Even in conjunction with weather satellites, forecasters would be deprived of the complete profile of the atmosphere above the ocean.

"The basis of a good forecast is a good observation," Rod Winslow said. "And that's what the ships provided. An instrument can't take the place of a man."

Nonetheless, EB-07 proved to be the final blow for the weather ships. On September 30, 1977, the Coast Guard cutter *Taney* turned her stern to ocean station Hotel and laid a course for home. There was no relief ship to take her place. Her departure marked the end of the Atlantic Weather Project and closed a bold chapter in America's maritime history.   ∞

Though Don Kent retired several years ago from WBZ, his forecasts are still carried on some New England radio stations. No one person has ever been as much a symbol of New England weather as Don Kent, and we reprint this profile, first published in the May 1974 issue of *Yankee,* to give readers a behind-the-scenes look at the everyday life of a TV weatherman.

He's Still Selling the Weather

BY STEPHEN C. ALTSCHULER

One clear New England spring day back in the late 1920s, Donald Kent sat in his third-grade classroom staring out the window. His teacher approached with a scowl and asked what he was doing.

"I want to be a weatherman," he said. On fishing trips to the Cape, his father had sparked his interest by explaining that the moon, the stars, and wind direction had an effect on the fish and when they would bite. "I'm watching the flag blow in the wind and the weather vane on that barn."

Now some schoolmarms might have taken drastic disciplinary action at that point. But fortunately for young Kent, his teacher must have sensed something: She made him the class weatherman! Of course, she might have figured this was a worse punishment than the ruler—forecasting New England weather is about as easy as astrophysics.

"There's more weather contrast in New England than any other place," Don Kent said as we chatted in his small office at the WBZ studios in Boston. Signs around the room read "Beware! Weathermen Inside" and "No amount of planning will ever replace dumb luck."

"New England is on the storm track for all kinds of things," he continued. "Chicago doesn't get hurricanes, but we do. They get tornadoes, but so do we—like the Worcester tornado." He went on about the Gulf Stream 150 miles offshore, about arctic air ripping down from the north, about contrasts in temperature, humidity, and dew point, and about upper air troughs of vorticity. "Potential energy" and "action" were the words he used to describe the situation when these factors mesh to produce a full-blown New England storm. The upper atmosphere certainly knows no energy crisis.

"The important thing about New England is that we're close to the source of abundant moisture," Kent explained. "We're sitting on a time bomb all the time, especially in the winter."

It was 6:00 A.M. on the morning of Christmas Eve. Don had left his Weymouth home at 4:50 and arrived at the studio at 5:20. Monday was the most difficult day for forecasting because he had been away from it for two days.

It was a clear, cold day, but there was a storm approaching, and Don was busily collecting data for his 6:55 broadcast. The facsimile machine cranked out constantly updated upper air maps from the National Weather Service (NWS). The teletype spit out temperature and weather information from all over the country. The Coast Guard weather ship patrolling the storm corridor from the Virginia coast northward teletyped its

219

Don Kent, the dean of New England weathermen, broadcasting from his home in Laconia, New Hampshire. Kent's studio is just large enough for him, his desk, and the computers that relay the latest weather maps and information to him.

periodic surface and high-level atmospheric information. Two sets of reports linked Don Kent with people up and down the coast and throughout New England. One was from a group of 50 to 60 ham radio operators who formed the Radio Weather Net in the 1950s. (Don joined them in 1961.) Every morning at 6:30 one of the operators reads over the air the collected weather observations from New England and along the Atlantic coast.

The other firsthand source was reported by phone from a woman in Chelmsford, Massachusetts. Every day since the mid-1950s Ruth French had gotten up at 6:00 A.M. to call ten weather observers in northern New England resort areas. Don called her at 6:45 to get reports that the teletype either didn't handle or clicked out much later. "She gives me all the information I need—like how much snow fell during the night, how the blackflies are biting, how the trout fishing is at Echo Lake, and how the surf is running at Bar Harbor—all this sort of thing."

"I feel that the way to make weather mean something to people," Don continued, "is to have it related to the things that are happening in season."

At 6:46 Kent was like a halfback in motion, and at 6:50 the ball was snapped. He rushed to the radio booth

to tape a forecast to be heard at 6:55, then to the television studio to ready his map. On this day, as on most other days, the prediction was good for some but bad for others: first a clear, cold, starlit Christmas Eve, then clouding up Christmas Day, then a warm trough of moist air from the Gulf of Mexico to bring a rainstorm. The ocean water temperatures were running six degrees above normal, and cold arctic air was retreating from the tropical onslaught.

After the broadcasts, the pace slowed to a canter as Don swabbed the map with a wet sponge. He didn't have much time to breathe, as his next television show was at 7:25, but while he was checking the teletype and computer updates, I asked him about some weather theories of my own. Rainy New England winters greatly annoy me, and during the previous winter, along with this winter to date, almost every storm had turned to rain in southern New England. The northern sections had plenty of snow early last winter, but up to this Christmas Eve day, all of New England had bare ground along with unfrozen lakes and ponds.

"No, the Gulf Stream hasn't shifted," Don replied to my prime theory. "You've got to have cold air sitting right over the Gulf of St. Lawrence, and you've got to have the upper winds come down like this and come up like this (he swirled his hand in a counterclockwise movement) and then a low pressure gets going here (he pointed to the Gulf of Mexico) and takes off in our direction. But, you see, we don't have that."

After the 7:25 broadcast, the private line in Don Kent's office started ringing. Northern ski operators were in a bit of a panic.

"We've got a tough, tough, tough, tough situation here," Kent told the ski resort operator. "The unbelievable is . . . looks like it is going to happen. Yeah, super warm air has already moved halfway up the Mississippi Valley. It's now raining all the way up in Missouri and the temperature is in the fifties. . . ."

As he was talking, I noticed that beside the phone, in a very handy location, was a current copy of *The Old Farmer's Almanac*. Could Abe Weatherwise have something to do with all this? I knew that Don Kent and Robb Sagendorph [former *Old Farmer's Almanac* editor], though good friends, had had a running argument for years about weather forecasting. Was Kent finally convinced that the *Almanac*'s secret weather formula was more reliable than all his scientific hardware? Not really.

"I tell people that anybody anywhere has just as much chance of making an 18-month guess—just as much chance of being right—as *The Old Farmer's Almanac*," asserted Don, returning to our conversation. "But I recommend that everybody buy the *Almanac* because it's filled with thousands of useful facts— many of which I refer to every day. The one thing that is least trustworthy is the weather forecast."

Kent admitted—and his critics agree—that many times he has had difficulty forecasting 6 hours ahead, so normally he limits his forecasts to 48 hours. He usually refers to a forecast beyond 48 hours as an outlook, and anything more than 5 days as guesswork.

Of course, when watching a TV weatherman, people usually ignore words such as "outlook" and "possibly" and "chance of." You see, a weatherman is actually Zeus reincarnated, occasionally casting thunderbolts, churning the seas, and whipping the air into a stormy frenzy. A Wednesday forecast of "and possibly a chance of rain or snow Saturday" becomes "Hey, I heard it's going to snow Saturday."

"The important thing in this job is credibility," Kent said. "But honestly, there are some people who believe every single word I say as if it's gospel. I mean it scares me. It's amazing." As one of the station engineers quipped after Don gave his forecast on the air, "God has just spoken."

For those whose goal in life is to be omnipotent,

that must sound like an enviable position. But it does have its problems. A TV/radio weatherman—particularly one whose name is synonymous with New England weather—is always on center stage. When he's right, he's expected to be right and so gets little praise; but when he's wrong, he wears the mark of Cain and bears the brunt of snide remarks and contemptuous sneers. My neighbor related that Kent sat a few rows down from him at a Patriots game one Sunday and was "reeling" under a barrage of jibes, indignities, and insults from the surrounding spectators. These are things that *The Old Farmer's Almanac* and other less visible meteorologists do not have to go through. When they are right, they're praised—and when they are wrong, they're ignored.

Don Kent is aware that many people plan their day around his forecasts, and it is very important to him that he not let these people down. He almost reinforces the view that he has some control over the weather, that despite the chameleon quality of New England weather he should always be accurate. The day after an unpredicted rainy, cold day, he came on the air and extended "my apologies for the miserable day yesterday." He's been involved in weather predicting all his life. It's his career, his hobby, his passion. He knows what he's doing, and he's disappointed when he's wrong. "I'm embarrassed when I say something in all sincerity and know people believe me and they plan to do things, cancel trips or do something based on my statement, and then something goes wrong."

Relating it directly to his family, he explained one reason why his four children (three sons and a daughter) never got interested in weather forecasting. Smiling easily, he said, "My wife used to believe my forecasts, and she'd send the kids off to school. They'd be all bundled up in their foul-weather clothes and their rain boots and slickers on a cloudy morning because it was going to storm. Well, those were the days before the weather ship, and the storm would go out to sea. And they'd come home after school with the bright, warm sun out. Other parents who didn't care that much (about the prediction) sent their kids out with no extras, and they'd come home laughing at my poor kids."

Obviously, Don is not such a zealot that he is humorless about his errors. To those who say he's wrong all the time, he answered, "There's no job in the world where you can be wrong as much as a weatherman and make such good money at it."

But the fact is, Don Kent is right most of the time. For those of you who plan picnics after he predicts rain, you'll be interested to know that Mr. Kent is 85 to 90 percent accurate. It's the glaring mistakes, particularly in winter, that cause people to lose faith. Despite the high accuracy rating, about half of the many letters that come to Don Kent are negative. And a number of those are abusive and unsigned. "When they're nasty and do sign their names," Don said, "I write them and invite them in here. When they see all the stuff I have to work with, they become my best friends."

But many letters are quite positive. He showed me one from a class at Mansfield (Massachusetts) High School that researched Kent's forecasts for two months. They reported he was 91 percent accurate. "Someone thinks I'm right!" he noted.

It was nearing 8:25, and the pace quickened. Don examined the latest NWS computer prediction and upper air charts. His forecast was his own, based on a multilevel look at the weather. He never puts complete faith in the computer, as some meteorologists do. "The computer's like a Ouija board," Don said. "Sometimes

To prepare his forecasts, Kent gets regular updates on wind and temperature patterns around the country.

the National Weather Service's five-day forecast changes every day."

He spotted an air pressure variation in the atmosphere above Missouri that he felt confirmed his prediction that rain was on the way. Warm air fed from the Gulf of Mexico was wedging its way north. "Look at this warm air coming up here," he pointed out. "It's 10 degrees Centigrade—that's 50 degrees Fahrenheit one mile above the ground. And look here—20—you never see 20; that's 68 degrees Fahrenheit one mile up. What hot air that is! But when you've got cold air at higher levels moving in over the warm air, that makes it unstable. . . . Do you see how interesting this is? It's exciting. And when you've got the knowledge of how to use it, you can't wait for the next map to see what's happening.

The pattern was set. All information confirmed his prediction. Don ventured a three-day forecast that he felt was "a sure thing"—bold words for a New England weatherman. (The forecast was accurate.)

After the flurry of morning broadcasts and tapes, Don set aside half an hour, starting at 10:15, to take phone calls from the public. In this brief interlude of relaxation, he sipped his coffee and related how his career had progressed.

After his father whetted his interest in weather and his third-grade teacher provided an outlet, Don read the few available books on weather and continued his announcing into high school, where he'd give pre–football game weather forecasts over the North Quincy High public address system. Upon graduation, he did a five-minute forecast on a small Boston radio station while studying business administration and salesmanship part time at Boston University.

An important break came in 1937 when the U.S. Weather Bureau offered a course under MIT meteorologist Dr. Hurd Willett in air mass analysis, the technique of studying upper air patterns. This type of analysis is widely used today but was very new in the 1930s. Kent took this course two nights a week and studied salesmanship three nights. "This was a unique combination of being a salesman and weatherman," Don said. "And I'm still selling weather."

With the start of the war, he was initially rejected for service because of a heart murmur, but he eventu-

ally wound up in the Coast Guard and volunteered for weather training. With his prior training and experience, he began teaching the course and advanced rapidly.

"When I came out of the service in December 1945, as an officer, I went around to the radio stations in Boston and they all said, 'Why should we pay you to do a weather forecast; we get it from the government free.' " So he entered his brother's rug business and waited until 1947 for his break into a weather career.

A small radio station in Quincy, WJDA, had just started operation about the time a hurricane was racing up the coast. They asked Don Kent to talk about it, and the response from the listeners was so enthusiastic that they hired him part-time at $5 a broadcast.

He did that and sold carpets for the next four years, "and then the Boston stations all started making offers, and I took the WBZ job because I could still stay in the rug business and use broadcasting as a hobby and a supplement." So WBZ provided him with equipment at his South Shore home and office, and Don Kent went on the air in 1951, known only as Weatherbee the 'BZ Weatherman.

After four years of obscurity, "I quit on a Saturday on radio as Weatherbee and on Monday, July 10, 1955, I came on as Don Kent on WBZ-TV."

"How do you remember these dates?" I asked.

"Oh, I remember well. These are big things in my life. This is a hobby, remember. This isn't a business; it's a hobby."

It was getting close to noon and the midday news—Don's final broadcast for the day. There was a partial eclipse of the sun on this day, and station film photographers had taken some good shots of the event. Director Davis had told Don to expound on eclipses for about 20 seconds, so he consulted his handy *Old Farmer's Almanac* for the needed information about the next eclipse. He gathered his material and began his dash to the television cameras, pausing for a moment as he looked out over my head. "It still pays me to look out the window before going on," he said.   ∞

America's Pioneer Radio Weathercaster

E.B. Rideout, at the mike.

Like Don Kent, E.B. Rideout started his career as a meteorologist in grade school, when he was given the task of observing the weather, keeping records, and reporting to the class. Also like Kent, he reportedly kept a copy of *The Old Farmer's Almanac* close at hand during his later years of weather forecasting, though not (he said) to predict the weather.

Around 1908 Rideout, then working as a typesetter in a printing plant, discovered the weather map posted in the Boston Post Office and was bitten by the weather bug again. He started making daily visits to the office of the U.S. Weather Bureau in Boston and soon became friendly with all the workers there. Due to a staff shortage during World War I, he even had the opportunity to fill in at the bureau as a weather observer, returning to his printing job after the war.

In 1925, Rideout finally got the chance to pursue his passion for the weather full-time. A ten-month-old Boston radio station, WEEI, invited him to give a couple of brief talks about the weather over the airwaves. Regular forecasts and commercial sponsorship followed, and soon E.B. Rideout became an institution, his voice a station trademark.

At the time of his retirement in December 1963, Rideout had completed more than 55,000 broadcasts in his 38-year radio career. Today he is honored as America's pioneer weather forecaster and is represented in this book by his 1966 article for *Yankee,* "The Day the Weather Bureau Was Right."

—*Larry Willard*

ENVOI

The Weather

BY MARK TWAIN

ADDRESS AT THE NEW ENGLAND SOCIETY'S
SEVENTY-FIRST ANNUAL DINNER, NEW YORK
CITY (DECEMBER 22, 1876)

I reverently believe that the Maker who made us all makes everything in New England but the weather. I don't know who makes that, but I think it must be raw apprentices in the weather-clerk's factory who experiment and learn how, in New England, for board and clothes, and then are promoted to make weather for countries that require a good article, and will take their custom elsewhere if they don't get it.

There is a sumptuous variety about the New England weather that compels the stranger's admiration—and regret. The weather is always doing something there; always attending strictly to business; always getting up new designs and trying them on the people to see how they will go. But it gets through more business in spring than in any other season. In the spring I have counted one hundred and thirty-six different kinds of weather inside of four-and-twenty hours.

It was I that made the fame and fortune of that man that had that marvelous collection of weather on exhibition at the Centennial, that so astounded the foreigners. He was going to travel all over the world and get specimens from all the climes. I said, "Don't you do it; you come to New England on a favorable spring day." I told him what we could do in the way of style, variety, and quantity. Well, he came and he made his collection in four days. As to variety, why, he confessed that he got hundreds of kinds of weather that he had never heard of before. And as to quantity—well, after he had picked out and discarded all that was blemished in any way, he not only had weather enough, but weather to spare; weather to hire out; weather to sell; to deposit; weather to invest; weather to give to the poor.

The people of New England are by nature patient and forbearing, but there are some things which they will not stand. Every year they kill a lot of poets for writing about "Beautiful Spring." These are generally casual visitors, who bring their notions of spring from somewhere else, and cannot, of course, know how the native feels about spring. And so the first thing they know the opportunity to inquire how they feel has permanently gone by.

Old Probabilities has a mighty reputation for accurate prophecy, and thoroughly well deserves it. You take up the paper and observe how crisply and confidently he checks off what to-day's weather is going to be on the Pacific, down South, in the Middle States, in the Wisconsin region. See him sail along in the joy and pride of his power till he gets to New England, and then see his tail drop. *He* doesn't know what the weather is going to be in New England. Well, he mulls over it, and by and by he gets out something about like this: Probable northeast to southwest winds, varying to the southward and westward and eastward, and points between, high and low barometer swapping around from place to place; probable areas of rain, snow, hail, and drought, succeeded or preceded by earthquakes, with thunder and lightning. Then he jots down this postscript from

225

As a resident of Hartford, Connecticut, Samuel Langhorne Clemens (Mark Twain) had ample opportunity to be both entranced and appalled by New England's capricious weather.

his wandering mind, to cover accidents: "But it is possible that the programme may be wholly changed in the mean time."

Yes, one of the brightest gems in the New England weather is the dazzling uncertainty of it. There is only one thing certain about it: you are certain there is going to be plenty of it—a perfect grand review; but you never can tell which end of the procession is going to move first. You fix up for the drought; you leave your umbrella in the house and sally out, and two to one you get drowned. You make up your mind that the earthquake is due; you stand from under, and take hold of something to steady yourself, and the first thing you know you get struck by lightning. These are great disappointments; but they can't be helped.

The lightning there is peculiar; it is so convincing, that when it strikes a thing it doesn't leave enough of that thing behind for you to tell whether—Well, you'd think it was something valuable, and a Congressman had been there. And the thunder. When the thunder begins to merely tune up and scrape and saw, and key up the instruments for the performance, strangers say, "Why, what awful thunder you have here!" But when the baton is raised and the real concert begins, you'll find that stranger down in the cellar with his head in the ash-barrel.

Now as to the *size* of the weather in New England—lengthways, I mean. It is utterly disproportioned to the size of that little country. Half the time, when it is packed as full as it can stick, you will see that New England weather sticking out beyond the edges and projecting around hundreds and hundreds of miles over the neighboring States. She can't hold a tenth part of her weather. You can see cracks all about where she has strained herself trying to do it.

I could speak volumes about the inhuman perversity of the New England weather, but I will give but a single specimen. I like to hear rain on a tin roof. So I covered part of my roof with tin, with an eye to that luxury. Well, sir, do you think it ever rains on that tin? No, sir; skips it every time.

Mind, in this speech I have been trying merely to do honor to the New England weather—no language could do it justice. But, after all, there is at least one or two things about that weather (or, if you please, effects produced by it) which we residents would not like to part with. If we hadn't our bewitching autumn foliage, we should still have to credit the weather with one feature which compensates for all its bullying vagaries—the ice-storm: when a leafless tree is clothed with ice from the bottom to the top—ice that is as bright and clear as crystal; when every bough and twig is strung with ice-beads, frozen dewdrops, and the whole tree sparkles cold and white, like the Shah of Persia's diamond plume. Then the wind waves the branches and the sun comes out and turns all those myriads of beads and drops to prisms that glow and burn and flash with all manner of colored fires, which change and change again with inconceivable rapidity from blue to red, from red to green, and green to gold—the tree becomes a spraying fountain, a very explosion of dazzling jewels; and it stands there the acme, the climax, the supremest possibility in art or nature, of bewildering, intoxicating, intolerable magnificence. One cannot make the words too strong.

From Mark Twain's Speeches *(New York: Harper & Brothers Publishers, 1910). Reprinted by permission of Harper & Row.*

Photograph
and
Illustration Credits